Spiritual Logic

Spiritual Logic

Behind the Power of Words & Beliefs

Energy's Universal Language

Artisans
of the
SPirit

C. Shadow Fox & Lee Two Hawks

ISBN: 979-8-9924423-0-4 (Paperback Edition)
ISBN: 979-8-9924423-1-1 (Hardcover Edition)
ISBN: 979-8-9924423-2-8 (Ebook Edition)

Cover Design: Mark R. Freeman

Artisans of the Spirit

DEDICATION

This book is dedicated to you, the seeker. We stand with the utmost gratitude and respect to each of you as you turn the page and perhaps find a new chapter in your life. We are honored to share our journey with you. Lest we forget- all roads eventually lead to illumination no matter how dim the street lights appear.

CONTENTS

TESTIMONIALS

~"Remaining open while reading this book is the Key. Please consider allowing these two gentle souls to hold your hand on a path you might not have considered. The inspiration here is just for you, dear soul, to pick up and joyfully run with. It's fun to read, and it works. Manifest!"

Sarah Nelson
Owner: Grandma's Organic Garden. Avilla, Indiana

~"Our relationships and awareness of others have to do with our relationship with ourselves. Becoming aware of your innermost navigational system is the power to create harmony, fun, and wisdom. The thought-provoking concepts of Shadow Fox & Lee Two Hawks will assist you in smoothly transitioning from resistant blocked energy to a beautiful flow of inspired ideas."

Jackie Francis
Owner: Ashville General Store. Ashville, N.Y.

~"This book is a wake-up call with an enlightening interpretation of our thoughts, words, and actions, how we use them, and how to better ourselves; very powerful. I love the book and will recommend it to others."

Wayne Lemish AAS, Indiana

~"I think about how often children see a view of a subject I have never considered. They are not yet confined by a belief system and are open to view naturally. This book will empower me to move toward a higher understanding of self and others. I will use it as a tool, rereading it often as I journey."
Robin Allen West,
KY Service for Veterans Chairman

~"This book is a clear, helpful guide to self-empowerment through spiritual guidance. Changing our thoughts and words can change our lives and bring a positive wave of change to our Beautiful Mother Earth. I commend and honor Shadow Fox and Lee Two Hawks for their unconditional love for all life.

Shadow Fox and Lee Two Hawks are committed, wise, spiritual teachers. Sharing their extensive spiritual knowledge and walking their talk with Grace has helped many others on the spiritual path, including myself. They are genuinely divinely guided. This new book is a shining example of their commitment to humanity and Spirit. It is of utmost importance for all humans living on the earth to understand how powerful their thoughts, words, and intentions are. Will we create or destroy the beauty, love, and joy in our lives? Or on our planet? Understanding how to move from our center of God-given power can make a difference in our quality of life."
Carla Morningstar M.A., LMT. Reiki Master, Minister Universal Life Church
Owner: Healing Waters Wellness. Ithaca, N.Y.

~"If I could share why someone should pick up, read, and apply the information, I would say-- Trust that you were guided to pick up this book! Shadow Fox writes with truth. The language is clear, upfront, and accurate. The information is transformative."
Morning Star. Virginia Beach, Virginia

~"Shadow Fox and Lee Two Hawks are excellent Messengers of The Light, who specialize in the nuances of energy. Speaking in the language that another comprehends allows understanding and harmony to exist. This comprehension will enable nations, businesses, families, people, and individuals to live melodiously.

They have a beautiful song resounding within that draws people from all backgrounds. Their teachings employ humor and emotional wisdom. In my deepest moments of grief, Shadow Fox and Lee Two Hawks led me out of the darkness into The Light through a simple changing of words and thoughts. We can design a harmonious life by using higher vibrations, free from reacting and repeating unpleasant circumstances. Effortlessly and quickly, these two experienced teachers guide their students through quagmires into infinite manifesting."

Rev. Carmen Quiñones
Order of Melchizedek Priest
Usui Reiki Master and Musician

~"This book gets right to the point, showing how to stay in tune with the Universe and live the life you desire. C. Shadow Fox and Lee Two Hawks did a wonderful job conveying the importance and the power behind your words and beliefs. This is life-changing information."

Master Red Sarber. White Crane Gung Fu.

UTILIZING THIS BOOK

Overview

This guidebook is a content-oriented, multifaceted source for energy awareness, expanding consciousness, transcendence, and manifesting. It should not be read cover to cover but chapter by chapter, giving honest reflection in and of our lives. Some chapters might resonate easily, while others may challenge you. By design, it's a safe place to think, to reevaluate actions, words, and deeds. Helping people find their own 'tuning fork' for self-validation, expression, and expansion. The importance of aligning with Laws constructs harmony, thus reducing friction and conflict within our lives. Readers can gain the ability to create efficiently, effectively, and effortlessly at higher vibrational energies. Understanding how energy facilitates our realities creates freedom to manifest from a seat of power where harmony, healing, and miracles become a by-product.

The Layout

Chapters begin with a story from a life experience, enhancing the concepts and showing some erroneous decisions, each building a foundation for understanding the Governance of Laws, and ends with key points. They guide a reader through the precept of how common words enslave us through resonance. It then moves into focused thoughts for healing, with a more in-depth expression of beliefs. Not to convince but to validate your own power. These are all-inclusive of how words, thoughts, and beliefs create and resonate from the etheric octave of Spiritual Logic.

How to work with its guidance

As a manual for dynamic living, Chapter Two is an exception from the rest of the book; Energy's Universal Language lays the foundation and dispels the elusive fillers people define as energy. Take your time with this chapter. It immerses us in understanding energy and its components that can be used as a reference point.

A chapter is dedicated to tools and techniques, providing opportunities to apply the teachings presented from this energy awareness. We have all experienced 'trial and error,' and now there are 'ways and means' to reduce our learning curve. Take your time and experiment with the suggestions.

Expanded Results

This information has the power to heal divisions and develop healthy social norms. When spiritual laws abide, humanity will most surely hasten an illumined society filled with great minds and loving hearts. Discover the power of words and beliefs which construct with a force of symmetry, avoiding conditions that enslave us with limitations, discord, and illness, individually and to that of Nations. Perceptions are our only limitations.

Journey Well ~ Artisans of the Spirit.

ACKNOWLEDGMENTS

There is a fluidity of content presented with a wise and experienced understanding of the human dilemma. This wisdom reveals how choices are made, what forces enter a choice, and what role belief systems play in directing our lives.

This work was a combined effort 'featuring' Shadow Fox and, in a minor manner, Lee Two Hawks. Shadow Fox is the primary voice. I am the shadow mumbling this or that- mostly grumbling, 'Aren't you done yet? She is the driver. I am the navigator who doesn't read maps; I design them. However, she delivers a message far better than she drives. So you might call me the backseat driver on this journey, securely buckled in.

All kidding aside, our thanks go to Sarah Nelson, White Dove Crow, Carmen Quinones, 'Nancy,' Diana Bishop, Jacquelyne Trieber, Mark R. Freeman, Mr. and Mrs. Michael Dean Edwards, who took this journey with us. Their insight, sharing of wisdom, laughter, patience, and encouragement helped manifest this book. To our family, we thank each of you for riding along. The depth of our love can find no words for expression. Finally, our immense gratitude for our Ascended Masters' Assistance is beyond measure. Their quality of perfection is reflected in this writing. Any flaws in the book are ours; we are human.

Journey Well. Lee Two Hawks & Shadow Fox

CHAPTER ONE

A PATH

A Child's Curiosity

*E*verything started with a simple question to my father: "Dad, why do adults talk about love yet don't act like it or show it? Like they say one thing and do another?" I treasured these moments-- these provocative dialogues with my father-- because I could ask him anything. However, he rarely gave me a direct answer to my questions; instead, he helped me find my own. He'd question how I came to a specific conclusion or redirect my efforts with a frustrating "Try again" or sometimes "That's stupid." as a response. My mind wandered, expecting the usual "That's stupid," when my father's voice pierced the silence: "Are you wondering why most people don't say what they mean or mean what they say?" I replied, "Yes, I think so." Dad answered, "Great, we'll tackle love later cuz it is all related."

1

With that, my journey of discovery unfolded before me. From nine years old, the following teaching would saturate my whole being. I had noticed that when people prayed or wished for something, the result wasn't quite what they intended. This observation was validated when a family member mentioned how he prayed for a wife, a gift from above. After marriage, he felt he had opened a present for someone else entirely. So, what was prayed for? This was the reason for our discussion on that momentous day.

So, this simple query to my father started a dialogue of thought. He expressed to me that we are our words and deeds. We are what we speak, and in doing so, we create our character by which others will recognize us. My dad stated, "If you are honest with yourself and others, people will know you to be an honest person. It's what you send out or bring forth. "Discouraged, I countered, "That's easy. Everyone knows that-- it's common sense." He then corrected me, "You ignored or missed the last part. It's what you send out or bring forth that counts! Consider this: "If a tree fell in the forest and no one was there to hear, would it still make a sound? (Berkeley) Please think before you answer. Really, give it some thought." He paused, then added, "The secret is found here with the sound of the tree's impact, so what is being sent forth?"

I answered, "Yes, the tree would still make noise, even if no one could hear it fall." He then asked, "How do you know this? Who would listen?" Dad was encouraging me. "I'm not sure how I know; I feel it. I can imagine the tree's impact and waves of sound spreading out on the ground, up to the heavens. The animals would hear and feel its sound and, perhaps,

God." For a moment, I saw a look of acceptance and pride, which quickly disappeared.

Finally, Dad cleared his throat and shared, "The waves of the impact sent out are, in essence, our sound each time we speak or intend something. Most people are unaware or remain asleep when they talk. They do not pay attention or understand how their sound is sent into the universe. Perhaps people are so accustomed to not being heard they speak without realizing the universe is always listening. Our voices are our instruments. Sometimes we are in tune, sometimes not."

Due to my father's teaching, I began my mission to discover how the universe hears us. If our voices are our instruments, how can we stay in tune? What causes sour notes, or why do we get out of tune in the first place? These were my childhood 'causes,' and nature answered many of them. But, each answer directed me to another, more significant question. At the time, I had no idea of its profound impact and importance for my life's journey. So I must frankly state, "Thank you, Dad, for showing me a path; I love you!"

Our results in life will flow from the energy within laws, whether by thoughts, words, or focused intent. However, nuances in our 'human logic' and perceptions can imprison us with struggle and strife. As a youngster, it wasn't easy to reconcile what was taught in school or religious studies regarding human logic or beliefs, mainly because it didn't reflect what I could see, hear, or feel from nature. Finally, in maturity, I found Cosmic and Universal Laws, which offered me terms to define what I intuitively knew as energy. This helped shift my perspective from human logic to spiritual logic, creating a life of balance and harmony.

Please make no mistake: in my search to understand Cosmic, Universal, Natural, and Spiritual Laws, there were times I was in harmony with these concepts; sometimes not. I constantly tested and qualified new ideas from my guides, angels, and nature. As a child medium, tuning in was easy for me; however, as an adult, being in tune would challenge my learned belief systems. I established that I lost whenever I denied, resisted, or rejected this energy from laws.

My experience in this realization is what I would like to bring to your awareness. Throughout this book, I will address some nuances of the laws, such as how they function when we request something and how we step into chaos by not being aware of them. My focus is gently shifting your perceptions, understanding, or awareness to concepts that help qualify words and develop an intent that carries a higher frequency in harmony with the laws. Thus, overall, evolutionary thinking can help remove discord from our lives. Remember, your perception is your only limitation.

Path of Least Resistance

Words resonate. The vibrations our voices, minds, and hearts initiate express the First Cosmic Law of Synthesis: sound. We resonate. A difference between spiritual and human logic can be demonstrated by qualifying how some words and beliefs resonate or sound in the etheric. We speak or communicate daily, yet we overlook how it vibrates in the heavens. The language of the Universe can remain elusive until there is a glimpse into the abstract concepts that rest within the etheric realm. Recognizing and aligning with the governing law of energy reduces the friction in our lives. We begin to speak from a seat of power. This power allays the unconscious, unintended results we create in life.

The design is simplistic, with constant reminders of its function. These teachings are commensurate with the Second Cosmic Law of Economy. My focus concerns a substrate of this Law, better known as The Path of Least Resistance. This Law means energy expenditure *is minimal, with nothing wasted. There is no friction or opposition. Everything is exceptionally efficient, effective, and effortless.* In other words, nature flows efficiently and effectively with the least effort. Nature demonstrates this principle with its masterful cohesion. From animals and water to weather and quantum physics-- our multiverse flows effortlessly. We are all influenced by this Law. However, humans choose to insert friction and resistance; it's nature's way of teaching us to evolve our spiritual side. The logic, perceptions, and intent we carry may well be the path of *__most__* resistance as we persist, unaware, in speaking this friction into our lives. What we resist will persist. Who among us is listening to their tone, their resonance? Who's paying attention to their expression or creating with beauty?

"Speech is literally a great magical force, and the adepts or white magicians, through knowledge of the forces and power of silence and of speech, can produce effects upon the physical plane" (Bailey, A Treatise on Cosmic Fire 981)

What Will You Learn?

In the past, our culture and educational system programmed us with this phrase, *"what you will learn,"* which still resides within our mass consciousness. If you search the internet, it is inundated with *'pay this, and this is what you'll learn'* websites. I've chosen this phrase to illustrate a point and to show you a different view, an alternative way to look at a word and its meaning. Many speak without much thought or understanding of the deeper essence within terms. Let's get real here; we've all been doing this since childhood. What are we honestly saying or creating? The word **learn** does not carry any specific belief system by itself. However, when we attach additional concepts or use *"learned"* in the past tense, this word can become immovable within a belief. Such as, "I have learned it this way or that way." or "I believe it this way." All beliefs are learned. The very nature of those responses denies the teaching or information; thus, it closes the door to further absorption, understanding, or modification.

"What *you will learn...*" vibrates with a command, judgment, and assumption. There's no way to know what an individual will accept, reject, use, apply, absorb, or integrate; these are all assumptions. Are they not? Due to past exposure to learning and life experience, individuals will learn at their level of ability. Other words, such as to *present, demonstrate, offer,* or *share,* will convey a more accurate representation of intent and reduce friction.

This phrase is *intended* to show the benefits or results a person could gain. So why not just say that? The course offers results in__, or This exercise demonstrates__. We can provide information on a topic or subject and hope others can grasp the idea for understanding, or we can mandate absorption- for testing.

If we apply logic, consider this: If someone offers a course or information, can anyone genuinely state with *full authority* to another person or the Universe what they will learn? Is this the arrogant tone we'd like to send to the heavens? What have you learned if you attend a class and cannot process the covered material? What are the possible feelings one might have--could they be disempowerment, disappointment, discouragement, or unfulfilled expectations? One little word choice changes the resonance. One little word has the power to ignite principles from the Third Cosmic Law of Attraction and Repulsion. It should be stated that all energy radiates from the Three Cosmic Laws of Synthesis, Economy, and Attraction and Repulsion. These laws will be explored in greater depth in the coming chapters as we uncover the harmony behind all creation.

What beliefs or words have shaped your experiences so far? Are they in harmony with the life you wish to create?

As you read, a gentle reminder is to keep an open mind and save some room for growth. We have all learned from different sources and perhaps have come to believe in a certain way. Although this field of study may be new to you, or you've worked with it and are even proficiently advanced, there are words of wisdom for anyone. You may find a missing puzzle piece or challenge your position on something that sets you free. In any capacity, please continue with your own research; we offer ways and means to help achieve peace, balance, and harmony in your lives.

There are many paths on this life journey; this is but one. As with the application of any of the spiritual logic presented, the benefits can be:

- Identify inadvertent errors that enslave us.

- Consciously speak from a seat of power by reducing friction.

- Qualify intentions and beliefs using checks and balances.

- Create efficiently and effectively with vibrational energy.

- Recognize how energy creates our realities.

A Universal Language

Speech through words, resonance, and efficiency means nothing until we combine them with a cohesive ingredient called energy. The Universe has a language, but what do we know of it? How can we thrive without being fluent in its customs or behavior? It's sufficient to say we will continue to make mistakes until we understand. Envision yourself on an undiscovered island, and you do not know the culture or language of the people. Perhaps you could convey that you're hungry, cold, or tired, but that would be about it. You might survive but won't thrive until you understand their ways. The Universe listens, answers, and delivers results to us all. Within these pages, you will find out how it is done effectively.

We'll include how to align and resonate within Laws through speech, focused intent, and belief systems. Suggestions are given to the meaning in the etheric realm for some common everyday words and their antidote. Additionally, you will be presented with the spiritual/etheric logic of laws through examples of friction from daily events. If there is no awareness of abrasion, how can we stop or alter it? Why should we care?

When combined with beliefs, the Governance of Law and its Principles act as a system of checks and balances, guiding our actions and choices. Any esoteric or metaphysical Laws stated are condensed

8

from many different sources. For example, volumes could be written on one Cosmic or Universal Law. This condensed form was done to simplify an understanding of their action and flow, cohesively aligned and constructed for what we bring forward. Therefore, no one should consider the information on any law presented complete or comprehensive in this work.

Friendly Disclaimer: Words, beliefs, and intent carry meaning. They also include vibration, rhythm, and frequency; we can choose what we prefer. It is a matter of allowance, conscious awareness, and spiritual development that will define the outcome for your desired results. We offer only information. If your perspective is from a scientific, philosophical, or spiritual background, know we cannot prove anything. Applying the principles presented can alter previous results you've received, thus perhaps your proof. Take from it what you will. The concepts of energy we offer are universal.

Wrap Up

As we reflect on these teachings, remember that the principles introduced here are only the beginning of our journey. Each step forward will deepen our understanding of the laws and their transformative power. This chapter has offered a glimpse into the power of words, intent, and Universal Laws. As we step forward together, may you realize that you are both the creator and the instrument of harmony in your life. Remember, your perception is your only limitation. Let this journey guide you to align with the Silent Code of Life and manifest a reality imbued with purpose and peace.

Over all, this is much more than a guidebook—it's a roadmap for navigating life with clarity, grace, and purpose. The chapters speak directly to readers wherever they are, whether they're stepping onto this path for the first time or are already exploring it. Tuning into energy and understanding Universal Principles reinforces the overarching goal of helping humanity reconnect with its essence and find harmony.

So, what is energy, you ask? It's the access and delivery system from the multiverse. Stay tuned.

Key Points: A Path

- Words and intent create the foundation of your reality.

- The three Cosmic Laws offer a framework for harmony and balance.

- Perception is your only limitation; shift your view to shift your reality.

CHAPTER TWO

ENERGY FLOWS

Ayla's Laugh

*I*t was one of those marvelous laid-back days, mid-afternoon. Shadow Fox and I were sitting in the living room, deliciously obtuse to the cares of the world. The day was ours to savor, relax, and listen to the dulcet tones of Vivaldi's violin concerto in D minor, floating in the air, softly, comforting. Ahhh, so lovely.

Then, oh, then – wow!!! The skies cracked, the earth split, and the wind howled. Ayla, whom we called Sweet Thunder, came rushing down the stairs, spewing vitriolic verbal curses. The air exploded with her fevered rhetoric. This was the thunder without the sweet. I never knew a human voice could be so loud, nor so harsh, or that angry. Her eyes were even shouting, flashing with intense distress and dismay, 'My sister...took my makeup, my favorite shirt, my...I will tear her room apart, shave her head, and break every bone in her body...I have to get to work...ohh, that little...'

Well, weren't we surprised! Our sweet Ayla...where has she gone? Shadow Fox and I sat on the couch in astonished disbelief. So this, our Sweet Thunder, being vile and obstreperous, burning the very oxygen out of the air.

Then, for all of three seconds, she was silent. She looked at her parental units and saw the look on our faces of stupefied disbelief and concern. Ahh, then the laughter began. She plopped down on the stairs with a roar of belly laughs, bringing tears in a profound recognition of how she looked and acted. The absurdity of the situation, how we looked, so aghast and befuddled, how she had appeared with her hair flying, eyes blazing. Well, the sun came out, and together, we shared a laugh; a more profound understanding was at hand, and Sweet Thunder was back.

Ayla discovered a valuable asset: laughter. This was a lesson and tool she would use for the rest of her life. As for her sister...well, let's say a justifiable recourse was administered.

As a result of the principles we emphasized, our children had the benefit of identifying energy and its nuances early, so it was not a foreign language to them. They knew life would always present opportunities to explore. Ayla especially enjoyed applying her knowledge and expanding her capabilities through energy. As a language, they could become proficient in its application once they understood the fundamentals.

Ayla's experience reveals that awareness of energy can transform our lives. By observing our emotions and finding humor in their intensity, we can restore balance. The Universe speaks in energy; moments like these teach us to listen and respond in harmony. At this time, Ayla was experiencing the nuances and recognized a 'big elephant in the room' that was fundamental; its name was energy, and she ran smack into it. Let us unveil what seems so elusive.

Finding Common Ground

In essence, energy is the Cosmic Multi-dimensional Universal language of all that exists. Whether it is an object, innate raw material, living organism, thoughts, or emotions, all are influenced by and through energy. This force can be subtle, vibrant, or robust. Any interplay or exchange we have, such as the smell of grass being cut, admiring the beauty of autumn colors, or a gentle smile between strangers, is the language of the Universe. These signs and symbols are reminders that help us navigate life and stay in the flow of balance.

Building upon this understanding that everything is made of energy. Albert Einstein knew that, eventually, science would have to explore a metaphysical dimension to realize its full potential. When esoteric or metaphysical perceptions are interwoven, doors to the unknown open, and mysteries dissolve. By becoming aware of and accessing this delivery system, we can reclaim our authority to self-govern and transform our lives with balance and harmony.

We can avoid errors that create discord by becoming aware of this creative force and considering a couple of Laws to form a foundation to move forward. Can we find common ground within an esoteric, metaphysical perception related to the Laws of Thermodynamics, Quantum Physics, or Quantum Mechanics? And could this field of science reveal a theory of human consciousness known to the ancient sages? Is there more to discover in a realm unseen that affects our daily lives? Such questions lead us to explore what lies beyond the tangible world-- this logical, intelligent force is energy.

At times, energy is referenced in conversations, such as raising the planet's frequency, something that resonates with us, or having good vibes. Even statements like, "The energy in the room was so thick, you could cut it with a knife," are often elusive fillers. Words people use to describe something they vaguely sense but can't delineate. These phrases are sometimes thrown around casually, yet they point to a deeper awareness rarely explored or understood.

Unfortunately, many people get stuck with unintended and undesired results by not acknowledging or observing the intelligent force surrounding them, becoming numb to its presence. Yet, within this numbness lies an opportunity—a moment to awaken to the profound connection energy offers, bridging life's seen and unseen dimensions. So, what is this language? What is the interplay between us and this force, and how can it serve us?

This raises the question: How does energy affect and influence us daily, and how can we work with it? The good news is that no one requires a degree in science to understand it. We can recognize these elements with different perceptions, opening a doorway to greater awareness and alignment. This chapter offers concepts to begin that exploration and step into the flow. Please take your time with the rest of this chapter. The goal is not to reach the last page but to contemplate the process and essence.

Special Note: Chapter Two stands apart from the rest of the book. While it serves as both a foundational and reference chapter, introducing the principles and components essential for understanding the Universal Language, the remaining chapters expand on these concepts in more approachable and practical ways. Readers are welcome to revisit this chapter to reflect on these teachings and deepen their understanding.

Let's begin with the metaphysical, esoteric activity and meaning of energy.

The Law of Energy

It is an ambient, intelligent force that carries information, influencing and directing through vibration, rhythm, and frequency. It acts as the universal access and delivery system, enabling all things—seen or unseen—to be defined through expansion and contraction. At its essence, energy is spirit or life, and spirit or life is energy, holding the foundation of authentic power.

Energy relates to motion and action, encompassing magnetic, electrical, gravitational, and active intelligence. It cannot be extinguished, only transformed. As a neutral force, energy is neither inherently positive nor negative; its qualification by thoughts, words, and actions determines its ultimate influence. Focused Force relies on active intelligence to determine the direction, such as in healing.

Qualifying Energy

By consciously directing energy cohesively with Universal Principles, we align our thoughts with actions, words, and deeds, fostering harmony and balance. In other words, qualifying energy enables us to transmute it into forms that serve our highest purpose. Transmutation is that endeavor that allows us to master and control our energy, transforming our lives.

Energy's Above, Below and Within

As we explore the nuances of energy, let us see how its presence connects us from above, grounds us below, and flows within—serving as a guide to alignment and harmony. Energy flows through the Cosmic, physical, and inner realms, interweaving what is above, below, and within. These cues help us align with this Universal Flow.

- **Governing Laws:** Aligns with the Cosmic Law of Construction, including the Laws of Synthesis, Economy, and Attraction & Repulsion, governing harmonious creation.

- **Above:** Energy flows in the stars, a rhythm guiding all life—are you in tune?

- **Below:** The earth grounds us in nature's cycles—do you feel its steadiness?

- **Within:** Your breath and emotions reveal energy's presence—what are you resisting?

- **Simple Reminders:** When energy is applied correctly--you're in the flow.

Parallels & Positions

Much in the world goes unrecognized as an energy source influencing all of us. If everything is composed of energy, it includes our thoughts, aspirations, and even the circumstances that shape our lives. The following categories are often overlooked: scientific, mental health, wellness, spiritual, biblical teachings, color, and even time. Yet, they profoundly influence our resonance and sense of harmony.

Each of these categories can be sectioned into three positions. For example, sound, light, and matter are typical terms used with energy. Yet, these three terms can be positioned from resonance into vibration, rhythm, and frequency. The same applies to the other categories. Within Natural Law, water is expressed as a solid, liquid, gas, or vapor. In mental health, our daily exchanges manifest as thoughts, intentions, and emotions. We can consider the alignment of mind, body, and spirit for wellness. Within the Christ Consciousness, we see the declaration: 'I AM' the Way, the Light, and the Life. The biblical parable of planting seeds references the soil or heart. Thus, it illustrates three positions: path, rocks, and thorns, encouraging us to seek fertile ground. Our primary colors, red, blue, and yellow, will also find a placement in this framework.

Another illustration is time, expressed as past, present, or future, which can be framed or measured by our thoughts. Each example will be shown in its position relative to vibration, rhythm, and frequency to help you discern distinctions. After each law's description, these categories will be presented in a neatly organized box for your reference. An exception is made for Energy as a Totality, which will be explored at the end of this chapter.

Energy's Three Fundamental Components

When studying a foreign language, beginners start with pleasantries like "Excuse me, Thank you, and Goodbye." We will begin the same way with this Universal Language but with a vast difference. As we become aware of these components, which are not elusive fillers, they will allow us to engage in conversation far beyond pleasantries.

Within the Laws of Energy exist vibration, rhythm, and frequency—fundamental components resonating across multidimensional realms. These three elements are interwoven, intertwined, and interdependent, working as a cohesive cluster that defines how energy operates universally. Identifying these energy components and their activity can reduce friction within our lives. Furthermore, results can manifest efficiently because these elements become *principles* that resonate from all Cosmic, Universal/Solar, Natural, and Spiritual Laws. These three components or elements are the trinity that we all innately sense. This is why prominent religions incorporate some form of a trinity in their specific focus. However, to my knowledge, religious leaders have yet to address why this universal structure is so prominent. Quite simply, it reflects the three Cosmic Laws that govern energy and existence.

We can see these powerful components interact with our innate intuitive nature every day, whether through the rhythm of our breath, the vibration of our words, or the frequency of our emotions. These elements shape how we experience and influence the world around us. This interplay is so fundamental that it even appears in modern practices, such as marketing, where three descriptive words are used to enhance a message. In our personal lives, we rely on three-word phrases to convey concepts, ideas, or issues, such as I love you, I miss you, or please come home.

The Law of Vibration

Governing the speed at which energy flows, shaping and maintaining stability. This law directs the expansion and contraction of energy, which are essential for harmonic balance. All matter and energy are in constant motion, vibrating at varying speeds. As the gateway to creation, this law determines the swiftness of delivery based on the energy we qualify. To harness its power, we must cultivate equilibrium, balancing our thoughts and actions with poise. (An easy reminder for vibration is speed.)

Vibrational categories are as follows:

Vibrational Parallels and Positions:

Wellness: Mind, **Body** & Spirit. (Physical)   The Breath: **Inhale**

Mental Health: **Thoughts**. Thoughts shape perception and stability.

Consciousness: **Unconsciousness** – the automatic, instinctual level of awareness, where actions and reactions are habitual and unexamined.

Scientific Energy: **Matter** or particles. Water: **solid**
Primary Color: Red

The 'I AM': Resonates as **The Way—Body**.
Parable soil/heart: Aligns with **The Path**, where energy begins to direct itself but lacks full reception. (**Ears to hear, yet deaf.**)

Time Positional: **Past** reflecting the stored energy of all that has come before. If our **thoughts** are focused primarily on the past, it can create feelings of **depression**.

(Cosmic Law of Attraction & Repulsion governs motion & stability)

Let's examine this Law's activity and how to work with it. All things have a vibrational motion by contracting and expanding. The lower vibrations are sensed as still, heard as soundless, and felt as density. Low, dense, and slower vibrational energies cannot enter higher vibrational regions unless they accelerate to match that faster speed.

Conversely, the higher, more rapid vibrations can enter the lower, thus, by default, raising that vibration. This process cannot be seen, heard, or felt within our third-dimensional reality until an expanded consciousness evolves. (–see frequency.) Have you ever entered a house or a building, and your spidey senses were activated by the eeriness or to be careful around a particular person? These are vibrations influencing our fight-or-flight responses. That intuitive spidey feeling should be listened to and respected.

Within the Law of Vibration, we have three choices as a qualifier. We can *contract and lower the vibration, leave it alone to remain the same, or expand and raise it.* This is done through our actions, words, or deeds, a cluster or grouping of human impulses. These include thoughts, emotions, and beliefs. We can also assign or qualify these clusters as positive, neutral, or negative, which can become a judgment. Suppose we elevate or expand the vibrational rate. In that case, the results with the lower frequencies will be consumed, and the experience will change. The cluster of these human impulses we produce must undergo this transformation process. However, we are naturally inclined and impulsed to the higher frequencies of this process, but are we listening? When we remain at the lower-contracted, denser energy, we'll repeat life's lessons; thus, change in our circumstances will appear to us as slow in our physical realm.

There are many ways to raise or change our vibrational energy, such as prayer, meditation, music, or laughter; more will be shared throughout this book. Referring to our story, Ayla, our Sweet Thunder, tried to enter our peaceful space. She was fully energized with righteous anger, holding a solid density. This is why she did not fully enter the room. Ayla ran smack into a higher vibration. She found stability when she observed her 'parental units' stunned

19

by the vigor she threw all over the place. For her, she saw the humor, allowing her to regain her dignity and refocus her day. Laughter can be the best medicine and a great teacher.

Vibration Above, Below and Within

As with all energy, vibration flows through Cosmic, physical, and inner realms. Working with vibration and not against it helps us stay attuned to its dynamic motion, guiding us toward balance and creation.

- **Governing Laws:** Aligns with the Cosmic Law of Attraction and Repulsion, demonstrating the movement and flow of vibrational energy.

- **Above:** The universe listens to the vibration of our actions, words, and deeds—how could it be hearing you right now?

- **Below:** The results in your life—harmony or discord—mirror the thoughts you are sending out. What is the world reflecting back to you?

- **Within:** Are your thoughts resonating with the highest and best for all? What are you sending to the world, or how are you directing your energy?

- **Simple Reminder:** Vibration is speed or velocity.

Full stop: Rest, reflect, and contemplate on the material given before moving on.

Can you identify recurring thoughts that influence your vibration? How do these thoughts raise, lower, or stabilize your energy?

Cautionary Tale: Rigid Thinking. For those with black-or-white thinking, it blocks the flow of creative energy. Where could you embrace the gray to create more balance in your life?

Law of Harmony/Rhythm

This Law is a Universal Equilibrium. It governs the Multiverse's flowing order and rhythmic consistency, preserving precise balance. It ensures that energy remains in constant motion, inherently cyclic, and acts as a bridge between etheric and physical realms. This law underscores the Universe's precise timing, enabling the cohesion of various manifest actions and aligning them in a synchronized flow.

Harmony is the goal, rhythm is the cohesion, and activity is its pulse that sustains motion. This principle operates seamlessly across all dimensions of existence, anchoring the balance necessary for creation and transformation. (A simple reminder for Harmony is precise, flowing order. Rhythm is inertia or motion.) A few aspects for consideration as follows:

Aspects & Elements with Harmony

Please bear with us as we move forward because these elements are essential. Residing here is the secret sauce for manifesting that mostly goes unnoticed or unrecognized. Even Nicholas Tesla, when he described energy, did not mention rhythm or harmony. Yet, the Law and these aspects play a pivotal role in how we see, interact, or create our realities and how nature functions. There is an interwoven rhythm we unconsciously draw from and a power to behold when we consciously create from it. This energy is delivered with perfection unless we qualify otherwise. Harmony is the goal, and rhythm is the cohesion, with perfect timing. (The following three descriptions are not mathematical but written as a fraction, nor are we discussing music theory; they are for illustration purposes for common ground.)

Three Aspects

$$\frac{Harmony}{Rhythm} = \textbf{Resonance}$$

Middle C in music is used metaphorically as a bridge for equilibrium, and a rest delivers volumes of information within its silence. When there is silence and peace within the body, healing takes place. If we consider two different rhythms, they could be challenging to harmonize. Prime examples for everyday life can be reflected by fighting and conflicting beliefs or love and compassion. So, if our focus is always fighting, we'll receive more of the same; harmony, therefore, is misplaced. The essence here is that love embodies the truer Resonance.

Law of Correspondence: As above, so below.
Lord's Prayer: On earth as it is in heaven.   =   **Positions**

Positions reflect our alignment with spiritual or human logic, offering a way to correlate Universal Principles with personal experience. Choosing positions of above, below, or neither gives us this correlation. Which expression or position do you resonate with more? The Law of Correspondence or The Lord's Prayer. They are the same expression.

Spiritual Logic: Macro or within.
Human Logic: Micro or without. = **Consciousness/Awareness**

Spiritual Logic reflects the macro or inner world; human logic mirrors the micro or outer world of illusion. These dual realities shape how we create, either from 'fear and lack' or 'love and abundance.' Everything vibrates, yet to manifest harmoniously, there must be a consistency, a pulse that aligns our intent with the universal flow. This is an expression of awareness.

These fundamental aspects, such as resonance, positions, and conscious awareness, will be expanded upon throughout this book.

These are only a few micro references to the macro totality of a quantum synthesis. Look to **Harmony/Rhythm** as the #1 go-to when we experience pain, suffering, or blockages. It is easier to identify and offers us solutions.

Harmony/Rhythm's categories are as follows:

Harmony/Rhythm Parallels & Positions:

Wellness: **Mind**, Body & Spirit.   The Breath: **Pause/ Rest**
                  The **Mind** fosters coherence and adaptability.

Mental Health: **Emotions.** (Mental & Emotional bodies.)
Rhythm is experienced through emotions, which pulse and shift like waves.

Consciousness: **Subconsciousness** – the layer of awareness where stored patterns, emotions, and intuitive flow shape our interactions and responses.

Scientific Energy: **Sound**/waveforms   Water: **liquid**
Primary Color: Blue

The 'I AM': Resonates as **The Life-- Breath/Blood**.
Parable soil/heart: Aligns with **The Rocks**, which allow growth but lack
deep rooting. **(Heart open or closed)**

Time Positional: **Present.** Time aligns where rhythm allows for alignment
and synchronicity in life. If our **thoughts** are focused primarily on
the present, we step into **harmony and the flow** of now.

                  (Cosmic Law of Synthesis governs balance & flow)

Briefly, let's examine this law's activity and how to access it. The harmony of thought, mind, and consciousness with those around us and the harmony with spirit are required for healthy mental development and spiritual unfoldment. When all is in balance and harmony, power is generated correctly. Manifesting becomes a by-product of perfection and timing. Being out of tune will cause an imbalance, and there will be reduced energy and strength. This imbalance can create illness and dis-ease due to stuck, stale, and stagnant energy.

How can healing with light and sound energies become effective in a healing process? Simply, it reestablishes the Universal Equilibrium within our bodies. Humans can remain on this path of most resistance, unaware of this flowing order and position.

The Law of Harmony/Rhythm is a bridge that impulses innate *emotional responses* as triggers, a subtle push or nudge from the Universe. Our Multiverse will always send an impulse to get our attention. Many have felt an impetus or a driving force that stimulates us into action, like a nagging feeling to give someone a call for no apparent reason. Ayla was also impulsed to stop and not enter our space. Could she have bolted down the stairs and continued her rampage? Yes, of course. However, by not being numb and sensing the energy around her, she felt the impulse to stop. This transitory action allowed her to regain her composure.

Like our heartbeat, this energy represents a pulse; music can illustrate these emotional triggers. What song played when you first fell in love or when tragedy struck your life? Within a few notes of a song, our focus can shift to that experience. It triggers a remembrance. Such was the case when Ayla was dying in the hospital, and her sister played a song. If I hear that music, I am transported back in time to the hospital, reliving the highly charged emotions.

By the way, pain is how the Universe gets our attention, telling us that something is out of alignment or we are out of tune, thus not in harmony.

Harmony/Rhythm Above, Below and Within

Harmony and rhythm resonate through every realm and should be our first go-to when assessing anything. The multiverse listens, so become aware of how you're being heard. Here are simple clues to help you tune into their presence.

- **Governing Laws:** Aligns with the Law of Synthesis (Sound), uniting diverse elements into cohesive patterns. These are observed in waveforms and cycles within nature, such as tides or seasons.

- **Above:** Joy lifts us to a higher rhythm. Are you aware of how emotions elevate or block your flow?

- **Below:** The rhythmic crashing of waves or the steady hum of a river reflects nature's balance—can you feel its harmony grounding you?

- **Within:** Are your emotions stable, or are you easily thrown off balance? How do they create harmony or discord within you?

- **Simple Reminder:** Harmony is Universal Equilibrium— precise order in rhythm's motion. Our positions will influence us.

Full stop: Rest, reflect, and contemplate on the material given before moving on.

How do your overall emotions reflect harmony or disharmony within your life's rhythm?

Can you identify patterns that nudge you to tune in with this resonance?

Cautionary Tale: *Emotional Imbalance. Strong emotions like anger or fear disrupt life's harmony. Do you notice patterns of dissonance in your thoughts, actions, or intentions that call for balance?*

Law of Frequency

Frequency defines sound, radio, and light waves according to their cycles per second (Hertz, cps), representing a range of qualitative vibrations determined by the energy output of the source. Frequency can vary from low to high and shapes the energy's expression. It provides the basis for movement and rhythm, transforming idle speculation into a higher purpose. It's the inner stimulation of the astral or mental bodies moving from inertia into expression. This progression forms a driving force for involution (internal exploration) and evolution (external manifestation). This Law urges us to seek why we are here and what our purpose is.

In both the physical and etheric realms, frequency is a measure of sound and light, often abstractly referenced as differing 'octaves' of consciousness, mindfulness, and spirit. Its electromagnetic resonance stimulates a deep-seated desire for self-discovery, purpose, and growth. This dynamic encourages a shift into higher awareness, facilitating harmony and balance by aligning with Universal Laws.

Frequency's categories are as follows:

Frequency Parallels & Positions:

Wellness: Mind, Body & Spirit. (Astral & etheric bodies.)   The Breath: Exhale
  Spirit: The spirit transcends the limitations of the material realm.

Mental Health: Intentions
Through our intentions, frequency is experienced by intuition and perception, elevating awareness.

Consciousness: – Conscious the active state of awareness, choice, and expansion into greater understanding.

Scientific Energy: Light, photons.   Water: vapor or gas
(Frequency corresponds to light & intuition carrying information across time & space.)
Primary Color: Yellow

The 'I Am': Resonates as The Light- Spirit, illumination, guiding consciousness toward enlightenment.
Parable soil/heart: Aligns with The Thorns, which entangle energy, creating interference, preventing full reception. Sometimes growth is hindered by discomfort. Transformation requires movement out of our comfort zones. (Eyes to see, yet blind.)

Time Position: Future, symbolizing potential, evolution, and limitless possibility.
 If our thoughts are primarily focused on the future, it can create feelings of anxiety.

(Cosmic Law of Economy governs light & expansion)

A fundamental frequency activity is for and of expansion. Working with this energy is an exploration. Exploring a spiritual consciousness involves raising our vibrational patterns to a higher frequency by shifting our thinking and helping us co-create in our everyday lives without wasted energy. This is a form of mindfulness; love and laughter can be excellent modifiers for transformation. Frequency is responsible for our inner desire for exploration and questioning or can motivate us to change the status quo, getting us out of our comfort zone. At times, it can feel uncomfortable. Resolutely, we can gain control of the world around us in a simplified fashion without causing harm. The intensity and anticipation of new love can elevate us to a higher frequency.

Intuitively, we are impulsed to seek a deeper spiritual existence. Is this not so? Ayla realized this within a moment, knowing what power it held. A slower, angry, emotional state intending to cause harm to another would solve nothing. She shared this valuable tool of laughter with her friends, humorously referring to her experience as "The Parental Units." In addition, this expansion allows us to perceive and understand the knowledge and wisdom contained in the higher harmonic frequencies - the informational highway of energy. (A simple remembrance for Frequency is the highest and best for all without harm.)

Oh Sister

*O*ur *twenty-five-year-old daughter lay dying in the emergency room of an accidental overdose. In the wee hours of a September morn, we were escorted out of the E.R. They were moving her to a specialized Intensive Care Unit.*

We all stepped outside for some air, waiting for the nurses to settle Sweet Thunder in the I.C.U. and for our son and daughter-in-law to arrive. The atmosphere had a supercharged numbing energy, and every conceivable horrific emotion was in play. The five of us, my husband, youngest daughter Red Dawn Lighting, her boyfriend, and Sweet Thunder's husband, piled into our red Tahoe. The consequences infiltrated us with the realization of what would be, encompassing us with a very low, slow, and condensed vibration; everything seemed motionless.

Our children used music to communicate and keep in touch with each other, and this moment was no different. As we sat in the vehicle, a deafening silence prevailed. Red Dawn Lighting pierced the silence, "Mom, check out this song." It was **O' Sister** *by City and Colour. (Green) Its beautiful sound filled the air to a captive audience during a highly emotional state. There it was, this song now written in indelible ink upon my heart and coupling this memory with the death of our child and a sister.*

Grief is bad enough, but driving down the road, this song would suddenly come on the radio. Bam! I'm back at the E.R. parking lot, reliving an excruciating experience. I would not allow this song to be a cyclic trigger controlling me. I could change the frequency and emotional memory by shifting my focus. Sitting at the computer, I played this song repeatedly, letting the tears come until I couldn't cry anymore. I remained seated and continued the process, listening to **O' Sister** *repeatedly, reframing and softening the remembrance. Each time, giving as much love and compassion as possible to this song until I changed the resonance it held for me. I reclaimed my power by requalifying the energy surrounding this memory. This event and sitting in the Tahoe will always exist. But now I can listen* *without the emotional trigger and upheaval, allowing me to stay balanced and in harmony.*

This experience illustrates how powerful intent and reframing can transform even the most challenging memories. Reframing and softening memories through intent aligns with the Law of Frequency as it raises emotional resonance and transforms energetic patterns.

Frequency: Above, Below and Within

Frequency flows above, below, and within, aligning us with an expanded awareness of higher octaves. Energy speaks to us through understanding its precise activity resonating with our intent. Here are some clues.

- **Governing Laws:** Aligns with the Cosmic Law of Economy, which emphasizes efficiency and minimal energy expenditure. This Law impulses the discovery of who we are and influences our evolutionary path.

- **Above:** The universe listens to the vibration of our intentions—are they guiding your evolution toward your highest purpose?

- **Below:** The results in your life reflect your frequency. Are you aligned with growth and awareness or caught in discord?

- **Within:** Are your thoughts and emotions resonating with the highest and best for all? What intention are you sending out into the world?

- **Simple Reminder:** Frequency is the highest and best for all without causing harm.

Full stop: Rest, reflect, and contemplate on the material given before moving on.

Are you consciously aligning your intentions with the energy you wish to project?

What small shifts can you make to balance your thoughts, emotions, and actions?

Cautionary Tale: Analysis Paralysis. Overthinking or requiring constant validation disrupts energy flow, leaving intentions stagnant. Are you caught in a loop of doubt or indecision that prevents you from aligning with higher frequencies?

Interwoven Nature of Energy

A key to life is recognizing how to integrate these energies, thus changing the motion/rhythm by creating an orderly, harmonious flow within your life. As with any situation, focusing on one element, such as vibration, can create an imbalance within our lives. Remember, these components are interwoven, intertwined, and interdependent with equal and precise measurements. The Universe will get our attention through pain and suffering merely to get us to recognize the other aspects of energy. Perhaps it impulses us to seek a higher frequency as a path to resolution or the bridge of equilibrium. It is ever the involution and evolution. The harmony connects all the worlds of manifestation and includes Natural Laws.

The diagrams below are expressions to find meaning with Frequency in our spiritual growth and development. This component seems more elusive and abstract than the others. Consider frequency as our consciousness or a moral code of conduct, which must at some point align with laws, as above, so below. It is the constant impulse for Love, Oneness, and our evolution as a species.

Spiritual Pattern of Growth or Development

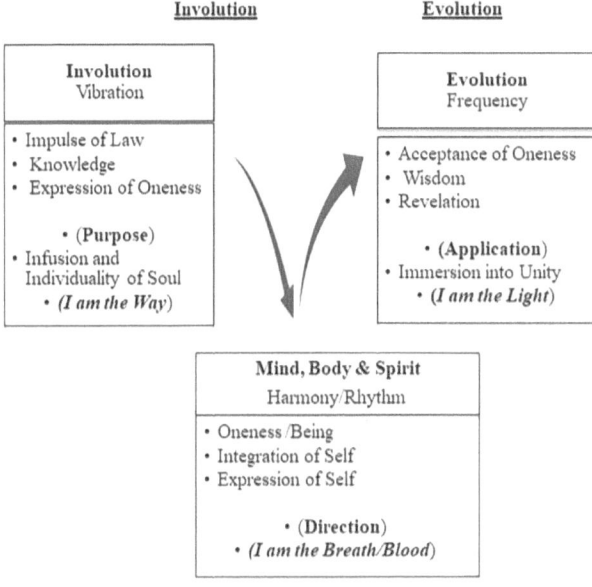

This second diagram is a makeshift neutrality gauge to show the placement of vibration, harmony/rhythm, and frequency.

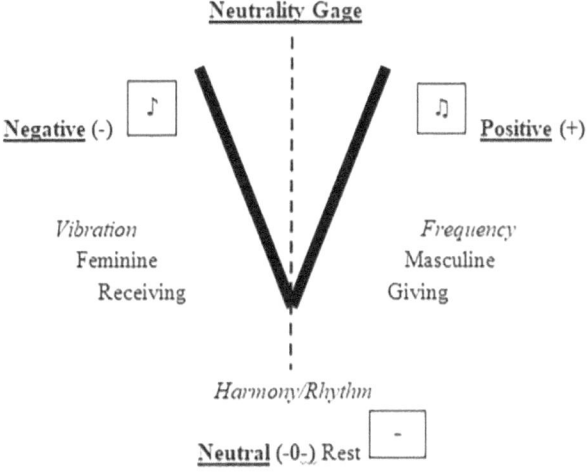

Energy's Totality

Having explored the components and laws of energy, let us now bring these ideas together to consider energy's totality—how vibration, rhythm, and frequency align to create harmony and transformation in our lives. In the final breakdown, let us reiterate the importance of recognizing energy as a language. Equal awareness of vibration, rhythm, and frequency brings balance. When we act on this awareness, harmony flows, opening up endless possibilities. Just as Ayla's laughter helped transmute dense energy into light, these principles offer tools to raise our vibration and align with the universal flow.

The categories regarding Energy as a Totality, with its parallels, can be expressed as follows:

Energy's Totality Parallels & Positions:

Wellness: When Mind, Body, & Spirit are **equalized**, all function cohesively, creating **wholeness**, transformation and manifestation. It is **The Breath of Life**.

Consciousness: **Superconsciousness** – The highest state of awareness, where all aspects of energy are synthesized into **Divine Understanding**. Consciousness is our **Seat of Power** for co-creation, aligning with universal flow and intent.

Energy Components: Vibration, Harmony/Rhythm and Frequency, when equalized and balanced, we access the **Cosmic Flow**.

'I AM': Resonates as, **The All—Infinite Potential**, encompassing all expressions of creation.

Parable Soil: When our heart, ears and eyes are **open**, we have **fertile ground** to create abundant blessings within our lives.

Color: **White**, representing the totality of energy and information. When refracted through a prism, it reveals the **Rainbow**, symbolizing the full spectrum of creation.

Laws: When we are **in tune**, manifesting can become a **by-product**.

(The Laws of Construction govern creation, transformation & manifesting.)

Please remember none of the descriptions for energy have to be committed to memory. Instead, allow the concepts to settle naturally as you begin to notice how they operate in your life. The essence of energy lies in its experience—not its definition. By simply observing and tuning into the resonance of your intentions, you'll find the alignment begins to take root effortlessly.

We can all sense their existence. Innately, we recognize when patterns repeat in our lives. These repetitions are opportunities for you to evaluate which energy components or categories might be missing or overlooked. Consider whether mind, body, or spirit could be misplaced? We are all creators, perhaps more potent than our minds can conceive. We create every moment, consciously or unconsciously, through our thoughts, feelings, and words. Energy and its Governing Laws surround us; there is no escape from this reality. My life's lessons are strewn with indelicate mishaps, but they've shown me how to align more gracefully.

Cosmic Laws

Energy is not random; it moves according to principles that shape all existence. The Cosmic Laws—Synthesis, Economy, and Attraction/Repulsion—govern how energy manifests. They were mentioned along with the Laws of Construction within parallels and positions. We will explore these more deeply later, but for now, simply recognizing their presence helps us align with the greater flow. For understanding these Laws is not required at this stage; awareness of their existence is sufficient.

Wrap Up

As we conclude this chapter, take with you the understanding that energy, in its totality, is both our guide and our mirror. Through alignment with its principles, we unlock the path to balance, growth, and harmony. As we reflect on the energy flow, we see how its totality—vibration, rhythm, and frequency—brings balance and harmony. This understanding sets the stage for embracing the Cosmic Laws and aligning with the Silent Code of Life.

The physical energy chart below shows that results have different timeframes in the etheric. This difference is due to physical matter, friction, and awareness. If there is any discord in your life, it's friction, plain and simple. When we experience disharmony, conflict, or upheaval in any aspect or area of our lives, we are not aligned with energy or its Laws; friction and discord thrive.

The Energy Flow Chart: *Energy is Always in motion.*

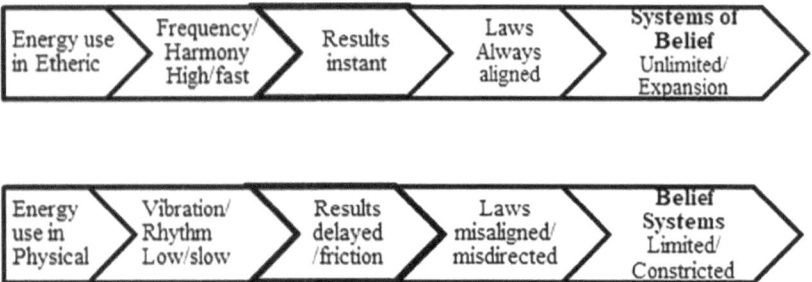

This flow chart shows that the etheric results are instantaneous because Laws are always aligned. In contrast, results are delayed in the physical world due to friction, misalignment, or misqualified energy. I aim to help bridge this gap and show you how to get 'in tune' with these laws.

Energy's Totality represents the harmonious balance of vibration, rhythm, and frequency. These elements, when aligned, create fertile ground for manifestation and growth. Together, they form the silent code of life, where each component interweaves with the others to produce a unified flow of energy that shapes our reality.

Vibration is the speed and motion of energy, rhythm provides balance and flow, and frequency defines the resonance that directs expression. When these elements are understood and aligned, they become the guiding principles of all energy interactions, leading to balance, healing, and harmony.

Moving forward, for easier reading, I will not prefix vibration, frequency, or harmony as "Law." However, these Laws of Energy are like our immune system—always active and quietly working, whether we are aware of it or not. Laws are always working in the background.

The next chapter will focus on how these principles manifest in the natural world and within ourselves. Observing nature and reflecting on our perceptions can uncover profound truths about our position within the Universal flow. The journey continues as we move from understanding energy's components to applying them, allowing us to navigate life with greater clarity and purpose.

Key Points: Energy as a Universal Language

- Energy is the language of the Multiverse: Understanding its activity allows us to step into its flow.

- Equally balanced, each component enhances our full potential to guide and transform our lives.

- Consider comparing categories such as mind, body, and spirit with vibration, rhythm, and frequency. Is one more dominant than the other in your life? Or are your thoughts focused more on the past or worried about the future?

- Rhythm is the easiest component of the three to distinguish. We innately know when we are out of balance.

- Each energy component will become a Governing Principle for all laws, enhancing their specific function or focus.

CHAPTER THREE
A PREMISE

Our Rt. 224

*S*ome years ago, before smartphones or Google Maps were comm onplace, my husband, Lee Two Hawks, and I were to attend an event in Ohio. We were fully prepared with the address and a physical paper map, the kind that never seemed to fold back to its original position. He was driving, and I was to give directions. Nothing extraordinary with this setup, or was there? I live with dyslexia. I have found ways to become proficient at negating some of its effects, so we continued.

We were driving south on our designated route. We continued driving and driving and driving some more when Lee Two Hawks awoke from his slumberous thoughts and asked how much further? In my haste to answer, I told him we were looking for Rt. 422, which should be near. It would be in about five minutes or so. Well, we could not find Rt. 422. We turned around just before a viaduct and headed back toward a pond we *had passed, but there was still no Rt.422. We changed direction again, southward bound, driving around this beautiful pond for the third time.*

By now, Lee Two Hawks' voice started to have a slight edge. My face was surrounded and buried in this large accordion map. I was turning it this way and that way so he would know I was really, actively looking. Unbeknownst to me, this activity solidified that I had no idea what I was doing. I was the navigator, after all, subsequently checking and re-checking. I knew we were not lost. It was the right road. It was our location in question.

As confidence dwindled in my map-reading abilities, it started to rain. Lee Two Hawks suggested we pull under this viaduct to look at the map. The very same bridge we saw before we turned around. As he slowed down to pull over, we simultaneously looked up at the road above and saw a small green sign on the overpass that read Rt.224. Did I mention it was small?

My husband immediately takes a deep breath and asks, "Sweetheart, is that Route number we are looking for 422 or 224? I noticed a little amusement in his voice and replied, "Yeah, it's Rt. 224 ". Well, to my credit, Rt. 422 crosses the highway, about sixty miles further south. We were only a few miles from our original position when we began this drama. He said sweetly, "What a lovely large pond. Wasn't it? Are we ready to go?" I estimate it was more like a small lake, but that's beside the point. A half-hour later, we arrived safely at our destination. Phew! We were grateful for those few minutes to calm our thoughts and settle our energy.

This experience is one we share for the humor. Sometimes, we refer to the 224 as a personal reminder that perhaps we're too obtuse or a reevaluation might be in order. However, the scope of this experience carries a much deeper meaning. Neither one of us blamed the other for the circumstances we created. Our illusion was that we, quite possibly, were lost. Lee Two Hawks was driving and decided to reevaluate our position based on my ability to confuse letters and numbers. My error was that he was right.

It wasn't until we stopped and looked up that we found our answer.

The thrust within this body of work is to encourage you to stop, look up, and rethink what you are sending forth. We create the situations we find ourselves in, one way or another. The intent is to get you to see the illusions, which reveal themselves through the energy of Laws. The illusion is that we have no control over the events that manifest in our lives. It is how we think and react to any situation. If we never look up, the sky and the heavens will remain but strangers. The catch '22' or, in this case, the 224, is that it is sometimes necessary to reevaluate our position; our perspective is to see a larger picture. An expanded view is our navigation, and the destination is within.

Laws are the Governance, its Principles are the guidelines, and Energy is the access/ delivery system. If you are open to receiving differing views, your power comes to light, with the authority to bring it forth with wisdom. All answers are within you.

Every situation we find ourselves in can be seen through the lens of kindness and compassion. Why or how this can be done is quickly answered by resonance. Both of these words flow harmoniously with all laws. The easiest way to realize and experience this is to utilize the skill of becoming the observer.

Let's observe what happened during our trip from a perception of energy. A few errors occurred. Point blank, neither stopped long enough to assess our environment, and we allowed an expectation to slip in. Undeniably, we expected an obvious road sign on a pole, yet missed the observable pond. Unfortunately, what is not seen is often right in front of you. No roads were going over a body of water. We missed all the signs, literally.

Neither of us expressed what we were thinking, being lost or not. Instead, we became concerned about being late, which creates feelings of anxiety that only feed into the lower frequencies. Talk about stirring up nasty energy. We were out of balance, and our rhythm was off. Instead, we should have brought our attention to the present moment. We were fine. We lost sight of the larger picture.

How many people could slip into anger, fighting, doling out accusations, or engaging in road rage when events such as ours happen? What a scary thought for a mild irritation. So many are quickly sucked into a lower vibrational field and don't recognize it as it is happening. This lower energy we experienced was recognized and felt. Yet, we did not fully engage in it.

There were areas where we remained grounded and aligned regarding Laws. In doing so, neither spoke sharply to the other nor placed blame. We did not jeopardize our relationship by causing harm to each other. It may have been a frustrating development we created, but we never lost sight of our love.

The moment we saw the road sign above, we recognized our erroneous thoughts and actions in this unguarded moment; shit happens, then you move on. So we released the built-up tensions, giving this event no opportunity to ruin our day.

Spirit or the Universe will use every opportunity to shift our awareness and help us step into a more harmonious frequency. This has everything to do with the Law of Economy. This moment of looking up symbolizes the essence of spiritual logic—shifting our perspective to see from a higher vantage point. This experience is not merely a navigation story; it establishes a premise for understanding how shifting perspectives allow us to see beyond the immediate—much like the essence of spiritual logic itself.

Spiritual Logic: *is a framework for understanding and interpreting life through the lens of Universal Laws and the etheric realm.*

Unlike human logic, which is grounded in duality and imperfection, Spiritual Logic reflects universal energy's absolute precision and perfection. It aligns thought, intention, and action from higher vibrational principles, enabling harmony, balance, and resonance. Spiritual logic invites individuals to perceive beyond physical limitations, fostering a connection to the oneness of creation.

The World Around Us

As we move forward, this chapter will be in two sections, with key points at the end of each section. The first is to become aware of how we think by positioning ourselves more in tune with nature. If we pay attention, nature gently guides us to remain balanced. The second section deals with speech. Words are potent, and understanding how to speak things into existence becomes a key.

If something is out of balance, look to the Universal Equalizer of Rhythm. Its Harmony will reveal a solution through resonance, position, or awareness. With this premise in mind, let us explore how spiritual logic operates from the macrocosmic level—revealing patterns, opposites, and the guiding laws of the universe.

Section A

Spiritual Logic From The Universe

The following are suggestions to help stop the enslavement or imprisonment we inherently know and feel. Finding our more authentic-self unconsciously shifts our awareness into the etheric, where harmony and balance reside.

Could you find value in becoming free from compulsive behaviors, such as living with fear and worry or being in survival mode? What if you could approach challenges in your life differently? Could we step away from those imprisoned thoughts we send out, only for them to return to us? It starts by perceiving or sensing the world around us, and if you choose to do this, perhaps this time, you'll choose to align and be in tune with nature. All of nature follows laws and gently reminds us to remain in its flow.

Positions

Our human logic or perceptions are not the same logic, point of view, or resonance the universe supplies. Spiritual Logic can be expressed through the resonance of words and the Yin and Yang of opposites. As a position, Spiritual or etheric logic can also be conveyed through the progression of our Human Life Cycle. For example, how do **we interpret** the birth of a child? We view this as a New Life. Formally, we understand that Life progresses.

We are born. We have experiences/learn. Then we die.

However, we also have a Spiritual Life Cycle, interpreted as a New Opportunity with a completely different view.

Life cycles are often perceived linearly—birth, life, death—but this perspective limits our understanding. From a higher spiritual view, these cycles are seen not as beginnings or ends but as transitions, much like moving from one room to another in the same house. What we call "birth" in the physical world is perceived as a "death" from the spiritual plane, a descent into physical form and limitation. This dual perspective reveals the richness of our existence and the importance of alignment.

To illustrate, consider the caterpillar's transformation into a butterfly. The chrysalis may seem like the end of its journey to the earthbound caterpillar. But from above, it is seen as the butterfly's true beginning. This duality—how life appears from above versus below—reminds us that harmony is achieved by recognizing both perspectives. By aligning with this higher understanding, we reduce the friction of life and embrace its natural rhythms. This 180-degree intangible perspective is vital to understanding our spiritual cycles, and in one way, it can be expressed as follows:

Life Cycle Progression Chart

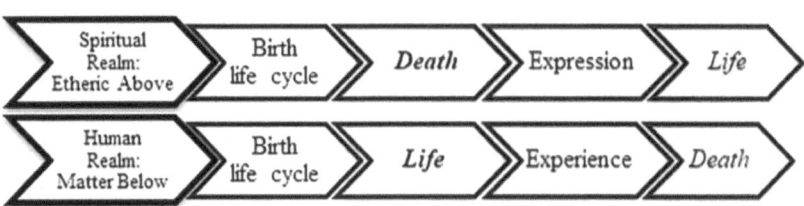

If you notice, the spiritual realm is the exact opposite progression of that in the physical realm regarding birth; it is a 180-degree perception or concept. My Master Guide Keegane once told me, "You (humanity) view birth as a new life; we see it as a death. This opposite concept is because souls waiting to be born vibrate so fast in 'heaven' or the etheric realm; it is considered death to slow their vibrational rate down. Reducing the speed required to enter the constrictive, imprisoned physical body of matter is painful. We choose this painful experience of birth for the opportunity to express our essence for who we truly are. These souls ready to be born are sacrificing their freedom to find expression in your physical world." (Keegane) Each one of us went through this process as we were born.

My guide's perception supports the Laws of Energy and Laws as a totality. Nothing stated is in violation. Furthermore, its view supports the involution/evolution with frequency. In this case, shifting our point of view changes our position. Thus, we move our awareness into a more harmonious rhythm from above.

Our ability to find expression is, at our very core, our essence, which drives us to explore. Innately, the frequency of our spirit is love and is our utmost expression. However, most of us are stuck within the constraints of our experiences and perceived limitations here on the Earth plane. Accessing this potent authenticity is a primary key to what's conveyed as your power comes to light, with the authority to bring it forth.

The ability to have your 'quality' resonate outward is equivalent to the sound waves of the tree. There is a principle known as sympathetic resonance or sympathetic vibration. It is also known as a harmonic phenomenon, where two similar tuning forks will respond or resonate with the vibrations of a harmonic likeness. We can physically experience this same principle as empathy. When we experience empathy, we match that vibrational frequency for a short time. The idea is to be in harmony as we experience life and realize our potency. Harmony and balance will occur when we vibrate with the Cosmic and Universal Laws, thus empathizing with the

Multiverse. This Silent Code of Life is a harmonic resonance that requires a basic grasp of the Universe's spiritual logic. (-See Glossary)

Observing Nature

Apologies if we triggered a belief system within you. If we ruffled some feathers, please know everything is working perfectly. Perhaps this triggering feeling can become a gauge for you. It's simply a positional understanding. Please note that for those who may have difficulty accepting the previous explanation of life cycles, this awareness is just a 180-degree concept. Opposites reflect a universal balance to which nature will respond, and the quality signifies this balance. We cannot have one without the other. The Law of Harmony/Rhythm can validate this.

Other natural illustrations are of our physical bodies concerning opposites or signs of duality. We may not be aware, but our eyesight initially registers on the retina upside down until the brain transforms the image. Another example is the yin/yang concept expressed in our human form by being self-centered in contrast with a Centered-Self. (We all find ways to express ourselves.) Another view seen from the human or physical world of energy is that when we speak, it is mainly said with imperfection. However, everything is perfect in the higher frequencies of the etheric or spiritual realm. In this context, perfection and precision are interchangeable, each reflecting harmony and exactness within these higher frequencies. Feel free to substitute perfection with precision. Are we that reflection, or are we the source? Imperfection or Perfection is something to think about. We can create from fear or love.

Opposites in nature

Nature calls out to us, enticing or reminding us to pay attention and establish a bird's eye view. Many signs are given every day to remind us to change our point of view and our perception. If you seek, nature answers. A fascinating example is that we can witness this 180^0 effect by observing a large body of water during inclement weather. If we pay attention, we can see the color of a dark stormy gray sky reflected with a lighter gray hue of the water. For a pale blue sky, it's dark blue water. As for the concept of color, it has opposite hues. The concept of birth is opposite views.

Speaking of bodies of water, in our Rt.224 episode, Lee Two Hawks shifted his position when he stated, "What a lovely large pond." This signaled his gratitude for nature, and the drama was over.

One last point

It is important to note that 'The light' recognizes no opposite or opposition; this is the most profound 'Truth' of perfection from the highest perspective in Cosmic Law. It becomes a cohesion, not an opposition. Therefore, anything that is not of 'The Light' is consumed by it. Perhaps you've heard this referenced in church or other studies. It resonates with the Law of Vibration. If no limitations were integrated into our beliefs, we would be free from all constraints. Without limitation, the speed at which we manifest quickens exponentially. Unfortunately, this knowledge has remained elusive in humanity's consciousness, and very few will apply this wisdom in their daily lives. If we realized light carries no opposition, in an expanded view, we would no longer have illnesses, agony, war, or discord; these are human creations.

In tangible ways, we can experience and validate this wisdom from the Universe in our physical world. Please consider, as we open a door from a lighted room to a darkened room. Does darkness enter, or does light flood in? Light's energy is active. Darkness is passive energy. This is the reason it recedes from the light.

We use opposites within Natural Law to express abstract ideas, raising our vibrational energy or our conscious awareness. Abstract and intangible concepts are simpler to disclose when using a tangible lens. By living in this physical world of duality, the goal is to access the spiritual world of Oneness. Opposites are only a building block for understanding and leading onward and upward. Our position or the 180^0 viewpoint helps create alignment in our lives. Have you noticed that the Law of Harmony/Rhythm and its aspects are interwoven throughout this chapter? (-Resonance, positions, and awareness.) Miracles happen when we see as the angels do.

Having explored some of the foundational principles of spiritual logic, as compared with nature, we now turn to its practical application—how aligning with energy's resonance can reduce friction and discord in our lives. Just as looking up provided clarity and direction on Rt. 224, embracing Spiritual Logic offers clarity in navigating life.

Key Points

- Observing natural patterns helps us align with universal principles, reducing friction and achieving balance.

- Nature and the universe invite us to view life, death, and existence from an etheric perspective, challenging human logic.

- Nature follows all Laws.

Section B

Logic's Application

Reduce Friction through Resonance

Let's consider how the logic of energy aligns with natural patterns. When we resist the flow, we create tension and obstacles. For example, friction occurs when opposing forces meet, but we can reduce this resistance by adjusting our perspective and intent. Aligning our thoughts and actions with the universal flow transforms struggle into synchronicity, allowing life to flow more easily.

The practical application of Spiritual Logic begins with mindfulness. When we are aware of our thoughts, words, and deeds, we can evaluate whether they resonate with the harmony of the universe. This awareness is a tool to identify discord and consciously realign with balance and purpose. The results are profound, with increased clarity and a deeper connection to the rhythms of life.

Words, words, and more words; what are we sending forth?

As we transition from understanding Spiritual Logic, we'll explore the practical application of energy alignment through speech and intent. Words are potent, and understanding how to speak things into existence becomes a key. This is especially essential when coupled with emotions or beliefs; this awareness alone can serve us all. This is where many get caught, as unintended and undesired results often arise.

How can we communicate effectively through the use of energy? Simply shift our conscious awareness into the frequency or resonance closer to that in the etheric realms. Then the magic happens. We are, therefore, reducing friction and opening the doors to new experiences.

As a premise, let's consider or observe the resonance and more significant meaning of Dominion and Control as a verb. While human logic often seeks to dominate outward circumstances, spiritual dominion begins within, focusing on self-governance. These two words are not necessarily used in everyday conversations. However, their connotation is expressed through our actions, deeds, and intentions. We will find that our **Human Logic of Imperfection** and understanding of both words utilize the energy to **dominate and control others** globally and personally. This is of a lower vibrational resonance. Nations take over lands through force, claim authority, and regulate cultures and religions. The results are war and revolt. People try to control their partners, employees, and others' human rights, individually dominating situations or events and governing conversations. The results are war, fighting, struggle, and strife. However, when viewed through the lens of spiritual logic, dominion and control transform into tools for self-governance rather than external dominance.

We can observe a difference when our focus shifts to the **Spiritual Logic of perfection** and resonance. Both of these words take on another aspect of meaning. The spiritual use of Dominion or Control is only **for the Governing of Self**. Having self-control would be the ultimate goal or, in this case, perfection. Our authority means we have dominion over our emotions and actions and conscious control of our focused thoughts. To do so otherwise would not serve a higher purpose. If this understanding could be integrated into our conscious awareness and acted upon, wars would end globally and individually. By shifting our focus to self-mastery, we align with the universal flow, eliminating resistance and fostering internal and external peace.

The most profound meanings of these words carry power simply by our positioning. From an expansive perspective, a harmonic resonance holds a higher vibration and frequency. Thus, we eliminate errors by serving our highest and best intentions without causing harm. Conversely, this premise equates to what was revealed in the first chapter regarding the phrase "What you will learn," which carries a lower-slower vibration and frequency. We create from our position of resonance, being in tune or not. We can manifest from love or fear, above or below.

Just consider how we, humanity, try to control our lives by forcing or mandating others to adhere to a specific belief or action. This focus is on the outer world of life, not the inner world. There are many control dramas, such as manipulation, micromanaging, justifying our actions, holding expectations, and creating disempowering laws. Similarly, we can recognize greed for the few at the expense of the many within some business or corporate structures. As a result, disharmony and friction arise until we can choose which position to master. Recognizing and relinquishing these dramas empowers us to choose harmony over conflict, reflecting the spiritual resonance of dominion and control in its purest form.

So how would these control dramas serve anyone for the highest and best for all? There is nothing but harm in the long run. Energy is a language, and we can use language as energy. (Harmony/Rhythm.)

Speaking is a force: Qualifying

Every spoken word sends an energetic ripple, affirming or misaligning our desired outcomes. Recognizing this impact empowers us to align our words with the harmonic flow of the Universe. Energy always obeys the law and is in motion; it is neither positive nor negative until we qualify and focus on it. When a direction is intended or spoken, a result will occur. We design everything through and by our authority. Most of humanity has forgotten this and has taken this life-stream for granted without thankfulness.

We have become numb to these flowing principles. Humanities focus is on the *'outer world'* of life - that which we are not. Many will continue to create their experiences through turmoil instead of constructing from the world within. We all choose to direct perfection or imperfection daily; this is the process with vibration and a qualifier. The simplest is recognizing how the two most powerful words known in the Multiverse will create our reality. They are "I AM." Speaking is a force and can be qualified through energy. Every spoken word is a declaration of energy, an affirmation sent to the Universe. Recognizing the power behind words allows us to co-create with intention rather than by default.

The 'I Am' Awareness.

The most potent tool in this process is the I Am declaration, which carries the weight of Divinity and resonance in motion. This foundational awareness bridges the gap between intention and manifestation, offering a tool to consciously direct our energy. When we speak, anything following "I AM…" creates that Divinity and remains in motion! It would be wise to commit that to memory. Our 'I AM' declaration is a powerful force sent out to the heavens, and it is a stream of light energy set in motion, following all Laws. When we say, "I am happy, healthy, or blessed," we speak that energy into existence, our world of expression and experience.

In the same way, when we say, "I am sad, hurt, or sick," it is still Divinity in action; it is how you qualified and directed this energy into your life. This simple declaration will be how perfection or imperfection will be realized and lived. The **qualifier** of that last 'I Am' statement is for you to remain sad, hurt, or sick. You will continue to experience this friction until you stop and change it. So many people inadvertently receive unintended results by misdirecting and misqualifying a simple format. When we misqualify our I Am statements, we inadvertently affirm limitations. For instance, saying "I am stuck" reinforces stagnation. But when we declare, "I am finding solutions," it opens the door to progress.

I will not sugar-coat this teaching. The following is an example of drawing creativity from the outer world of imperfection. Consider this one example of a non-constructive misqualification with friction; there are many. What not to say would be, "I am an alcoholic, or I am a recovering addict." These statements create a limiting pattern and a misdirected qualifier that remains harder to correct. As if it were written in stone. Worse yet, it can set up a limiting personal belief. These statements of imperfection serve no one in a healing manner and can create opposition. There are many reasons these phrases for recovery were introduced, all with good intentions, helping people become accountable for their actions. Yet, I'll ask you, where is the Divinity or healing that follows I Am? A curative means is non-existent with, "I am an alcoholic or recovering addict." When does recovery end? Never? Would that not be a limiting premise?

More significant results would manifest quickly with a simple alteration. Should our focus rest on the disease or condition, only to continue? Or should we focus on the solution and freedom from the disease? What healing results are sought, for do we not have complete dominion over these choices?

The trick is understanding how we speak discord or friction into our lives. We can produce the desired effects and results more quickly by adapting a premise; there is no limitation. I am not limited by a condition, or I am a master of my world/ life, which is a redirection or reframing. This would initiate the design process for healing. It also reverses the unintended focus. Do we say I am cancer? Does that not sound absurd? It doesn't flow, resonate, or feel right. Neither will -I am an alcoholic- if you consider it. The medical community is saying alcoholism is a dis-ease. So how can we say we are the dis-ease? We have become numb to this resonance. We are not a condition, an illness, a position, or a profession. These are activities; it is not who we are.

Mastering our words is the first step toward mastering our reality. Each declaration can uplift, empower, or detract depending on its alignment with universal harmony. Freedom from the enslavement of repetitive behaviors comes when we are willing to self-correct our perceptions. Here are a few powerful suggestions for those who struggle with this or any other dis-ease, condition, or situation. These declarations are of a higher vibration and easy to integrate into our vocabulary:

- I am open or willing to heal.

- I am seeking or asking for forgiveness.

- I am stronger than this addiction or situation.

- I am re-creating myself.

- I am responsible for my actions.

- I am here for the opportunity to heal, gain strength, or encourage others.

I 'AM' verses I feel.

Our words not only describe our experience but also shape our reality. The choice between I feel and I am illustrates this power vividly. While "I feel" reflects a passing emotion or state, "I am" carries the full weight of creation, resonating deeply with the Universal Laws that govern our being. There is a difference when we identify a feeling. I feel excited, sad, or in pain; notice 'I Am' is not a prefix. With these statements, energy is short-lived, not as powerful, and will not continue unless we focus on it. In this format, it is related to empathy, which is vitality borrowed. Sympathy is the acknowledgment of a limitation that carries lower vibrational energy. So, if there is something you wish not to continue, beware of your qualifier. We are all playing in this game of life; an essential guideline for setbacks or upheavals is how quickly we traverse and not remain within that lower vibrational frequency.

In all sincerity, utilizing the flow that creates Divinity's Perfection is simple; even children can use it. The speed at which you can alter how you experience life will be faster than it has taken me to write this section.

Recognizing what follows 'I Am' will serve you well; it is Law and our authentic expression. The first initial step to working with your 'I Am Presence' is identifying you have one. Through the 'I AM,' you gain your freedom. When we declare "I Am," we position ourselves with a state of being that transcends the moment. This alignment is why such statements hold immense power. Christ knew and mastered this Law of Life when he said, "I AM the Resurrection and the Life." (John 11:25.) The expression in his statement commanded the full power and dominion of the Universe; the result thus reversed death. His declaration resonates with all Laws. Imagine that.

When we declare I am an addict or I am an alcoholic, we inadvertently bind ourselves to the very condition we seek to overcome. This is the premise of dominion; take your pick, above or below.

This teaching is Law in action, showing you the power to create simplistically without discord and friction through Harmony/Rhythm, which is the easiest of all three energy components to discern. It has nothing to do with any human-made institution or its programs. Humans make errors; energy does not. Therefore, a fundamental foundation or awareness of Laws is essential to reduce our exposure to mistakes and unintended results. What follows your 'I Am' statements most often? Do they affirm your highest self or align with limitations you've unknowingly adopted?

Who are we when no one's looking?

When no one is looking, sometimes not even ourselves, our shared humanity reveals itself in moments of care, love, and quiet connection. In these unseen moments, we strip away the layers of societal roles and expectations, uncovering the truth of who we are at our core.

I'd be remiss in my duty if the following information isn't shared; in some not-too-distant future, this premise will play a fundamental role in our evolution. My only intent is to bring it to your awareness.

Humanity is enticed by Life and Living. Whether intentional or without awareness, we are working towards a goal of commonality, a group endeavor. We are pursuing a more extensive vision as we move from the personal to the recognition of our synthetic relation to the social construct. Our interrelation becomes the higher function and our commonality.

Yet, this innate connection often clashes with external forces. Societal expectations and the constructs of mass consciousness create friction, defining us by achievements, roles, or appearances rather than by our essence. Society mandates and creates friction without insight, which promotes misunderstandings about who we are. This friction arises when we forget the deeper truth of our being, allowing labels to cloud the resonance of our authentic selves. Focusing on positions or activities is the outside world of illusion. As an alternative, we should focus on how we express and conduct our lives, our being-ness.

We interpret what someone does for a living with who they are, for which there is a vast difference. If I were to ask, "What do you do for a living?" Most will answer, "I am a doctor of____, I am a therapist, mother, accountant, ditch digger, etc." Society functions and craves all those diplomas on the walls, not what is within the heart. When evaluating someone's qualifications, do you consider their heart, integrity, and authenticity as profoundly as their diplomas or titles? How might shifting this perspective affect your interactions and choices?

We can carry integrity and compassion or deceit and vengeance. (Serving-self or self-serving) Yet, we only seek and interpret those pieces of paper to represent trust in those who have attained vast knowledge in a chosen field. We pursue this information from others to perform a job, but we do not seek their internal influence. This mass focus remains on the outside world of human creation, not the inside world of the creator. This collective consciousness focuses on activities of life, not the Law of Life. If we had a 180-degree vantage point, our value system and the importance of who we are would change.

The 'I Am' is who we are. Being a therapist or CEO of a company is only a byproduct, an activity. It states nothing about the quality of a person we might work with. Here is the division, the numbness, to which we have become accustomed within the human consciousness. Everyone holds positions as a mother/father, sister/brother, or daughter/son. We are all a child of someone. We were born. In the highest reality, we are children of Law and Light. The Law of Life is energy ever-flowing. If we do not change our point of view, tune in to ourselves, or recognize the flow of energy, we remain strangers to this inner power of creation. However, we can rediscover our true resonance by tuning into the flow of life and stepping beyond these societal labels. Aligning with the Law of Life brings us back to a state of authenticity and balance, empowering us to align with the more significant rhythm of the universe.

In closing, imagine an orchestra. Each person is responsible for a specific effect, tone, or rhythm. Essentially, bringing everyone together into a coherent entirety requires a conductor. The conductor applies procedures and principles of music to bring forth harmony, synchronous rhythm, and governance of quality. This metaphor is a minor equivalency of how Laws and Principles guide and direct us. Yet, as each individual does their part, they must look up to the conductor for direction, changing their point of view. This is expressed as Harmony. The conductor's role mirrors the Governance of Universal Laws, ensuring each part harmonizes into a unified whole. When we attune ourselves to these principles, we, too, become conductors of our own lives, orchestrating balance and resonance. If the universe is always listening, what message are you sending through your thoughts, words, and actions?

Wrap up

Laws are the Governance, their nature creating a universal avenue to perfection. Principles are our guidelines, the causal elements of effect and affect. Energy, the access and delivery system we use, moves through vibration, rhythm, and frequency. These Laws of Energy contain a language and culture we coined the *Silent Code of Life,* and everything presented thus far aligns with these Laws, some of which have yet to be disclosed.

The Catch-22 of life lies in numbing our senses to force and energy. Once this consciousness is reawakened, we enter the avenues of harmony and perfection, recognizing the interconnectedness of all things. In their subtle form, expanded awareness of the Laws of Free Will, Correspondence, Reciprocity, Attraction, Forgiveness, and Abundance help qualify and bring direction to our lives. These Laws offer checks and balances, enabling us to better understand ourselves and the energy we project.

Visualize these Governing Laws as a spider's web or an ecosystem. Each Law connects and supports the others, triggering harmonious action in unison. Or consider them an echo system, an environment of sound containing all voices in resonance. Many of these Laws seem like common sense, yet their inner workings often remain a mystery.

Recognizing this unity and connectivity within the Laws allows us to replicate their principles in our relationships and environment. Perfection, as understood from the etheric, requires this unity. Through alignment with the Laws, we embrace the quality of purpose and proper execution of spiritual design, stepping into our highest potential.

Just as a spider's web holds its intricate structure through interconnected strands, the Laws function as a unified framework. When we align with them, we achieve balance and co-create our realities

ARTISANS OF THE SPIRIT

with precision and purpose. Each word, thought, and intention carries the potential to resonate harmoniously with the universe.

As you reflect on this chapter, ask yourself: What message am I sending to the universe with my words, actions, and beliefs? Let this question guide your path toward conscious creation and balance.

Your authority lies in the ability to partner and co-create. This partnership is freedom, joy, and expression. All energy readily seeks a declaration, a qualifier; it is the Divine Perfection of Love. Thus, I AM manifest. I AM complete. I AM healed.

Key Points: Spiritual Logic's Premise

- The Catch-22 of life lies in numbing our senses to force and energy.

- Spiritual Logic: as a 180-degree shift from human logic, it redefines how we perceive and interact with energy, life, and Universal Principles.

- Anything following 'I AM' creates that divinity.

Chapter 3 wrap up

This material marks a pivotal moment with the introduction of Spiritual Logic, a 180-degree perspective that shifts positions from limited human logic. This chapter invites readers to observe how nature reflects universal truths and encourages alignment through positions. In Section B, Spiritual Logic is explored in depth, highlighting the transformative power of words, particularly the 'I AM' statements, and how intentional speech creates resonance and harmony. These concepts lay a foundation for conscious navigation and alignment with universal principles.

Chapter 3 Key Points

Section A. Observer and Nature's Guidance

- Spiritual Logic of perfection versus Human Logic with imperfection, 180-degree premise or concept.

- As observers of our lives, we can view things differently from above, with an expanded view. This expanded perspective allows us to see the interconnectedness of all experiences, revealing opportunities for growth and balance.

- Nature gently guides us with harmony and rhythm. We can learn to align with nature's rhythms through observation, reducing resistance, and embracing flow.

Section B. Self-Governance and Power

- Recognize the opportunities with Self-Governance- dominion and control. True dominion begins with self-mastery, empowering us to lead our lives from a place of balance and intention.

- Self-correction/reflection are qualifying factors for position. Nature gently guides us with harmony and rhythm. Reflection allows us to recalibrate our energy, ensuring our actions align with universal harmony.

- Speak from a position of power, I am consciousness. 'I Am' complete. The I Am statement is a declaration of alignment, shaping our reality with precision and purpose.

CHAPTER FOUR

CONCEPTS

Scars

*T*wo weeks into a frigid January, I had a lucid night-mare. I awoke sweating, trembling, and weeping, unable to identify a specific person whom I loved. Nor was I able to return to sleep that night. Exactly two weeks later, this prophetic dream was repeated. In the morning, my life and very being were changed.

There was one of the worst fires with loss of life our town had ever known. Reality bites; tragically, all the critical points of my dream happened. A fire occurred two blocks from where we lived. The firefighters used axes to break the windows. The person I could not identify in Dreamtime was my boyfriend, Billy. Billy's mother lost her son, father, brother, and three-year-old niece. The pain this family experienced was astronomical.

Our community was in shock. I was hurt, angry, and lost, feeling alone and isolated in this vast empti-ness. There was no understanding of anything revealed *from this prophetic dream. Knowing I would be ridiculed without end if I spoke about what was shown to me, mainly by those who claimed to love me or were my friends. This reality of harsh ridicule and isolation is what many people experience, and we have learned to be silent. So I chose to bury this dream and hurt deep inside me, hoping it would never come to light. Confusion set in. Why was this dream given to me? What was I to do, suffer helplessly in silence? How could I move through this grief process and be truthful?*

The trauma of psychic survivor's guilt set the foundation and direction my life would take for a while, almost eight years. Anger set in due to inexperience, ignorance, and expectations. I fired my guides and angels, yelled at God, and deliberately chose the opposite of any intuition. My choice was oppositional defiance to everything I knew to be true and accurate about life, energy, or love. Survivors' guilt, either actual or psychic, can have devastating effects. It altered my self-worth, and I learned to hate myself, being cruel and judgmental, thus causing pain to others. Dimming that light inside me took work and dedication.

Years later, it occurred to me that I had misqualified my dream's intent. The message was to be a personal blessing and an opportunity, not to alter or warn my loved one. Fortunately, this misqualification allowed me to experience life's darkness, conflict, and discord. All the while, I was trying to escape from myself, Creator's love, and to ditch all this energy nonsense. There came a lesson, an awareness that escapism from the law of energy didn't work and never would. I became increasingly tired of misery, so I changed my mind about life. This ignited the light within, which taught me to love myself again.

There are great joys. There are great tragedies. When is our authentic self revealed? Scars are slow bleeding, not totally sealed against a memory.

After passing through this lesson, it ultimately became the journey of my life's purpose. This event has allowed me to teach from the errors made. Sharing this story is not for me to relive it but for you to step into healing in a broader sense. It is that of creating, manifesting, and living a life on and of purpose.

This experience allowed me to speak from a seat of power and qualify the vision in a proper context. Each concept that follows was used to re-create my reality. I had chosen to live a miserable, demoralizing life for a while. My life and inner beliefs were rebuilt extremely fast. Perhaps not easy to do, but it was simple. When speaking of balance or harmony, I know its resonance and that of its opposite energy. Understanding how to create effectively helps bring healing into the physical, mental, and emotional bodies, which I have done and still do. Emotional scars can run deep. The experience shared with Dreamtime may have triggered some people. Please know your journey is honored, and the emotional scars can heal. Embracing this healing requires stepping into a place of illumination and empowerment. In this place, we can authentically create with intention and power.

Speak From A Seat Of Power

Speaking from a seat of power begins with an awareness of our energy, where our words are not just expressions but forces that shape reality. Three fundamental concepts create from behind the scenes or background. They are our qualifications, vision, and attention. Our words reflect the harmony or discord within us. Aligning our thoughts and emotions with our intentions ensures that what we speak resonates with universal truth. These concepts are similar to vibration, rhythm, and frequency because they are always engaged. Yet, few consider these concepts or components of energy as options when applied to life or manifesting. The force that directs all will remain with our thoughts and emotions. When we can perceive these intricacies, life gets a little easier. When we speak from alignment with Universal Laws, our words resonate with coherence and creation, transcending human limitations.

Humanity continues to create dissonance, limitations, and imperfections. These are misconceptions that can be healed. Therefore, when we are done experimenting with misery, there are alternative perceptions we can apply to live efficiently and harmoniously. We will examine a few Laws with a different focus, aligning our qualifications, vision, and attention by creating healing and cohesion. Let us consciously choose words and intent that uplift, heal, and align with the highest resonance, speaking not from habit but from the power of intentional creation.

Universe Delivers Through Laws

The Universe operates with precision and is guided by immutable laws governing energy, intention, and manifestation. Aligning with these laws unlocks the pathway to living in cohesion with the flow of creation. To illustrate alignment with laws and familiarize the spiritual power of words, I'd like to bring your focus back to the vantage point of 180-degree with Spiritual Logic. We tend to take for granted that our point of view is the only perception available. We create from this human position of understanding, i.e., by saying, "I 'want' a new car, or I 'need' a new job." We interpret and understand these statements as requests, something to get or manifest. It's common sense. Correct? With these requests, the Universe does not assimilate into *our* understanding or belief. It will deliver, but only from its' vantage point, that of above, that of energy resonance and perfection.

In the words of Lao Tzu from the Tao Te Ching,

"Not knowing of the eternal leads to unfortunate errors." (Stenudd) www.taoistic.com

The Law of Abundance: *Simplistically, it means the Universe supplies all our requirements for life, including the infusion of knowledge from the subconscious to the conscious awareness. There is enough for all, from the unmanifest to the manifest. Any and all possibilities exist, whether positive, negative, or neutral. This Universal Law <u>does not recognize lack</u> in any form. To do so would be an oxymoron- voiding the law. This is the Law's Governance or function.* Remember, the light knows no opposite or opposition.

Concept: Qualifying

What's the fastest way to be out of alignment or 'be out of tune' with abundance? It is to introduce 'want or need' into the equation. Why? Both mean lack, create friction and enslave us. Words carry frequency, rhythm, and vibration. These are of low deficient qualities, slowing timeframes for delivery. Remember, vibration deals with speed. So, right off the bat, we are creating from a position of lack, an oxymoron when applied to abundance. Qualifying is a form of focus or position with checks and balances. When manifesting, it is a form of understanding the Law's function and choosing to create within its flow, not against it. Energy is our access point, and our choices are imperfection or cohesion.

Consequently, The Universe will not assimilate to our understanding, so when we use 'want or need' in **any** fashion, we will continue wanting or needing it. Bam! Nowhere in this sentence, "I 'want or need' a new job, or car, etc.," has anyone asked to receive such. To illustrate how our qualified intentions are processed by Universal Laws, imagine receiving these recorded messages from the etheric desk of abundance. These playful examples show how the universe reflects our energy back to us, either as a cycle of lack or as alignment with abundance.

For fun, here is an individual overview from above. It's a recorded message from the multiverse with soft violin music playing in the background. *"Greetings from the etheric desk of the abundant universal store: Your requested continuance for 'wanting/needing' (blank) is noted. We'll send your request to the attraction and the mercy department for further review and processing. Please note you can resubmit an explicit definitive request as a 'receive or claim order.' Until then, please continue to wait. Also, note that your request has been answered."*

Round and round we go. Will it stop? Nobody knows. This is the endless cycle of lack when we misqualify energy through 'want or need.' My question to everyone is; how does it feel to 'want' or 'need'? How does it feel to claim and receive? There is a vast difference in vibrational energy between the two.

I have eliminated these words from my vocabulary unless I make a point or qualify them as I've just done. When written, I close them in with single quotations, so there is no forward movement in creating friction. At the same time, removing these words has altered my thought patterns. I might *like* or *require* something, but I lack for nothing. I know I can create anything and claim it when and if I choose. I give **no energy or focus** on the equation of lack or a limitation; to do so would not serve a higher purpose and would constrict someone else's ability to co-create. Using these words places us in misalignment with other laws, creates friction, and slows the delivery of our desires. Our human desires often carry the vibration of 'lack or need,' creating friction. By recognizing this and choosing alignment with abundance, we allow the Universe to deliver in coherence with its perfection. Consider how a court case can be won or lost hinged on a single word.

If people would alter and qualify their request with, "I *desire* this new car/job." Your results would be efficient, effective, and effortless. *"Greetings, dear one: This is your notification from the etheric desk of the abundant universal store. Your desire to receive your new car/job has been processed and sent to the attraction department; everything's in place for early delivery. Thank you for playing!"*

When aligned with the energy of receiving, the Universe responds efficiently and effortlessly.

The difference with powerful words that create alignment will reduce dissonance. The catch-22 is between the logic we humans understand and the logic our Universe delivers. Delivery is how the Universe answers. Could you imagine this premise applied consciously to the Law of Attraction? Meanwhile, the Universe is patiently waiting for us to decide what we would like. More 'wanting' or receiving?

Power of Intention

Intention is the energetic blueprint of creation, where thoughts and focus combine to direct energy into manifestation. How we perceive resonates with how we receive. Some people whose consciousness remains seated in the physical realm of human logic dismiss the previous teaching by responding, *"It's the intent that counts."* They don't envision a broader scope because they have learned and believe this statement is true. I could agree the intention is fundamental, but allow me to ask a simple question. Is intent not a strategic set of thoughts, words, or feelings to obtain a goal? Is it not a silent dialog? If questioned, "What is or was the intent?" We would have to think about it to express that intention to others or the Universe.

We filter and process with feelings, words, or symbolism, which remains as language and a force. We still *think* with mis-qualifiers, such as 'want' or 'need,' a position of lack. Perchance, in the first chapter, do you remember me mentioning a family member who prayed for a wife? He received one, just not who he envisioned or intended. By requalifying or reframing, *"It's the intent that counts."* It can change the accuracy, frequency, and speed of delivery. Responding from a consciousness seated in the etheric, a more accurate statement with greater resonance and clarity would be, *"It's the results that count."*

Concept: Attention or Focused Intent Using Laws

Words or verses hold tremendous power within our intentions and consciousness, sometimes creating unintended mishaps. U-in-verse can create your universe with lightning speed. Have you ever said, "That was not my intention, or it's not what I meant?" Intention by itself is given in broad strokes. Let's bring our attention to **Focused Intent,** which amplifies thoughts, desires, and results. Consider how much **time** and energy is devoted each day to the ideas or conversations we deliver. All about our tribulations, relationship issues, dis-eases, injuries, worries, and fears. Are these complaints genuinely desirable? Is our intention to repeatedly experience these tribulations? Perhaps not.

Law of Reciprocity: *briefly means what is unequal, unbalanced, or inharmonious must be equalized, balanced, and harmonized. Hence, an exchange has to be equivalent to the nature of what is given to be beneficial. Under this law, it returns in equal force. Thus, provide only that which builds, for anything less will only compound itself. That given through actions, words, deeds, thoughts, or intent returns to you unchanged until it aligns with Divine Will, Divine Love/Wisdom, and Divine intelligence.* (What you send out will be returned in kind. So, whatever you say and do will eventually return to you.)

In referencing the story, Scars, I used this Law of Reciprocity to continue punishing myself during my destructive years—what a horrible storm. However, I also changed the qualifying factors to recreate my self-esteem, thus envisioning a greater purpose. Using this Law, I changed what I sent to the universe. I realized that whenever we speak about something wrong, we re-create it and anchor it firmly to ourselves or our beliefs, requiring more effort to release it. Thus, pain and suffering are optional. We choose how we're going to experience life.

Seriously, have we not noticed humanity's change in social norms for greetings? Have we become so disoriented to struggle that struggling is an acceptable way of life? We have all been on the receiving and giving side of personal tribulations. Anywhere we go, we'll overhear someone's misery. Conversations about who died, got divorced, lost a job, home, or health. Their entrapment is gossip. Their sad storyline sounds like a broken record, forming their painful identity, which becomes their mantra. Can you see or sense the rhythm? Can you envision their results simply by speaking suffering into their existence?

These sound waves are just like the fallen tree's reverberation. The uncomfortable condition we are trying to break free from becomes stronger. It becomes a negative feedback loop infecting ourselves and others. I was so guilty of this. Many then question, "Why me, or when will this end?" The answer is when you shift positions and think with an awareness at higher frequencies. Then, we can focus on our intent, bringing about results without unintended consequences. Please remember our words, thoughts, and emotions vibrate through the fabric of the cosmos, setting into motion the laws that shape our reality. To create with precision, we must align our inner world with the harmony of the universal rhythm.

When experiencing someone else's misery and personal tribulations, please form no opinions or judgments about others and remain neutral. Remaining neutral or detached is essential.

I silently state when I inadvertently find myself on the receiving side of someone's pain or trauma, "Creator, forgive them. They are unaware of what they are doing, saying, or creating. Send mercy and abundant blessings to them and the situation at hand." This blessing is a gift we can all give each other.

Make no mistake; I'm not being dismissive of trauma. It serves a purpose. Sometimes, we should discuss situations or events that happen in our lives. First, look to your motive; what quality are you sending out? Are you seeking a solution or trying to handle a situation differently? Then, discuss these events only with those who could offer assistance and not with some acquaintances at the store. Does your storyline carry love, blessings, or support for the person before you? Are you just talking to talk, re-experiencing, or re-creating pain and suffering? Or are you trying to heal old wounds or reevaluate deep scars that were triggered? Oh, my friends, please seek a view from above. It's where miracles are created.

We do not have to give admittance to the drama and trauma. Nor do we have to give permission or authorization for it to remain. A suggestion when someone asks, "How are you doing?" A powerful reply would be, "Thank you for asking. I am well," or any of the 'I AM' responses previously given. You can add any constructive events or how blessed you are. Think about the positive changes or results you would envision in your life. This is where the focus should be. Also, to reduce a dissertation and empower another, ask, "How is your <u>day</u>?" Again, we have control over this.

What would you like to send out to the heavens? How would you choose to be heard? Finally, we can speak from a seat of power, using speech to influence our reality and creations.

Concept Envision: Another Qualifying Law

Many laws are in play, and each upholds the same principles given as energy in chapter two. For checks and balances, a common-sense law becomes self-evident.

The Law of Cause and Effect: *Is a measurement from the beginning to the end of Life. It's a progressive record of working through life's lessons to be learned and mastered. It is known for raising human consciousness. The Law of Karma is one of its most noted aspects. This Law also governs the many branches of Natural Law. Causes are unseen. Effects are seen, felt, and experienced.*

Perchance, was that an expected explanation of cause and effect? Please feel free to incorporate other known definitions for cause and effect into the equation. They will resonate. Let's see how this law plays out in daily life. First, it helps to understand its structure and flow of energy. All events happen in a circular motion, even karma. Every effect has a cause, and every cause has an effect. There is no randomness or chaos. Every effect we see is caused by the Self. It is the responsibility of Self to see what causes and effects have been brought forward. Altering or changing the action, thought, word, or emotion brings balance and harmony. In the second chapter, you will find that this Law supports the Law of Frequency, impelling a greater awareness of self. (Involution/Evolution.)

Most people live by succumbing to stronger wills and thought patterns and are buffeted around in a storm of their making. As a result, they create their Victim Archetype. Understanding the Law of Cause and Effect will help calm the storms and align the Self in centeredness with balance. "What you sow, so shall you reap" defines this law. Therefore, we should only do what we can give cause to, and recognizing the effects will surely manifest per our motivation, intention, and desire. We no longer have to be imprisoned by karmic debt. We can break these cyclic chains to be free from the residual resonance. Forgiveness, by requesting and receiving, works wonders in its release.

Cause and Effect are so closely related to the Law of Reciprocity that it deserves mention. Between these two Laws, I found understanding from my destructive, angry period. This period of errors offered the most remarkable healings and teachings. Due to my emotional turmoil and scars, I was impulsed to resolve the cause and effects. The reason was my dream and carrying the guilt. The results were self-sabotage and being caustic. So, by deep diving into what I was manifesting, recognition came for life's application. It rests upon our mindfulness regarding focus and intention. It is *how* we think and speak. Our focus and intent will construct our reality, with or without qualifying anything.

The resolution: The Universe acknowledges our fixated or focused thoughts (to be) an experience or drama we wish to continue. Or we would not give it energy or focus.

Remember that nothing happens by chance; everything proceeds from something and is succeeded by something else. Nothing is independent of what has gone before, nor can it help but influence what is to follow. We should be aware that energy is neutral and can only respond based on what we consciously or unconsciously qualify and set into action. When we honor these laws, we reclaim our power as co-creators, designing a life that flows effortlessly with the currents of divine energy.

A gentle reminder: the Law of Abundance is always engaged, and it is a time for healthy mindfulness, a time for corrective measures of erroneous thoughts or feelings about healing. We can't see the wind, but we can see and feel the effects of the leaves that rustle. We can find and alter the causal effects we create with a bit of practice. Reflect for a moment—are your current intentions harmonious with your daily actions? Bridging this gap can transform potential into reality. We can access balance and harmony by acknowledging energy's components and function. Is this not healing? Can being healthy be a vision or an end result? Healing is not just the absence of dis-ease; it is the conscious creation of a harmonious state where perfection reveals itself naturally.

Now is the Time

Now is the time to honor the call within, to embrace the opportunity for healing and transformation that the present moment offers. What follows was originally not intended to be in this book. It is a perception of healing given to me by the Ascended Masters who have impulsed me to provide this information and place it in this chapter. It is delivered with no more or less than was given to me to be used as *seed* thoughts for healing philosophies. A Seed Thought is a focal point for thoughts and perceptions. For those who can feel the resonance and see your answer or find your error, blessings to you; know that prayers have been answered. If it is confusing, now is the time to seek answers, for opportunity awaits. Ask for clarity, and it shall be given.

In any case, a reread is suggested to process the information into small bite-size pieces. As you engage with these teachings, reflect on the physical and the layers of thought and emotion shaping your experiences. There could be a lot to process for some, or it may sound controversial. For others, it could be simplistic and straightforward. Perhaps addressing a physical illness is not on the menu today. Yet, our emotional and mental bodies exist, and if our thoughts are erroneous, so will be the result. Nevertheless, the following material contains principles that are interwoven from the thread of life. Let these words guide you, whether they resonate now or plant seeds for future understanding.

A Note on Discernment and Medical Advice

Warning: This information is NOT Medical Advice or intended as such. In no shape, manner, or form is anyone suggesting or inferring to stop any medications or medical treatments or dismissing any physical/mental complaints. Use discernment. We are not Medical Doctors. We are Artisans of the Spirit. Everyone can choose any, all, or none of what follows. We acknowledge the gravity of severe illnesses and hold deep respect for those navigating such challenges; in no way are we dismissive.

The following message carries a universal perspective, offered with profound compassion and intended for reflection. 'We' refers to humanity as a whole, and 'you' is intended to address the collective rather than any individual personally. From the Ascended Masters:

Healing Perceptions and Blessings in Disguise

"These perceptions are constructed and flow from many laws. This harmony is essential to note due to its curative power. What

73

follows carries no judgment or blame. It is a loving-healing view from above. These concepts tap into Active Intelligence; your bodies are designed to heal. Everything is created from feelings and the ideas surrounding them. These perceptions are a healing process with thoughtful discernment, reasoning, and logic. False human pride, personal opinions, and human disbelief are limiting. They keep humanity bound and chained to the human condition of limitation, thus locking the doors to healing. As you read, position yourself to remain neutral, refraining from exceedingly positive or negative emotions or opinions.

The Golden Key

The time will come when a person will either think or say, "I never asked for this illness," and yet it exists. So get excited because this is an awakening triggered somewhere deep inside you. The optimum word here is asked; the awareness is of healing.

Consider this- If you didn't ask for an illness consciously, then logically- unconsciously, you did. So, if your unconscious awareness could manifest disease without you asking. Then, your conscious awareness and thoughts have the power to reverse it. Do you know healing is possible? It is **how** you think about an illness or dis-ease. Dis-ease means the body is not at ease. Nothing can find expression in your life or body without your authority at the soul level. For an illness to exist within the body, it may serve you somehow. For example, it could be life lessons, finding strength, and compassion for self or others.

Does imperfection manifest out of fear? Dis-ease or illness affects millions. Man has created this discordant note that has entered the mass consciousness of humanity, which has been passed down through millennia. Dis-ease is still focused on because humans bombard each other with thoughts or ideas of imperfection. Consider your drug commercials. Can humanity envision and focus on the different outcomes of wellness? If we can envision disharmony or dis-ease as a learning experience or for expanding consciousness, it changes the outcome. This adaptation reduces any hold or power from dis-eases' discordant energy. The greatest pandemic of all humanity is discord. Fear, worry, and irritation only create limitations and imperfection. How much more time will be devoted to the limitations of human creation?

The human body records so much history upon and within itself. The energy within the body's cells has become dense from fear, pain, worry, and error in thoughts. This density restricts the body's ability to receive the nurturing light from which all life exists. If a *painful experience* has manifested in your life, misqualified energy was allowed admittance into your world, your sphere. Somewhere in the consciousness resides the misdirected application, either known or unknown.

This energy has snuck in during an unguarded moment, initiating its effects, and took up residence like an unwelcome guest. You do not have to continue to give permission or acceptance for it to remain. The dis-ease is serving you in some form, consciously or unconsciously, or it wouldn't exist. There are many reasons why dis-ease slips into our lives. The focus here is not on the deeper-why or how-to mechanisms. With the antidote of possibilities, there is the opportunity through thoughts and intention to heal. Processing these concepts for the Golden Key can start the curative power within you. Why settle for imperfection when perfection is the design? When inner peace exists, recovery and healing become a byproduct.

What we resist - will persist; this is law. Humanity wastes or devotes so much time and energy to anguish and suffering, whether in the physical, emotional, or mental capacities. Make peace with the condition that ails you. Has anyone thought of blessing the situation? Why bless it, you may query? A blessing immediately alters energy's vibration, rhythm, and frequency into a graceful universal equilibrium. What results do you desire?

In light of emotional upheaval, with situations, people, or circumstances, it helps to become amused. Amusement reduces angry judgments and their hold. Another powerful perception to consider is that of forgiveness. Forgiving the illness or condition also removes the power and attention given to it. When we fight something, it tends to fight back. This struggle implies a win-tie-loss scenario. Are we creating odds? If we fight or resist nature, nature's harmony will always win. How can anyone combat something that is erased or no longer exists? You can only battle something you have given your energy or attention to. Can you visualize you are healed and that it no longer exists in your field of vision?

Humanity uses the past, present, and future as a time*line*; ours is always now. Therefore, you also have heal, healing, and healed as a time*frame*. Healed means the issue no longer exists in the physical/ emotional, or mental bodies. This restorative action includes cause, effect, and record- which is karmic. Karmic cycles can be removed through forgiveness, both giving and receiving. If the record remains, its history can be triggered, or we can experience failed remissions.

- **Heal the cause:** admittance from an unguarded moment.

- **Healing the effects:** of misdirected energy within the body.

- **Healed:** eliminates the *record* both in the physical and the etheric bodies.

These Golden Keys of seed thoughts unlock all doors for curative means and break the chains of limitation. Who will open the doors to the possibilities and walk through to an unknown heaven? Who will focus their thoughts away from illness? Creating a relationship with our bodies through awareness can start the healing process. Consider these:

Dearest Ones, Can you see or feel the power and importance of imagination? Can you imagine that all your body's cells will respond to your thoughts and will? Will you shift perceptions into the beauty and radiance from this vantage point from above and within? Forgiveness and blessings are fundamental. Mind is the builder, and your thoughts create your reality. If you don't like what life has presented, change your point of view and the energy you give it. Learn to play with perfection. A mantra to incorporate is; I am well. I am blessed.

For Assistance

'Creator (God), hear my prayer, energize, and fill every cell of my body with your healing, loving light. Restore health, balance, and harmony within my thoughts and body so only your perfection remains. Forgive and heal these human qualities in error by removing any cause, effect, and record surrounding me. Bring to my attention that I might see this error so as not to repeat it. Help me to maintain and sustain your loving light of freedom within my heart. In my thoughts and intentions, I establish the essence of love eternally. Thank you for the abundant unseen blessings already on the way. A'Ho (Amen)'

Did you notice no focus was on dis-ease or illness in this prayer or request?

There are many healing modalities, such as sound and light energy. The imagination uses light energy, which works on the etheric energy body. It is a means to re-establish balance and harmony in the physical body. This Golden Key given to you is an effective use of ideas and perceptions. Thoughts and feelings will determine if we remain balanced and harmonious for healing to take root. Know it is the application of your thoughts that can assist and render healing or dismantle it. Determined Focus determines the 'timeframe' of delivery.

The Greatest modality of all is your 'I AM Presence.' There is no other. Now is the time to turn to your 'I AM Presence.' We stand in the Service of the Light and send Loving Blessings to all." With love, The Ascended Masters.

The understanding shared by my guides reveals that forgiveness does more than release discord—it clears the energetic records of imbalance, both physical and etheric. This teaching aligns with universal wisdom found in Saint Germain's "I AM Discourses" (Volume 3), where forgiveness is described as a divine law that dissolves discord and clears energetic records of imbalance, restoring harmony.

The Golden Key is a simple yet profound realization: alignment unlocks the doors to infinite possibilities and healing.

In _The Magic Presence_, St. Germain states,

"Life never struggles, for that which struggles is the consciousness which attempts to limit Life, and is but the interference with Perfection which is forever trying to come through. If the personal or outer self will just let LIFE flow and keep at peace the manifested result will be perfection- the Divine Way of Life fulfilled…." (King 273-274)

This profound teaching reminds us that healing and alignment come from releasing struggle. The following Seven Universal Tools are designed to help us do just that, creating a bridge to reduce interference and manifest balance. It does not matter what condition, event, situation, or issue people experience. Simply form a question with them to move through a concern or circumstance. These are just suggestions.

The 7 Powerful Tools from the Universe

Thoughts & Feelings: (They're not separate) Are mine aligned with energy? What position or logic have I chosen?

Allowance: Have I allowed my actions to hurt others?

Acceptance: Do I comprehend accountability and accept the lesson?

Adaptation: Am I adapting to new experiences?

Integration: Have I identified & embraced personal development?

Gratitude: Am I grateful, no matter how life presents itself?

Belief: Does this belief limit me or others?

These tools, grounded in the philosophies of Universal Laws, guide us to move through life with grace and precision, transforming struggle into ease and dis-ease into harmony. Using these seven tools also helps to qualify activities at higher vibrational energy. (Right-thinking & right–action) Thus, it can help a person augment a rapid expansion and reduce errors and dissonance.

One of the 'hidden' unconscious facilitations for illness can be karmic. It can be a redemption of past harm to another or self. For example, a chronic alcoholic may come into his next life with deficient kidneys or a poorly functioning liver.

In this life, we condition the next. Maladaptation or misqualification of energies deforms in some manner our physical, mental, or emotional health in this life or the life yet to come. Sharing, caring, and kindness – all conform to the Laws and, with due justice, modify karmic concerns. The accurate measure of health is the quality of our living. The kickback of karma in a well-lived life may intervene only in correcting past-life injustices. Dharma, or attending to earthly duties and responsibilities with loving regard, is equally a factor in health. Disbelief or apprehension concerning dharma, karma, or reincarnation in no way means that such events are not viable. You are certainly welcome to hold such misgivings, and that is o.k.

The phrase, Just let it go seems vague and unattainable at times. Many will struggle with 'letting it go.' But, the moment your focus changes to what you desire, it will transform your life. Ask yourself, is this drama self-serving, or is it serving-self for your highest and best? Is this an experience I wish to repeat or continue? If not, don't repeat it. If something causes pain, worry, or fear, give it no more energy; stop talking about it. My Grandmother would say, "I am too busy to get sick." And she didn't.

Please note: As we proceed, when '*end result*' is used, it is not redundancy or tautology, pun intended. Everyone receives a result. Results are based upon our thought patterning, usually with an unintended consequence. The 'end result' is implied with full awareness, for a desire to be fulfilled precisely as qualified and intended with perfection. A bigger picture is involved.

An Exercise: Where We Place Focus

Paying attention to how we sound or resonate makes all the difference. For practice, let's explore a quote from an anonymous person. Can you identify where the focus and attention are held in their request? Become aware of qualifying: Could this be negative, neutral, or positive in resonance? Was it created with the flow of energy and not against it? What might be a possible result? Hint: How would The Universe understand this request?

A person is seeking a mate and promises, "*...I'll honor your time with the same respect I give my own. No games, no gimmicks, and no guile. Just truth.*" (Anonymous)

At first glance, things seem to be ok. We have respect, honor, and truth. Hence, it was once suggested to use it in marriage vows. However, the way this is stated, there are unintended consequences in the making:

First: Can you see where a relationship with this person is founded on Conditional Respect? This respect is related to conditional love. It's the first thing said. What position is this statement produced from love or lack?

Second: No, no, no? The statement **focuses** on what s/he would not like or not do rather than what s/he **would like to receive**. Opposition is in the result. What is being asked or offered?

Third: Consider the emphasis on games, gimmicks, and guile. To begin with, this is a repeated pattern of pain, or it would not be in this person's awareness. So, it would not be stated if creating anew. How would The Universe understand this request?

Lastly: Who's truth, what truth? What if this person's moral truth is out of alignment with energy? Can it be seen where there is a dominating and controlling mechanism? (Dominion) It's there, look for it. We get used to interpreting what is implied but not what is specifically asked or what will be delivered.

The irony is that the results of this focus will attract someone who plays games and won't give him/her the time of day. Precisely as requested, per the focus. Could this be an unintended result? If so, rephrasing could sound like this: *"I will treat you with mutual respect and honor."* Focusing on caring, laughter, honesty, loving, or giving would bring significant results and magnetize the effort. Had this person validated or qualified their statement with even two laws, misalignments would easily be identified. Practice saying what you mean and mean what you say. Rethink, Reframe, and Rephrase. (Laws of Reciprocity and Attraction.)

We naturally engage the Laws of Reciprocity and Attraction by rethinking, reframing, and rephrasing. While the Law of Attraction is widely recognized, it's just one strand in the grander web of energy and Universal Principles we navigate. Let's briefly define it before moving forward to the broader harmony of the laws.

The Law of Attraction: *It is a Universal micro sublet law. Briefly described is the expressed force that overcomes inertia by applying will and desire. At the atomic levels, the vibrational resonance causes atoms to coalesce when of vibrational accord. Specific thought energies merge with like energy thought forms, i.e., hate, anger, love, or compassion. In the Physical, opposites attract (m/f). In the Etheric, like attracts like, thus the importance of shifting our awareness to 180⁰ positions. What's focused upon will manifest. (Like attracts like.)*

While the Law of Attraction operates as a force of alignment, our perceptions shape how we engage with and influence that force.

Let's examine how our perceptions guide or hinder the manifestation process.

Perceptions

We can all utilize a higher consciousness as a focal point to ensure any result we desire. The key is to know what your end result will be.

Allow me to explain because the following example might ruffle a few feathers. Others who see the expanded view can run with it and make it their own. Before I begin, please know the following story is neither pro nor con for a belief, action, or debate. It's a perception that can be held any way you choose; the following is mine.

Your perception is your only limitation.

A few students attended a gathering that my husband and I hosted. One student expressed how she was always prepared and on guard; she carried a gun and never left home without it. It was her protection. This individual works around animals and shady environments that could be dangerous. (Do these animals include humans? It's just a question.) With that, we listened to her point of view, which was mildly compelling to some.

A teaching opportunity presented itself. I then remarked that I found guns to give a false sense of security, and I do not own one. This student retorted immediately with modest irritation, "Are you telling me you are not going to protect yourself and your family?" I looked her lovingly in her eyes and said, "I never said that. You have interpreted what I said based on your position and beliefs. I was referring to a false sense of security. A gun does not hold power; it is the hand that holds it, and that power in my hand is directed a little differently." Lee Two Hawks interjects and asks the group if I should elaborate. All heads nodded in agreement.

By now, silence filled the room. Everyone was paying attention. I, therefore, acknowledged, "My power and security are within me. Why would I create a situation of lower vibrational energy that I would require protection from in the first place? We construct everything in our lives. I would not generate or give permission for anything requiring a gun to exist in my world. Therefore, have I not offered protection for myself and others? If a situation manifests in that form, I can transmute a different outcome immediately. Therefore, I remove and deny it from entering my world. No admittance." I finished with, "You may have a G-U-N, but I have G-O-D. I co-create without limitation."

This explanation did not sit well with this person. A couple of the students agreed. While still, others remained open in astonishment. A prevailing perception entered into their awareness. I asked all to reflect and consider what I was inferring. Where would they place their focus, fear or love? What atmosphere would they like to create?"

Questions were asked and answered that day. Generally concerning, common phrases such as Standing in your Truth, Your Seniority, and Your Seat of Power all reference the Authentic Self. However, the 'I AM Presence' is your being's Holiest, most powerful directional force. Therefore, my closing remarks to the group were, "I state what I mean and mean what I say. Our perception is our only limitation; remove limitations, and only your perception remains. Therefore,

*my focus will remain and reside here with my 'I AM
Presence' that never fails, and results are immediate.*

To be clear, as an amateur at best, I have fired many weapons and can feel the seduction with them. I can hit a target, yet I can't guarantee it would be the intended target. Does this sound familiar? We all get results, perhaps not the intended end result we desire.

With that clarification, let's finish up. Beliefs are potent, and it takes courage to challenge yourself to see a limitation and strength for self-correction. Disbelief, resistance, and denial close the doors to enlightenment and expansion. By changing the thought, we change the outcome. Likewise, when we alter our feelings, it changes our results. Changing both will allow you to create without limitation. Which position would you like to construct from love's perfection or imperfection, meaning lack or fear?

The weapon-wheeling student required time to sit with this new perception. She called me about ten days later and said she could now see and understand the lesson. She would now focus on creating an atmosphere where she could move freely from fear; no harm would come to her. Was protection and security not the end result she was seeking in the first place? Sometimes, new or counter ideas will take time to process. It's like buying new clothes; bring them home and try them on to see how they fit. To reach these higher levels of consciousness, we must know where we place or direct our focus. Finding and creating a resonance that differentiates our end results creates such freedom from limitations. (-See #2Resistance next chapter)

Wrap up

I state with full authority that I have seen, experienced, and achieved an awareness of energy that manifests lightning-fast, bringing comfort, peace, and healing. The primary key is an awareness of how the universe delivers, and the rest is elementary.

A simple error in misqualifying an event like my dream can always be an opportunity for an expanded view. It does not have to define us. Pain is used to get our attention that something is out of balance, usually found through rhythm. Look for the imbalance, and a solution appears. I found my Authentic Self by utilizing the premises, concepts, and Principles of Law. I no longer focused on hurtful events, nor would they dictate how I would live. Instead, I removed this limitation from my intent, focus, and any results I sought to explore. By envisioning it, I stepped into the light of radiance, love, and inner peace. I choose to be in tune with the flow of energy, thus manifesting and speaking from a seat of power.

Key Points: Healing Concepts

- Manifest with the flow of energy, not against it. Friction arises when we push against the natural flow.

- Your focus will manifest results, intended or unintended.

- Intentions resonate most powerfully when precise and aligned with the highest good.

- We create from positions of love or lack

- Pain and suffering are optional- Seven Tools

- Healing thoughts for healing

- Clarity on what your end result will be.

- Perceptions are your only limitation.

- The universe responds to our intent's clarity, not our fears' ambiguity.

CHAPTER FIVE

BELIEFS

A Story of Being-ness

*A*s I sat down for a self-hypnosis meditation class, a woman beside me asked if Lee Two Hawks was my husband. Cough, cough, "No, no, he is not. We are friends." I replied.

My thoughts began to race. What the heck? Not again. I had just sat down for class, yet here it was— the same question: "So, are you two together?" People kept asking, and it wasn't just me. Lee Two Hawks was fielding the same inquiries over and over. The sheer repetition of it was maddening. Couldn't they see the tension, the dismay, the sheer resistance between us? Neither of us wish to be around each other. Being near him felt like touching a live wire—jarring and electric, leaving me unsettled...

Yet, no matter how hard we tried to avoid it, this unspoken connection hovered between us, pulling us into interactions that felt more like collisions than meetings. The questions didn't just come from strangers; they mirrored something neither of us could admit out loud. We weren't in a relationship, but somehow, we were tangled in something that defied explanation—a magnetic force paired with an exhausting resistance.

Our friendship of five years was now shifting. Consistently, I felt those accumulative 'not-again moments,' accompanied by chills that I couldn't refute. Just because something was felt did not mean it had to be acted upon. We were obtuse and couldn't figure it out because being a couple was not a consideration. We didn't desire any part of it. No thanks.

My focus then returned to the class. Lee Two Hawks studied past life regression techniques and invited me to experience a different self-hypnosis technique. After learning the meditation, the class was separated into four small groups, and we each partnered with other students. Lee Two Hawks was on one side of the room, I on the other.

Each student took turns reviewing a past life. Essentially, we took notes for each other and had a chance to make a few of our own. Then, our teacher instructed the class to review our summaries and encouraged us to share any experiences, feelings, or observations.

Lee Two Hawks, as usual, volunteered to go first. There was that not-again moment as he shared his past life experience; chills ran up and down my body, and I became embarrassed to share mine. The randomness of our past-life experience played out like this, our cliff notes version:

*---**Lee Two Hawk's Journey:** "I am alone in a cold, dark, wet cave. I crawled injured, old, starving, and*

88

waiting to die. Life has been harsh, and death is calling- but I can't go- release does not come. It is painful. Oh, the loneliness, emptiness; I wish for death. But wait-- what is that... a light? I feel warmth and love.... I am not alone. The light is my release."---

My partner kept nudging me to share, elbow- ing me with wide eyes and hand gestures, clearly in disbelief that I wouldn't speak up. It was one of those not-again-moments, fully engaged. Finally, she blurted out excitedly, "She illuminated the cave, and you were not alone." You could have heard a pin drop. I felt the warmth rising in my cheeks. All eyes turned, focusing intently on Lee Two Hawks and me. "Well, you now have our full attention," said our facilitator, her voice calm but firm. She asked me to please share. Reluctantly, I did

---***Shadow Fox's Journey: "This is hard to describe. I'm me, but I'm looking out from me with a bird's eye view. I see this view from the back of a cave; it's lit up, and a man is curled up in a fetal position. I can hear him moan. I feel like this man is me, but it's not- I know because I have a view from the back of this cave. I am here - I am standing in the light. It's like I am the light. I feel a great giving of love to this man...I feel longing and anticipation. I'm here to accompany and help this man die."***---

After sharing my experience, a lingering feeling took root-- there was no me, only we. Like a scene from a rerun movie, I watched this man from the light, every part of me aching to embrace the pain he carried. Though I was separate from him, I was also *an inseparable part of him. Unbeknownst to us at the time, yet deeply felt on a soul level, we were fulfilling a connection that transcended conscious understanding.*

But, even as the depth of that connection lingered within me, I couldn't shake the frustration and confusion stirred by my ignorance and the insinuations of others. The Past Life meditation didn't help in the least. Theoretically, it actually ignited more whispers. As chance would have it, a dear friend from the community invited us for a group healing meditation the following week.

Her meditations on self-healing with seed thoughts weren't guided, so we could explore independently and journal afterward. Thankfully, we did not have to share. It was a legacy for our growth and development.

After the meditation concluded, people departed, but our host asked Lee Two Hawks and me to stay for a few moments. She looked at us and said, "You categorically don't know what's going on, do you?"

We exchanged glances, unsure of her meaning. "Let me put you out of your misery," she continued with a playful yet knowing smile. "What you two share is the energy of Twin Flames. Your connection isn't ordinary; it's the energy of creation itself, magnetic and undeniable. People sense it and misinterpret it as sexual energy because they don't understand the depth of what they're witnessing."

She paused, her tone shifting. "Once twins accept their twinness, they can spot additional twins miles away. Usually, they require a little assistance with understanding—and you both have suffered long enough. I get the honor of delivering a set of twins," she laughed.

Her tone became more direct. "Your twinness keeps propelling your acceptance of each other forward, even when you resist it. Shadow Fox, you experienced a virtual memory from the other side during your past life class. That wasn't a past life experience—it was the reality of spiritual life when you assisted your twin in releasing his physical body. It's a fragment of your shared journey, a glimpse into the profound bond that connects you beyond this lifetime."

She paused, her words more pointed. "This time, Shadow Fox, it was public. Get over it."

Our mentor continued, "First, twins take turns experiencing life—one here, the other staying in the etheric, lending assistance when required. Then, we learn to navigate life together, perhaps as siblings. This continues until we can live as a cohesive unit, fulfilling our mission. This is the first time in Earth's history that many twins are reaching for a successful resolution of their mission and duty. We are a rarity indeed. My twin and I could not coalesce. Thus, he chose the other side."

Neither of us moved, listening to every word. Then, laughing, our friend added, "I'm sure you've noticed that the deep, painful tugging stops when you're together. If one gets poked, the other feels it." At that moment, all the puzzle pieces came together. The unending questioning stopped.

Intuitively, she asked us to review our journaling from the evening's meditation. She already knew what we would discover: Lee Two Hawks' and my entries were word-for-word identical.

"Take this as a confirmation," she said. "Your journey is divinely guided, and your existential education has just begun."

This experience exemplifies the essence of Twin Flame-ness, teaching us how unity in duality serves a higher purpose. It is not about completion but collaboration, not about romance but resonance. Twin Flames exist to awaken, challenge, and guide humanity toward the harmony of spiritual logic.

Twin Flames

As Twin Flames, we should express what we are and are not. Our experiences disclosed thus far may seem unimaginable to some or unbelievable to others, and this is the point of demonstrating a unique expression and challenging a belief.

When Twin Flames first meet, they experience an undeniable energy—distinctive, powerful, and transformative. It's an encounter where time seems to stop, eons unfold, and the omnipresence of oneness leaves them speechless. In that moment, sparks ignite, and a connection beyond conscious understanding is revealed.

What Twin Flames Are Not

Contrary to popular belief, Twin Flame relationships are not solely romantic. While there is often a deep bond, Twins can exist as parent and child, siblings, or even friends. Many confuse Twin Flames with Twin Souls or Soul Mates. Twin Souls often represent intense love stories. While Soul Mates share recurring lifetimes in various roles, they form bonds of familiarity and support.

Misconceptions and Truths

To be clear, a person cannot find or un-find, for that matter, their Twin Flame. Each will be brought together through a magnetic impulse. The magnetic force of Twin Flames transcends physical will, drawing them together to fulfill a higher purpose.

The energy of Twin Flames is often misread as sexual because it is creative and intensely magnetic. However, it is not rooted in physicality but in the universal force of creation itself. This energy propels them forward when aligned, resolving internal conflicts and fulfilling their purpose.

Each takes turns navigating life—one incarnating, the other remaining in the etheric to assist. Over time, they learn to operate together, often as siblings or close companions, before finally uniting in a cohesive partnership. This process is part of a broader mission to elevate human consciousness.

The Path of Twin Flames

The journey of Twin Flames is rarely straightforward. They originate as a single spark of energy split into two entities at the moment of creation. This split occurs in the sacred heart flame, not the soul. Therefore, the fire drives them—the flames that burn with purpose.

We often say—and we mean this sincerely—we wouldn't wish being a Twin Flame on anyone. The gravity of this journey, with its duty, mission, and purpose, is immense. It demands more than just inner work; it requires a blending, a unity that challenges every aspect of who you are. It's not an easy path, and it's not meant to be romanticized.

As a qualifier, Twins will deny, reject, and dismiss their twinness. It's not just the singular inner work of one but the blending and unity of each other. Each has an internal duty to examine personal beliefs, and they must be aligned with each other and within the Law of Love; it's not fun. Fraught with challenges and uncertainty, they are not guaranteed success in one lifetime or another.

Referring to our story, did our relationship develop over only five years, or did we live many lives together? We knew Twin Flames existed, yet refused to acknowledge the potential we were one. Our erroneous beliefs caused so much turmoil that we chose to deny, refute, and run in the other direction as others have. Our belief system would not comply with what was to be. But then, those undeniable, not-again moments propelled us forward, and our ideas changed.

Did this story stretch the possibilities, alter illusions of love, or challenge your learned beliefs?

Moving into belief systems, this story sets the stage to challenge the constructs and limitations we accept in our lives. Beliefs are powerful forces that shape our perception of reality. By examining and requalifying our beliefs, we can align more fully with the truths of spiritual logic and transcend the discord of human logic.

The following two sections will guide us deeper as we turn the page from this personal story. Section A reveals the threads that weave our beliefs, often unnoticed, into the fabric of our reality. Section B invites us to explore the tools and techniques that realign these threads, bringing harmony and clarity into our lives. Together, these sections bridge understanding to application, helping us move from reflection to action.

Systems of Belief

Understanding Systems of Belief

This section introduces the foundational concepts of Systems of Belief, which are rooted in Universal and Cosmic Laws and distinct from belief systems shaped by external influences. The focus is on how Universal Laws create a framework for understanding and aligning our human belief systems.

Systems of Belief: *Is a concept that bridges the gap between what we know and what we hope to understand. It underscores how awareness and knowingness extend beyond individual constructs, resonating through the etheric to create harmony and alignment with Laws. A belief is what we do not know and is something we hold onto without certainty.*

"We live in a sea of influence, where every thought, belief, and word carries a resonance that shapes not just our reality, but the realities of those connected to us. Morphic resonance reminds us that these patterns, once formed, can be accessed

and amplified, influencing the collective consciousness."
(Sheldrake 23)

By understanding and embracing these resonances, we can transcend the limitations of belief systems and step into greater co-creation with universal energy. As presented in chapter two, the Energy Flow Chart below demonstrates how results manifest instantaneously in the etheric realm, reflecting the expansive and unlimited nature of Systems of Belief.

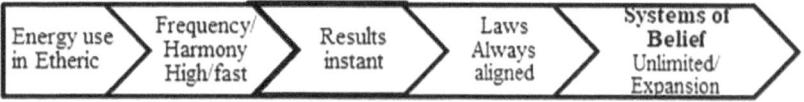

Do you remember that vibration is associated with speed? As a reflective measure, this knowing power is the number one reason everything in the etheric is in the present moment-- The Now.

These systems reside outside this constrictive circle of personal beliefs and value systems. The Governance of Cosmic and Universal Laws radiate through us, influencing even our core being-ness, which holds only light responsive to Law. This means our spiritual essence also responds to energy, impulsing us to reflect and act according to the precepts codified in Law. (Remember the Law of Frequency in chapter two? From its influence, pain becomes our signal or teacher that something is out of balance-- Involution and Evolution.) These energies are filled with grace, expansiveness, inclusivity, and co-creation without friction or harm. The universal flow knows naught but wise counsel and loving embrace. Law is your guidance; its light ever reveals the Path.

Belief Systems

A belief is what we do not know and is something we hold onto without certainty. Our beliefs, often shaped by personal experiences and societal conditioning, act as the filters through which we interact with universal energy. Yet, these filters can distort truth and harmony if not aligned with higher principles.

Let's explore beliefs about how we form them, how they serve us, and how we qualify them. This awareness helps when our emotional triggers are stimulated. For example, wars have developed due to moral values or hidden agendas. Why is one belief more valid than another? So how can we identify if our beliefs breach the energy of Laws? We can align more fully with the truths of spiritual logic and transcend the discord of human logic.

In contrast to the etheric, the physical flow chart demonstrates how Belief Systems become limiting and constrictive, shaped by external influences that disrupt alignment with energy.

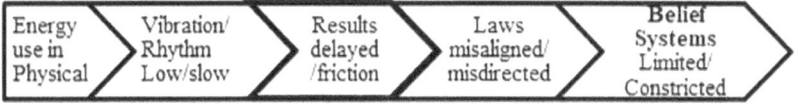

Beliefs are energy but can become inadequate due to misalignment with the flow of laws. As mentioned, a belief does not exist in the etheric because it is an uncertainty-- not a knowing power of life or laws. This is why humanity has been limited and destructive. While personal belief systems are often rigid, Systems of Belief offer a broader, universal framework that aligns with Cosmic Laws. This distinction—between personal beliefs is essential for breaking free from outdated perspectives. The Law of Correspondence plays a fundamental role here, which shows how internal misalignment manifests externally, guiding us to realign with Universal Principles.

Law of Correspondence: Nothing exists that does not have a corresponding attribute or aspect at a different vibrational level.

Therefore, anything manifested in this outer world must first be created in your inner world. Cause and effect are integrated within this law. Everything corresponds at differing octaves or bandwidths. (As above, so below.) Incidentally, this law is partly why vibration, rhythm, and frequency become Principles to the expressions of Laws. Because beliefs do not exist in the etheric, chaos exists here because there is no corresponding attribute.

Corresponding Attribute for Healing

Suppose we consider the belief in healing according to the law and its principles. In that case, it must first start in our inner world to manifest in our outer world reality. Healing our emotional, mental, or physical bodies begins with our thoughts and feelings. The possibilities are limitless. Either we can heal or we can't. These options come from our filters. Thus, to understand how belief systems take root and influence our perceptions, it's essential to examine the filters through which we interpret reality and the values that anchor them.

How Beliefs are Formed--Filters and Values

Please note we will continue to use the term belief due to its established status in humanity's terminology. Therefore, based on our Human Logic, our filters clarify, check resonance, and then balance new ideas before we lock them in our chakras. Chakras are where our hot buttons are stored. This filtering process is called Belief Systems, for which I call B.S.

Belief systems are learned through education, mass consciousness, culture, familial, political views, and religion. These influences are stored within our chakras and shape our identity and values. If humanity's ethical values resonated with love and harmony-- judgments, criticisms, and resentment would not exist. For example, these criticisms have causal effects, harming self and others because they resonate with selfish discord. Consider how low self-esteem causes self-injury. Quickly, racism is another exponent of misqualified filters remaining in the core values and mass consciousness.

Many identify who they are based on their experience with their learned beliefs. Group beliefs that are either cultural or religious can remain ingrained for generations. However, they do and will shift slowly over time, ever moving forward toward harmony. Outdated beliefs, such as having a child out of wedlock, no longer resonate with horror and disgrace. Also, with effort, we can correct our parents' mistakes when parenting our children.

Our filters, shaped by these societal and personal experiences, determine how we process new ideas and experiences. Yet, when 'out of tune' with the flow of energy, they can distort reality, creating discord within and around us. This brings us to the Law of Correspondence, which highlights the interplay between our inner and outer worlds, offering a pathway to realignment.

The Process

Whether inherited or self-formed, these belief systems shape how we interact with the world, often dictating the energy we project and receive. Consider how our B.S. interacts daily with the thoughts and emotions that govern our actions and character when comparing and evaluating new concepts. First, we will analyze information for resonance, assuming a truth, something known to us. Then, we'll quickly justify or validate the acceptance or denial of new information. In addition, our personality plays a role in this assessment. Rarely does humanity look to quality a belief.

Is this new idea harmonizing with a known 'truth' or a 'perceived' truth?

Here lies the error people make: Spiritual or Human Logic. Humanity decides without feeling if 'Truth or Law' resides there.

Most people give no evaluation based on checks or balances from energy, which the System of Beliefs/Laws provides us. Belief Systems create checks and balances using personal filters. In contrast, the System of Beliefs uses laws of energy as filters, creating checks and balances with a known perfect resonance. The previous chapter's exercise presented with 'Anonymous' reflects this dichotomy.

In totality, these Systems of Law encompass an expanded view. It is a knowing power of Life and Law. Why do beliefs not exist in the etheric? Beliefs are personal filters, not knowingness, and why we should align our values with energy. Our values and emotional triggers often stem from deeply held beliefs and sources of internal reality. We gain freedom from reactive patterns by aligning with Systems of Belief, the Metaphysical, and Natural Laws rooted in universal truth.

How Beliefs Serve Us

This segment for Sources of Internal Reality helps to identify our relationship with energy. As we gain responsiveness to the macro/micro dynamics of our thoughts or beliefs, we can more clearly assess our choices, behavior, and perceptions. This is why an emphasis was placed on the premise of Spiritual Logic. As a result, we uncover the freedom to create a life of alignment-- with joy, abundance, and balance as natural outcomes.

The diagram below illustrates how external influences shape our internal realities. By understanding this dynamic, we can begin to see the constraints belief systems place on us and move toward alignment with the Governance of Laws.

Sources of Internal 'Reality'

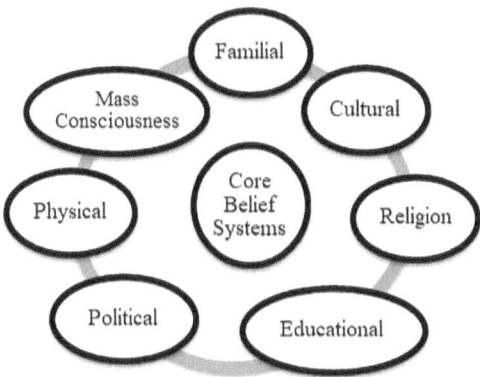

The entire multiverse resides outside this constrictive circle of internal realities. Therefore, Cosmic Energy and Karmic Influences impulse us into a pattern of enlightenment. Referencing A Story of Being-ness, these were the influences Lee Two Hawks and I were resisting. We were comfortable in our realities, not seeking or working towards our combined mission as Twins. Hence, until we understood our twinness, what we resisted persisted until we aligned with knowingness.

Our beliefs act as unseen architects, designing the frameworks of our reality and influencing the energy flows that govern our experiences. Individual core beliefs give value, serving as the compressed energy of outside influences, such as education and religion. These condensed values create a nuanced viewpoint or perspective of self or others. Events, circumstances, and environments become pivotal components that motivate one's expression, identity, and deeds, ultimately influencing mass consciousness. Sometimes, dissatisfaction drives people to seek alternative answers. The willingness to process and explore differing information or ideas shifts our understanding.

How we qualify Information

Once something is learned, however, redirecting it can be challenging unless it resonates closely with something previously known.

If it resonates closely, we can modify our original understanding and make proper adjustments.

These are the filters that qualify our learned beliefs. Consider the belief that our aura, containing the etheric, emotional, and mental bodies, is only within a few feet of our physical body. The aura could extend far beyond, challenging the limits imposed by filtered information. The non-threatening core belief is that we have an energy body or aura; the distance or radiance is in flux.

Developing our B.S. also creates our hot buttons. Hot buttons are emotionally charged energy that triggers anger. These triggers become resistant to any intuitive influence. Most individuals won't accept a 'truth' compared to one's accepted conviction or dogma. A saying comes to light; "Their mind is made up; don't confuse them with facts." This friction causes hot buttons to ignite to validate one's position. Anger also represents a response to feeling diminished; it is compressed energy focused on relieving an internal disruption.

Having explored the mechanics of B.S. and their impact, the next step is to actively engage in reshaping them and clearing our filters. By rethinking, reframing, and refocusing our beliefs, we can utilize the 3Rs, which offer a practical guide to recalibrate our perceptions and align them with higher truths. Recognizing the power of our beliefs is the first step toward transforming the energy they generate, paving the way for actionable change, explored in the next section.

Key Points: Belief Filters

- Belief Systems (B.S.) are shaped by external influences, such as culture and education, and act as filters for our experiences.

- Misaligned beliefs cause discord, while alignment with Universal Laws fosters growth and balance.

Section B
Transforming Beliefs

Belief systems act as frameworks that influence our internal and external realities. Having explored the personal and societal frameworks of belief, we now turn to how we can align beliefs with Universal Laws.

This section delves into the transformative framework of Rethink, Reframe, and Refocus—an intentional exploration of beliefs and their alignment with universal laws. The 3 R's—Recognition, Resistance, and Rejection—offer a structured approach to navigating the challenges of integrating new truths and expanding awareness. This framework provides a structured approach to examining and reshaping beliefs, challenging our filters and assumptions that limit personal growth.

Rethink, Reframe, and Refocus Beliefs

Having explored the foundational aspects of belief systems, we now turn to practical steps for examining and challenging them. Questioning our beliefs and what we know can feel uncomfortable.

Yet, we all survive them. Consider how, as children, we learned the truth about Santa Claus or the stork. Initially, the revelation may have disrupted our worldview-- but ultimately, after the anger clears, we adapted to a broader perception of reality. Having explored the foundational aspects of belief systems, we now turn to practical steps for examining and challenging them.

Challenging Beliefs

Core beliefs often reflect the compressed energy of external influences, such as cultural norms or education. Shifting these requires recognizing their origins and choosing alignment with higher truths. When we purposely examine core beliefs and trace their origins, we can assess whether they align and are in service to others. For example, the roots of Christian burial practices began with Constantine, who, after conquering a region, decreed that the dead be buried instead of burned. There were executions for non-compliance. Each passing generation lost the fear, and this mandate evolved into doctrine. So, does a Christian burial still serve our immortal soul? Were hot buttons just triggered?

While core beliefs shape our actions and interactions, they can also be exploited by hidden agendas that thrive on our vulnerabilities, revealing the darker side of belief systems. One of the worst manipulative, hidden agendas for a moral value is when a kernel of truth seems to validate a belief. A judgment then distorts, creating a false argument. This distortion is a sophism, becoming a Self-Serving agenda propagated by misqualified or misaligned motives. Truth within Laws does not have to be justified. If you're rationalizing a belief or value, perhaps it's time to rethink that position. Shall I mention the hidden agenda or horrors of Jim Jones in Guyana? Ask yourself: Who or what does this belief serve? Reflecting honestly on your motives and their alignment with universal principles opens the door to transformation.

Have you heard someone state that they believed they were doing something in the best interest of another? Then perhaps realize they were enabling? Yet, people judge, take action, and initiate a cause and effect without evaluating any spiritual laws. We are accountable for qualifying and aligning with love, peace, and harmony. Friction is of our own devices.

Keynote Speakers: Inner Voices of Harmony

Criticism, judgment, resentment, and labeling become our Keynote Speakers when beliefs are out of harmony. These voices serve as mirrors, revealing where transformation is required. Imposing judgments on others is used when people become threatened-- such as feeling diminished. Try listening to your intuitive Keynote Speaker when you're out of tune because judgment cannot exist in the energy of love. We can replace discord with balance, accountability, and love, which holds no resentment.

The keynote speaker's reflections emphasized the importance of discernment, a principle deeply tied to the Law of Truth, which invites us to align our words and actions with universal integrity. Law is truth. We can feel or sense it. I cannot emphasize this enough; many times, core beliefs and values we hold near and dear to our hearts are entirely out of alignment with Law. As a result, we tend to continue on and on with only a fragmentary understanding, losing sight of a comprehensive picture. Humanity experiences such agony because many continue with blinders on.

Agony is the end result of misalignment. Perhaps a more profound awareness is at hand, or an error in reasoning or logic is missed. Every time we experience trauma, discord, or anguish, it is our clue to see the bigger picture. These influences play over and over again until we learn the lesson. Each of us is responsible for self-correction. For those who dare to seek and question, freedom is yours. We have a choice, and if this choice contains truth, it will resonate with accuracy; we innately know we are guided to do this.

This metaphysical world we live in holds answers to life. But can people accurately assess from an uninformed source? It is not difficult to question our filtered beliefs. It is how we respond to the answers we get.

3R's- Aspects of Intuition

There are signs when you hear 'truth' or are presented with new information. We refer to them as the 3Rs: Recognition, Resistance, and Rejection, which are self-evident. Each of the three R's offers a pathway to deeper alignment with universal laws, highlighting where beliefs support or hinder growth. These are our filters for how we see the world around us. They can also help direct and align you to the vibration of law. Ask, and it will be given. You will feel it when information, ideas, or perceptions come into your awareness.

The process of aligning beliefs with universal truths often involves intuition. When presented with new information, perspectives, or people, we may experience one of three responses; Recognition, Resistance, or Rejection—the 3 R's. And yes, this includes when we meet someone for the first time. These responses act as filters, directing us toward alignment or highlighting areas that require deeper exploration. These signals can be understood through the intuitive feelings that alert us when something is aligned or misaligned.

By recognizing where our beliefs create resistance or rejection, we can shift toward Systems of Belief that resonate with higher vibrational truths, creating harmony in our lives.

As an added bonus, these 3Rs can simulate energy's components- Vibration, Harmony/Rhythm, and Frequency. For practice, consider how each of these components could find placement. I will illustrate using Vibration as speed for each of the 3Rs for clarity. Also, we can apply any of the 7 Powerful tools from the Universe from the previous chapter. Have fun by mixing and matching these concepts within your own reality.

Recognition

Recognition often manifests as an intuitive knowing or familiarity with a concept. This is the moment where a belief resonates deeply, creating a sense of clarity and alignment. Immediate recognition might sound like: 'I know that, though I'm not sure how, but I know.' These moments are signals that the belief is in harmony with Universal Laws. The Vibrational Speed- fast or immediate.

R1) Immediate Recognition: It's a peaceful-natural knowing feeling, a flow, an excitement within self, an intense curiosity. Some people experience tingling in their bodies, 'like the good chills,' or a magnetic resonance that feels natural. The Truth in Law resides here. We call this feeling an impression. (-See: Transforming Energy Through Beliefs in the following story.)

Resistance

Resistance is the space where the most significant growth occurs. When faced with new truths, discomfort often arises, indicating areas where beliefs or perspectives may require expansion. This discomfort is a natural response, signaling that the belief is challenging established thought patterns. Instead of avoiding resistance, leaning into it with curiosity can lead to profound transformation. The Vibrational Speed- remains the same.

R2) Resistance: Pay attention. There may be a higher vibration, nudging you to seek an expanded view and impressing you to re-examine a belief or learned behavior. The comfort zone comes to mind, or the feeling of being challenged. The key is to be open/clear to new information or inspiration. No one says to swallow hook, line, and sinker. (Jim Jones) Give yourself time to consider, reason, and place that new idea or belief up against Law.

(–See *Your Perception is Your Only Limitation*, in chapter 4.)

Rejection

Rejection is the conscious decision to stand firm within certain beliefs while remaining open to growth in other areas. This occurs when a belief or idea fundamentally contradicts core truths or mis-aligns with Universal Principles. For example, rejecting an idea that encourages division or harm may align better with higher truths. Balancing this rejection with openness requires discernment and ongoing reflection. Rejection is where limiting beliefs often arise. Question yourself whether this rejection stems from fear or a mis-aligned belief system. The Vibrational Speed- Slow

R3) Rejection: When knowing or sensing that there is a violation of law, Law of Love, or Free Will, for example, then stand firm within this rejection. Knowledge, wisdom, and checks/ balances from energy play a significant role in this case. Many of us close the door to a vista of possibilities or an expanded awareness through disbelief, dismissal, fear, or worry. This rejection is where B.S. gets in the way and holds us captive. It halts inspiration. (-See Chapter 6, Two Little Words, Different Worlds.)

Immediate Recognition allows us to notice a shift instinctively, Resistance signals internal friction, and Rejection highlights what's required to be released or avoided. Together, these act as a **keynote speaker** within us, drawing our attention to what matters most. By consciously working with the Three R's as a compass, we refine our ability to interpret intuitive signals for clarity.

Pause a Moment

Take a moment to reflect on a belief or idea that challenged you recently. Did you experience recognition, resistance, or rejection?

Consider how this response shaped your understanding and whether it led to growth or reinforced existing patterns.

We can 'clean' our filters by asking, intending, or allowing them to remain open. When this resistance or rejection happens, question who or what this serves. Does it serve the highest and best for all? What am I missing or not seeing? Is my belief so anchored and immovable, or am I immovable? Am I threatened by who I think I am? When resistance arises, notice it and stay open to new ideas; they may lead to a deeper understanding. Remember, beliefs can be limiting. Look for the limitation within a perception. As with any information, question if it carries the criteria of cause no harm. If not, make adjustments as required. I refer you back to the words 'want and need'; they no longer serve me for my highest and best or provide a greater purpose.

These principles were tested in my journey with Lee Two Hawks as we grappled with the challenges of twin-ness and the beliefs it brought into question. Our story illustrates how the 3 R's framework can be applied in navigating profoundly personal and transformative experiences. Our random moments became a glimpse into a Cosmic Consciousness we were unaware of. Although we tried to find meaning in this 3D world we physically live in, the error was that our individual beliefs still rejected our journey's path. Knowingness and acceptance were hard to find when struggling with yourself.

Transforming Energy

Spiritual logic in action is what I'd like to address when combined with a deep conviction of a belief and used within the guidance of Law. This process demonstrates how alignment with higher vibrational energy fosters transformation, moving from resistance to harmony. Consider the interplay of Laws that can help establish the desired end result. Higher vibrational energy (Light) will consume lower denser energy. Like attracts like in the higher etheric realm, opposites attract in the lower physical realm. (male/female). When our awareness is positioned in the etheric realm (as above), we bring the higher vibrational energy to us (so below) in the physical plane. Only we can harm ourselves; no deed of another can hurt us unless we give our power away; this principle is from the Law of Forgiveness. It involves permissions and allowance; this principle resonates with everything. Allow me to explain because the following example highlights this interplay or ecosystem for Laws and their Principles. It reveals how stepping into Systems of Belief transforms our perspective and outcomes, demonstrating the power of universal alignment.

This story is an experience that a very dear friend of mine had, and it will be presented here with her permission. I'll call her Nancy. Nancy had the wisdom of the interplay to which I speak.

Transforming Energy Through Beliefs (#R1Recognition)

Nancy's marriage of twelve years took a horrible turn. She cared for four young children, the youngest of whom was Stephen, who had special needs. She was in the kitchen when her eldest ran into the room, screaming, "Mommy, come quickly. Stephen is jumping on the bed, Daddy's sleeping, and Daddy has your gun."

Nancy ran into the bedroom, grabbed Stephen as fast as possible, and placed him in the hallway with the other children. She directed all of them not to move. She approached the bed and reached in to remove the gun from her drug-induced husband. Everything went downhill from there. A six-foot muscular man awoke in an uncontrollable attack mode. The effects of the drugs were in full gear. Nancy, at five feet tall, had the gun in her hand. He was hell-bent on retrieving it. A vicious, overmatched struggle ensued.

Nancy knew she had to hold on to her gun with everything she could muster. She was trying to empty the bullets while keeping her finger between the hammer and the firing pin. Blow after blow, Nancy endured. She was kicking him in the groin in an attempt to stop him, all the while hearing her children at the door

110

crying for Daddy to let go of the gun. She knew this would not happen on her watch. No way. Nancy did not slip into fear; her only action was not allowing any outcome other than her family's safety.

She called forth from deep inside her that 'mother bear strength,' feeling and knowing there wouldn't be any other outcome, period. She demanded in her thoughts that her husband would awake from his aggressive drug stupor. In a moment in time, there came calmness within her. A tingling awareness pulsed in her body, which words cannot convey. With one bullet left in the chamber, her husband let go of the gun and ran out of the house.

Nancy called the authorities and her mother. She had a broken hand and additional injuries to her face and body. Her mother helped care for the children as she healed, filed for divorce, and legally sold the gun. It was found out later her husband owed a lot of money to a drug dealer; that's why he had the gun with him.

Nancy's ability to align with energy demonstrates a profound understanding of the Laws of Attraction and Correspondence. In the heat of the moment, she faced her husband—a physically larger and stronger opponent, with height, weight, agility, and strength in his favor. Their conflict was between two opposing forces, and they had conflicting outcomes. Despite being outmatched in every physical sense, Nancy consciously redirected her focus. She chose not to meet force with force but to harmonize with the higher frequencies that naturally construct balance. This shift transformed what could have spiraled into a deadly outcome into a moment of grace and resolution.

Her story underscores how our belief systems can act as barriers or bridges. When we align with the Laws Governing Energy, such as attraction and synthesis, we allow for outcomes that transcend limitations. Nancy's actions were not just reactive but deeply intentional, demonstrating the power of focused thought and energy. She created a transformative result through harmony, not opposition, even in physical disparity. Some might consider this a miracle.

Please recognize that miracles are well within our expanded capabilities within Law and its action.

The Journey Within

Shaping Mass Consciousness through Relevant Questions

Until now, we've explored the foundational principles and their connection to the beliefs shaping our reality. The Journey Within invites us to expand those ideas, shifting to a more profound and exponential framework. For some, it may plant a seed; for others, it may reveal insights already resonating within. Either way, this journey offers an opportunity to explore the nuances of self-belief and the interconnectedness of all things.

In the journey toward higher consciousness, there exists a resonance beyond individuality—a field of unity from which all existence emanates and to which it ultimately returns. This field, often described in esoteric traditions as the ADI (Active Divine Intelligence.), represents the silent source of infinite potential. While the monadic self reflects our highest individuality, the ADI transcends even that, dissolving separation and embodying pure oneness.

For centuries, humanity has cycled through questions born of external conflict and ego-driven logic—questions that reflect the personality self rather than the higher self. These inquiries, rooted in the "world without," perpetuate inner conflict and reinforce the resonance of struggle within the collective consciousness. They are part of our mass consciousness, influencing the reality we experience collectively.

A student recently asked, "Are we robbing from the experiences of humanness as we journey within, or is this part of the chosen experience to realize?" This question reflects a dynamic we have faced for eons. While it acknowledges the profound nature of our journey, it also carries the resonance of separation. It implies that the act of inner discovery might detract from our humanity, as though the two were in opposition. Yet, from the perspective of spiritual logic, this question dissolves: the journey inward is not separate from human experience but the ultimate reflection.

Our questions should reflect our higher potential and aspiration, not our lower conflict. Questions such as, "What role does my human experience play in the evolution of my soul?" or, "How can I serve the greater whole?" contribute to a higher frequency within the collective consciousness. These are not merely personal questions—they are universal, resonating with spiritual logic and enriching the shared field of human thought.

By consciously crafting questions that arise from the "world within"—aligned with the I Am presence—we contribute to the elevation of mass consciousness. This shift is essential in the current paradigm; as we move from human logic to spiritual logic, we leave behind the merry-go-round of repetitive, unresolved conflict and step into a higher realm of collective evolution.

This shift also reflects the nature of vibration and its relationship with speed. In the etheric, everything exists in the present moment—'now.' This immediacy of the etheric realm allows higher vibrational thoughts and questions to ripple outward instantly, contributing to the collective field of awareness. When we ask questions that arise from higher awareness, we accelerate this process, drawing ourselves and humanity closer to the harmonious resonance of oneness.

The questions we ask now are not trivial. They carry a resonance that impacts the entire field of collective awareness.

Consider these guiding questions:
How can my actions contribute to the growth of unity and understanding?

What unique gifts can I draw forth to serve humanity's evolution?

What higher truth can this moment teach me, and how can I embody it?

These questions reflect a higher thought process that transcends personal limitations and opens the door to meaningful action. They move us beyond "how" and into "the why." They dissolve the boundaries between the human and the divine, illuminating a pathway for the inner and outer worlds to harmonize.

By embracing this shift, we honor both the human and spiritual aspects of our existence. We recognize that lifting these weights— our challenges, our conflicts—is part of the chosen experience, not a detraction from it. Through these experiences, we contribute to the flourishing of a unified humanity and the expansion of collective consciousness.

The Journey Within explores how aligning with the Governance of Laws creates harmony, balance, and expanded awareness.

Wrap up

Beliefs hold immense power, yet they do not dictate the existence of what is real. Whether we believe in ghosts, energy fields, or universal forces, their reality is not dependent upon our recognition of them. Energy flows through and around us, influencing every aspect of our lives, whether we acknowledge it or not. This awareness invites us to look beyond the surface, questioning how our beliefs shape our interactions with the unseen world.

Through transforming energy and challenging the status quo, as Lee Two Hawks and I have experienced firsthand, we learn that alignment with higher vibrational energies can dismantle old paradigms. The status quo persists when we resist change. But harmony emerges when we embrace transformation and align our actions with the laws governing energy. Awareness, forgiveness, and the willingness to shift perspectives open the door to meaningful transformation.

As we challenge the B.S. (belief systems) we step into the expansive power of Systems of Belief anchored in love, peace, and harmony. This shift is the key to aligning with the flow of universal energy and creating a life of balance. Integrating these insights allows us to observe our beliefs, reframe them with clarity, and align with the expansive flow of universal energy.

Key Points: Evolving Beliefs

- Belief systems can be reshaped through intentional actions like Rethink, Reframe, and Refocus.

- Resistance to new ideas signals growth opportunities.

- Recognition of universal truth fosters alignment.

Chapter 5 Wrap up

Chapter 5 delves into the profound influence of beliefs on our perceptions and actions. Section A explored how belief systems act as filters, shaping our experiences and aligning—or misaligning—us with universal truths. Section B builds upon this foundation by demonstrating how beliefs can be transformed through intentional internal actions, such as rethinking, reframing, and refocusing. These sections highlight the importance of recognizing limiting beliefs, embracing new perspectives, and aligning with higher principles with Systems of Belief. By consciously reshaping our beliefs, we foster growth, reduce resistance, and create harmony with the universal flow.

As we close this chapter, consider: What beliefs are you holding onto that may be shaping your reality? How might your life change if you allowed yourself to question them and align with the flow of universal harmony?

Key Points: Chapter 5

Section A. Systems of Belief

- Beliefs shape our perceptions and interactions with the world but can be limiting when misaligned with universal energy.

- Systems of Belief, guided by Universal Laws, transcend personal belief systems and create harmony.

- The Law of Correspondence reveals how inner misalignment manifests externally, urging us to realign with higher truths.

Section B. Transforming Beliefs

- The 3Rs—Recognition, Resistance, and Rejection—serve as filters to evaluate and align beliefs with universal principles.

- Transforming beliefs leads to harmony, healing, and a deeper connection to energy flow.

- The intuitive voice of the Keynote speaker is triggered when our beliefs, identity, or positions are challenged or diminished. We often respond to this threat with criticism, judgment, resentment, or condemnation.

CHAPTER SIX

TWO LITTLE WORDS, DIFFERENT WORLDS

Brown Cows

I was a young girl when my parents took my older brother Eric and me for a ride in the country to see the autumn foliage. My parents were engaged in a conversation in the front seat of the car, enjoying the outing. Unfortunately, the free time left Eric and me in the back seat to our own devices. As we passed a cattle farm, we could see the cows were going in to be milked. Immediately, I shouted, "Ooh, look, brown cows! Can we stop and get some chocolate milk?" Eric innocently responded, "Chocolate milk does not come from brown cows." I defended vehemently with, "Yes, it does. Chocolate cows make chocolate milk!" Next, we were in a brawl, kicking, punching, and pulling hair.

My Dad had to stop the car to break up the fight. For me, it went downhill from there. Sequestered between my parents, I nursed a fat lip, welts on my legs, a

117

few bald spots, a bruised ego, and learned about cocoa beans. My feelings were hurt; I chose to stick up for my uneducated and immature reasoning skills with brute force and willfulness.

Consequences? What are those? I could not see the larger picture or know it existed, nor did I care. The biggest and greatest lessons were yet to come. If memory serves, consequences were the theme for the year; many of my ideas were simply wrong.

Just because I believe something to be accurate does not mean it is. To stand so strong and defend a belief or justify an action when perhaps the greater truth is not even in the equation was a significant error. I was defiant and slowly realized this did not feel good. After my anger passed, I could examine new information, such as cocoa beans and brown cows.

So, how closely aligned are our belief systems to the Principle of Laws? This chapter offers an opportunity to apply tools introduced earlier, such as the three R's—recognition, resistance, and rejection. These tools can help you gauge your awareness as you reflect on the nuances of two simple words. You may feel a resonance or internal resistance/rejection; both are natural responses that reveal the emotional charge behind deeply ingrained beliefs. Clearing your filters and approaching this with an open heart and mind will allow you to tune in to these reactions and gain deeper insights into how your perceptions shape your understanding and energetic alignment.

Our belief systems are intricately connected to the resonance of our words. Like the brown cows, these words challenge us to reconsider what we've accepted as truth. For each term, I'll present information from three perspectives: above (spiritual logic), below (human logic), and within (the resonance felt in the physical body). This exploration will illuminate how the Universe provides only from its predestined logic and flow, highlighting the difference between human and spiritual logic.

Surrender in contrast to willingness. Both words create, but create what?

Two Little Words

Contrast: Observe Surrender

Can you recall your introduction to the word surrender? From where did it come? Was it your faith, political views, culture, or your education? The word surrender vibrates in the physical realm and body with lower vibrational energy. It carries friction, negates our power to co-create, abnegates responsibilities, and removes the freedom of choice. Surrender your armaments and your lands. Surrender to a greater authority and or surrender your life. For those who know the infinite possibilities, surrender has no purposeful meaning in the etheric. When spoken, its sound creates a discordant note of disempowerment and resistance. The definition in the etheric is to give your power away. In the physical body, the feeling to some is helplessness, vulnerability, and unease. While more challenging to detect, surrender reverberates with dissonance.

The intended meaning of surrender is often to give permission, acceptance, allowance, or release—all of which carry a higher vibrational precision on their own merit. Statements such as, 'I give permission for healing,' or, 'I accept a new perspective,' are far more powerfully effective. Yet, in the etheric, surrender conveys vastly different meanings, lacking these higher vibrational qualities and the precision required for alignment. Some people have justified and defended surrender's usage based on core beliefs, yet it remains as friction in the etheric. In an expanded view, surrender directly opposes the Laws of Free Will, the Path of Least Resistance, Correspondence, and Reciprocity. How often is this word used in churches when singing to God the Creator or for recovery from addictions?

A brief reminder concerning the Law of Correspondence: simplistically, it means, As above, So below. On earth, as it is in heaven. For the words given, if something vibrates here on earth, its energy will also vibrate in the etheric/ heavens, either in tune or not. We will still receive a result. But do we desire an end result tainted with friction or slower delivery?

Here is a 180-degree perception to consider for the word surrender. God/Creator has gifted us the power and authority to create anything. When we foul it up, do we not have the ability to reverse it? Can we not change our minds? Do we deny the gift of power and authority by surrendering it or even ourselves? For some Peaceful Warriors, even human logic does not compute with this concept of surrender. Many will never surrender their power to co-create.

Giving up or stopping the action is one thing that aligns with the Path of Least Resistance or recognizing the error. Abnegating responsibilities and throwing a gift back is another. Surrender-(verb): to give up one's power, stop resistance to an enemy or opponent, and submit to their authority and control. So is God-Creator, our opponent? Or our partner?

On the internet, I found definitions for surrender listed under spiritual contexts when they should be categorized as religious. To clarify the difference, being religious aligns with human logic, while being spiritual reflects the Creator's logic of laws. The definition describes surrender as 'a most loving feeling.' Here, I issue a significant caution and raise red flags. If one can recognize the spiritual logic here, embrace it. The loving feeling described is not surrender itself but the release that follows. Please use discernment and not blind acceptance. Someone mislabeled this feeling and misunderstood its resonance, tying intense emotions to an incomplete understanding. This misqualification can create significant hurdles. How many times must one surrender? Instead, directly seeking permission, acceptance, allowance, or release aligns with a higher purpose and avoids unnecessary confusion.

If surrender remains your moral code, please continue to use it. The heavens will not cease to exist. As authors, we are not seeking agreement or to sway an opinion but to offer insight. As we shift our focus to the concepts of willingness, consider this contrast and how it aligns with higher principles. Honestly reflect, as feelings will ultimately create your reality.

Contrast: Observe Willing-ness

As we observed the term surrender, let us contrast the word willing-ness. Willingness is a characteristic of the soul's impulse; it comes from an aspect of Divine Will. This term resonates with high vibrational energy and a higher frequency in the etheric realm. The word reflects Divine Will and holds to the Governance of Law without friction, transmitting a frequency that resonates easily with the principles and planes of existence.

Willingness will register in the physical body as upliftment, empowerment, and resolve. Which allows for acceptance, adaptation, or redirection as expressed in ideas, ideals, and purpose. It flows efficiently with manifesting. To willingly sacrifice your life, armaments, or lands keeps your power of free will and ability to co-create intact. It, therefore, is a choice with the alignment of energy, and the sound harmonically reverberates.

Consider willful, meaning controlling, stubborn, or determined. In that case, this word as action will carry a lower vibration to willingness but a much higher vibration than surrender. Willfulness is misdirected intent. Surrender is the negation of your power.

Willingness, however, bridges the gap between resistance and harmony, aligning us with Divine Will. It reflects a cooperative and intentional act, resonating with higher frequencies that invite cocreation rather than disempowerment. Where willfulness demands and surrender relinquishes, willingness allows us to participate consciously with what is, embracing flow and collaboration with the energy of creation.

What does manifest really mean? The powers to create, making something happen through visualization, imagination, or focus, like healing the body, to bring something from the unseen to the seen. Thus, we will it into our existence.

Become aware of what you manifest or will into your world. When all else fails, try this; I willingly accept, release, or give this situation to God/Creator. This carries self-empowerment. A grand design, is it not?

Two Different Worlds

The concept of 'Two Different Worlds' emerges from the vibrational gap between resistance and alignment, surrender and willingness. These worlds are not physical places but energetic realms that reflect how we engage with the Universe. Surrender, often mistaken as spiritual acceptance, can disempower us when it becomes an act of throwing our innate creative power back at the Divine as if rejecting the very gift of life and agency. Willingness, however, bridges these extremes. It opens the door to a higher vibrational "world," where we neither oppose the flow nor dismiss our co-creative role. Instead, we actively align with the spiritual logic of Divine Will. In this elevated frequency, our choices resonate with universal harmony, transforming discord into balance and revealing the profound distinction between the two "worlds" of struggle and flow.

Not to sound redundant, but the concepts and perceptions of Spiritual Logic regarding surrender or willingness are not expressed as a personal belief but as consciousness from an expanded awareness. It is from the resonance and influence of energy, which is Law. What will we choose to put forth as an expression of who we are? Will you say what you mean and mean what you say? Becoming

124

aware of this interplay can impact your life, spiritual development, and those you serve. Creating a partnership with governance helps align belief systems for the highest and best for all. When faced with uncertainty, willingness encourages us to lean into trust, fostering flow and adaptability. At the same time, surrender may feel passive or disempowered.

Things to ponder: Did you identify an emotional component for either of these terms? Did they resonate with recognition, resistance, or rejection? As our awareness expands, we can see where we place value and importance. We can alter our vibration by changing our position, such as being an observer or conscious co-creator. Words do matter. We can change our results by selecting powerful words that create and deliver.

What would happen if we threw out the term of surrender or willingness? Would it change who we are? Could the idea of never surrendering be held within a battle of our ego? It doesn't matter how we answer; our position will remain as permissions as our evolution unfolds.

The Why

My assessment of brown cows in early childhood and my defending behavior perhaps brought a giggle to the silliness of that belief. Yet, how often does humanity defend their religious beliefs or political views as I did with brown cows in childhood? Perhaps many may not resort to punching or pulling hair, but our influence, positions, and agendas can be harmful. I would still like to believe brown cows give chocolate milk. This shows how a belief can be so strong that we refuse to give it up even if it is invalid. A microcosm of this is individual fighting. The macrocosm is the warring of Nations. We can avoid perpetuating damaging repercussions by seeing resonance as a purview. Laws and their Governance may have to be explained but not defended. Oh, my friends, please awaken to the multiverse of energy we live in. Willingness is an active, harmonious alignment with Divine Will, guiding us away from resistance and into co-creation with universal energy.

Divine Will

The concept of Divine Will introduced here draws inspiration from the esoteric teachings of Alice A. Bailey, particularly her profound work in The Seven Rays of Life. These ideas have been simplified to align with the accessible framework of spiritual logic presented in this book. To put the term willingness in perspective and why there is an essential resonance with it, there is a macrocosm concept that I would like to address. First, we discussed Laws, and now I would like to discuss how Principles are our guidance. Within the fabric of this ecosystem or web of Laws, there is a seed thought or center. If we consider a spider's web, it vibrates and alerts the spider when an insect touches its net. Energy works much the same way; activation of one Law triggers all others. Principles radiate outward from this central point, which is the glue. Willingness is an active, harmonious alignment with Divine Will, guiding us away from resistance and into co-creation with universal energy.

This center point is considered a Trinity of Principles or Rays, consisting of Divine Will, Divine Love/Wisdom, and Active Intelligence. They are also known as the Laws of Construction. (-- See chapter nine.) These Principles are encoded and infused within our very be-ing; they are a part of us and of Laws. However, this concept presented in its modest format can't express the totality; it is massive, and our consciousness still seeks an understanding of God's Will or the Divine Plan. Therefore, the most we can reveal will be based on our spiritual development and evolution. However we can access information through the Energy of Laws.

To speak on Divine Will is one of three principles or Rays from which everything and all Laws of Energy flow. We move into universal harmony when we align our intention with Divine Will. In the etheric, there are also three planes of existence: Monadic, Atmic, and Buddhic. (Different octaves) Each carries aspects of Divine Will, Divine Love/Wisdom, and Active Intelligence. Even the prefix of willingness carries a part of the divine, so it transmits a frequency that resonates perfectly with the principles, planes of existence, and laws. Can we perceive the flow of perfection? Principles are Divine. It is easy to align with the Laws when we become aware of them, and then, we can gauge our efforts.

Bridging Willingness and Divine Will

Willingness doesn't merely soften resistance; it is the gateway to a higher vibrational state—a different "world" governed by harmony and alignment with Divine Will. Predestined energies, like the Cosmic Laws of Synthesis and Economy, form the scaffolding of the Universe, flowing effortlessly to uphold the Divine Plan. These energies are immutable, carrying the natural rhythm of evolution.

We align with these higher currents by stepping into willingness and qualifying free energies to serve our highest purpose. This alignment transforms struggle into flow and resistance into creation. Through willingness, we begin to sense the interplay of predestined and free energies, the Divine Order, and the profound implications of our choices.

Reorient- Recalibrate- Refocus with Principles and Laws

Perhaps to gauge our efforts, we can use tools like the 3Rs. These tools become a reorientation of values and viewpoints. Often, we are asked about Cosmic and Universal Laws. Which is the utmost, most influential, or first on the long list? This line of questioning shows a misunderstanding of Laws because people fail to qualify the Principles that drive the energy ecosystem.

To seek the most influential Law in our solar system, I would ask, Influential to whom? A more qualified question would be, Which one do we violate the most?

127

Can you guess which Law? It's been mentioned but not presented yet. Please play along for a moment. Here are a few clues.

Just as there was an emotional component with the words surrender and willingness, there is an emotional component to the subsequent Law. An accurate representation of our universe, first and foremost guided by LOVE, would be a law of utmost importance for self–governance and self-correction. This energy impulses everyone to our essence; it goes to the core or being-ness of who we are, allowing us to find expression. This Law lives in our Core Values.

In the etheric realm, this energy force is responsible for permissions. Permissions are given from our soul level, for our human experience, conscious of it or not. It's the Universe's checks and balances from our personality self and life lessons. Therefore, we must ask for intercession from God/Creator, guides, angels, and loved ones. Permissions are why we have prayers in the first place- we must ask.

Angels and Ascended Masters will not violate this law; to do so would not serve a higher purpose. This law reminds us that permissions, granted by our soul level, align us with universal checks and balances, ensuring our choices serve the greater good. Sometimes, praying for a miracle will not be delivered because it could contradict an individual's life purpose. If angels assisted, they would override the soul's will, thus, a violation.

Spiritually, breaking this law is a grander 'sin' than murder. Yet, humanity's ignorant and arrogant demeanor is still in its infancy and continually violates this law. Karmically, this is an excessive error that we place upon ourselves. Think about it; we go where angels will not tread.

You'd be correct if you answered that Free Will is the most violated law. **The Law of Free Will-** *Everyone has a choice and free will to choose it. You do not have to agree with someone else's decision or belief. Nor can your choice or belief be imposed upon another. This Law carries permissions, accountability, responsibility, and karma individually and that of Nations.* The Law of Free Will is an expression of the Law of Love. (Again, Angels will not violate this law.)

When we reorient and recalibrate our values and beliefs through The Law of Free Will, it immediately reduces the energy of human dominion and enhances spiritual jurisdiction. Yes, we can apply this law or not with our actions, words, and deeds; Karma and consequences remain. The Universe will send us corrections when required. Can you guess how? The answer is trauma, drama, discord, struggle, and strife. Suppose we do not consider the Law of Free Will within our belief and value systems. In that case, the results will remain with wars, revolt, agony, pain, and disharmony. This is the very law in question for violations of human rights. Where is the Divine Love? How might your life change if you recalibrated your actions and beliefs to fully honor this law?

Does not humanity give murder the harshest penalties, based on their value for them? Yet again, we are unaware of the penalties we will all face just because we refuse to allow others their expression and choices. Does society honor and provide value to free will? Or will humanity continue to step on free will? Just something for consideration, how do these resonate with you? Are they opposite perceptions of our core beliefs? If God/Creator gifted everyone with Free Will, then who are we to deny it to another person?

Wrap Up

Would it be worth the effort if we reorient or recalibrate ourselves, allowing the possibility of a larger picture to engender curiosity and grander vistas? Is not human nature so constituted as to seek the unknown, understand, and gain a firmer grasp of self-development? What if we applied this Law of Free Will to our human doctrines, beliefs, or societal laws? Could you imagine reducing control, greed, suppression, dominion, or war? Would it alter humanity's ethics or moral codes? The Law of Free Will resonates with Reciprocity and the Path of Least Resistance; it resides within all Laws impulsed by the Law of Love. We should remember that we are a functioning expression of the Universal Mind, including our will, purpose, and intent.

Can humanity not see an expanded view? For example, in the United States, each state, apart from the federal government, enjoys its own self-governance. Yet, many of these states deny their people the same opportunity for individual self-governance that they enjoy from the federal government. Is this not a demonstration of hypocrisy? If so, this reveals much inner work, particularly in the balance of giving and receiving. Just as the federal government grants states the freedom of self-governance, states should, in turn, empower their people to govern themselves. (Receiving/Giving.)

By choosing willingness over surrender, we open ourselves to the flow of Divine Will, allowing life to unfold gracefully and intentionally. In doing so, we honor our role as co-creators, embracing the possibilities that arise when we align with universal harmony. This is where the real work begins—living in resonance with higher principles to shape a life and world of balance, loves, and purpose.

Key Points: Two Different Worlds

- Feelings and beliefs resonate. Recognize how they shape our reality and influence alignment.

- Words carry the power to align us. Their vibration holds the key to harmony and intent.

- Surrender is a positional choice. It carries friction and negates our power.

- Willing-ness flows easily with Divine Will. As part of the title, it constructs or creates from perfection and precision.

- Reorient, Recalibrate, and Refocus through the Laws of Construction and Free Will. We can choose not to impose our will on others.

CHAPTER SEVEN

WHOM DOES IT SERVE?

Lee's Fedora Hat

*A*s a young man, I rode a bicycle to work. Navigating a large city's streets can be, at the least, hazardous. This early morning ride had nothing to do with heavy traffic, honking horns, screeching brakes, or irate drivers.

I woke up ornery, more so than a porcupine without needles or a pig with indigestion. Just plain ornery. I like hats. I wore all different shapes and styles, ritualistically selecting what I felt was right for the day. This day, I had picked an ornery hat, perfect for my ornery mood.

Riding to work and turning wide onto Southside Drive, I noticed a group of young men standing at the corner. Then I heard that direct assault on my hat. Ooooh – this isn't good, I thought as I curved back up to their corner. Nobody criticizes my hat. "Who said that about my hat? Who?" I demanded. There was a *stunned silence. Immediately, I thought, 'Hmmm, six or eight guys, yeah, I can take them. Take them all.' I repeated, 'Who?' The biggest guy – broad-shouldered, huge hands, with a smirk, 'I did. Whaddya gonna do about it?' he responded with not-so-gentle eyes. Let's see; he was at least 230 pounds of muscle, and I was 160 pounds and a bit scrawny. He had bruised my oh-so-fragile ego. "Over there by the trees, let's go, tough guy," was my ornery retort. Boy, was I gonna...*

He kicked my butt. Bloody nose, cut lip, the big guy kept saying, "Stay down, stay down." My pride demanded justice. At last, I staggered towards him. He backed off- laughing, "Enough, enough; you're hurt, man. That's enough!"

I got on my bike, shakily peddling the rest of the way to work. 'Yeah, I showed him. Yep, sure did. That guy ain't gonna mess with me no more.' My bloodied shirt was of a different opinion. My work buddies kept asking, "What happened. Are you o.k.? Man, you're really messed up." My humiliated ego responded, "I ran into a low-flying airplane." Or 'I got mugged, and they took my last dime." The truth was too much for me to bear. By the way, that guy and I later became friends. I learned he was a Golden Glover, training to be a boxer. And, no, he wasn't the person who had commented on the hat. My hat, however, met a rather ignominious end. It had rolled into the street during this episode and was no longer a fedora but would undoubtedly make a fine Frisbee.

Lee's story reminds us of the moments when our ego or emotions take control, prompting actions or beliefs that may not serve us. When Lee picked out that 'ornery hat,' his playful yet disruptive energy unknowingly shaped his day—just as we sometimes wake up on the wrong side of the bed and carry that energy forward.

Ego, unchecked emotions, and hidden motives can ripple outward, shaping our choices and creating unintended discord. Just as Lee's pride insisted on proving itself, we should pause and reflect on what drives our actions, motives, and intent. These elements work together, qualifying the energy we send into the world. By examining our impulses, we reclaim control over our emotional energy, learning to guide it consciously instead of letting it guide us.

We can choose differently than our first impulse with each inhale we take. It takes courage to examine our inner motives and a desire to change them if they do not serve us or others in a healthy form. When we become honest with what drives us to a particular action or belief, we can double-check to see its resonance. Our Keynote speaker can help enlighten and resolve numerous issues. A valid question we can ask ourselves is, "Who or what does this serve?" Was Lee Two Hawks only serving himself through his pride and ego? You would be surprised to see how this simple question shows where we are out of alignment, balance, and harmony. Honest reflection is required. Those who are so engaged with controlling others through manipulations, scheming, or defending positions for power miss the point where the authentic power is held—misguided, to say the least.

This brings us to the distinction between predestined and free energies. Understanding these qualifying guidelines enables us to align our actions with harmony rather than discord, ensuring that our choices resonate with Universal Laws and Principles. By mastering our emotional energy, egoic impulses, and intentions, we reduce the friction we unconsciously create and flow with greater clarity, purpose, and alignment.

Qualifying Guidelines

Predestined and Free Energies

The Universe operates through a blend of energies, those aligned with the Divine Plan and free energies, which await human qualification. Understanding this distinction is key to navigating the flow and aligning with the greater harmony of existence.

Predestined Energies are the immutable forces that shape and govern the cosmos. These inevitable energies are the scaffolding of evolution, ensuring harmony, balance, and order within all systems. They are untouched by human influence, forming the framework through which all existence moves. Examples include the rhythm of planetary motion, the innate drive toward self-realization, and the universal impulse for synthesis and cohesion. This represents both the macro and micro.

In contrast, free energies are fluid and malleable, shaped by individual will, thought, and intent. They are the building blocks of creation, responding to the quality of our consciousness, desires, and choices. They influence our experiences, whether we are aware of them or not. Predestine Energies are the framework, and Free Energies determine how we navigate within that arrangement. The interplay between these two forces—fixed structure and fluid potential—defines the spectrum of creation, guiding how energy manifests within our reality.

A Heads Up Before You Continue

These principles are not meant to be read for enjoyment or memorized, nor are they rules to constrain us. Instead, they serve as reference points—tools to help us qualify our intent, manifestations, and service. As we navigate energy, having a framework to reflect on allows us to refine what we create and align with a higher coherence.

As you explore the concepts in this chapter, you may begin to recognize patterns in your own life—moments where thoughts or intent felt blocked, misaligned, or created unintended results. This awareness isn't about judgment but about gaining clarity through the interplay of energies. Sometimes, all it takes is a shift in perception to understand why specific manifestations play out the way they do. Simply recognizing these laws in action can provide insight and direction. They are concise and structured in one place for you.

This is the dance of Divine Order, shaping the unfolding journey of all existence. It is a universal language that creates infinite possibilities and is of service to all. We can use it to qualify the energy we send and receive. It also serves as a framework for checks and balances. Explore and discover.

Predestined (Immutable Laws)

These are foundational, unchangeable forces shaping and Governing Our Solar System. They cannot be influenced but can be understood and aligned with in order to co-create. This is why the Multiverse will only deliver from its octave, not human belief or lack thereof.

Three Cosmic Laws: The Law of Synthesis: Governs unity and resonance, harmonizing all energies. The Law of Economy: Ensures energy flows efficiently, favoring the path of least resistance. The Law of Attraction and Repulsion: Manages cohesion and separation, balancing forces- (The Micro Law of Attraction is a mere reflection of this Cosmic Law.).

Laws of Construction: Principles or Rays from Divine Will: The foundational force driving intention and purpose in creation.

Divine Love-Wisdom: Creates balance through compassion, understanding, and unity. Active Intelligence: Governs the purposeful flow of energy as the architect of creation, destruction, and renewal, ensuring equilibrium and evolutionary progress. Free Will: Empowers choice, shaping consequences based on alignment with universal principles.

Other Immutable Laws: Law of Love: Governs harmony and the unifying force of unconditional compassion. The Law of Cleavages: Facilitates growth through destruction and reintegration. The Law of Life: Governs vitality and the perpetual motion of existence. Law of Forgiveness: Dissolves karmic energy, freeing stuck vibrations and promoting healing. **Nuances:** The Law of Abundance, Free Will, and the Universal (micro) Law of Attraction can be found within the Free Energies.

Free Energies
In contrast, free energies are neutral and malleable, awaiting qualification by human thought, intention, and action. These energies are not bound by a fixed purpose; instead, they respond to the direction given by individual or collective consciousness. When humans align their intent with Divine Will, these free energies integrate with predestined flows, creating outcomes that resonate with love, wisdom, and harmony. However, when misqualified—through fear, ignorance, or resistance—free energies create discord, friction, and stagnation, amplifying the illusion of separation from the Divine.

Universal Laws (Energetic Governance)
These free energies govern the universe's operations and **can be** consciously engaged through position and intent.

Law of Reciprocity: Energy exchanges must be balanced; what you send out returns in kind.

Law of Cause and Effect: Every action has an equal and corresponding reaction, whether physical, mental, or emotional, shaping outcomes (commonly recognized as karma).

Law of Free Will: Supports the ability to make choices while honoring their consequences.

Law of Harmony and Rhythm: Balances energy through cycles, fostering alignment and reducing friction.

(These are just a few.)

The Interplay of Energies

The relationship between predestined and free energies highlights humanity's unique role as co-creators within the Divine Plan. While predestined energies ensure the ultimate success of evolution, free energies provide the canvas for human expression, choice, and growth. This interplay exemplifies the balance between Divine Governance and the gift of free will. Through conscious alignment with the Cosmic Laws, individuals can transform free energies into powerful agents of harmony and manifestation, bridging the worlds of Divine order and human experience. Energy is a language guiding and shaping our lives. This understanding takes us far beyond pleasantries, inviting deeper conversations with the Universe.

Principles of Access and Application

These are practical guidelines for consciously working with energy to create harmony and transformation.

Law of Forgiveness: Dissolves karmic energy, freeing stuck vibrations and promoting healing.

Law of Frequency: Aligns higher vibrations with higher outcomes. (Like attracts like.)

Law of Abundance: Channels infinite possibilities and eliminates the concept of lack when accessed with clarity.

Law of Correspondence: 'As above, so below'—shows how macrocosmic principles mirror microcosmic experiences.

Law of Attraction: (micro) Operates through resonance, reflects the frequency of our thoughts, emotions and intent, drawing like energies into our experience.

(These are just a few.)

What are we qualifying?

These qualifying guidelines establish the foundation for recognizing the energies at play—those predestined within the Divine Order and those freely chosen through human qualification. Like threads in a tapestry, these energies interweave to create our lived experiences. To navigate this dance effectively, we must discern how to align our free will with the predestined flow, harmonizing intent, and action within the more lavish design. Through this interplay, we shape our reality while honoring the divine order.

To intentionally qualify the energies within this interplay, we must first explore the framework of service—how it manifests and what it reflects about our alignment. The distinctions between self-serving, service to self, and serving others are not only philosophical but highly energetic. They reveal the resonance of our intentions and the outcomes we create, offering a mirror to our place within the universal design.

Qualifying guidelines are not a concept or a demeanor of overthinking. Often, no thought is given before we take action. I'll remind you of the anonymous single person seeking a mate, navigating emotional upsets, or Lee Two Hawks' self-destructive tendencies driven by a bruised ego. Yet, when we become clear on our end result, qualifying takes only seconds.

We've established that some energies are fixed, shaping existence, while others are fluid, shaped by thought and intent. Recognizing this balance helps us qualify energy in our daily lives. As we move forward, we'll examine how intent, whether self-serving, serving-self, or in service to others—determines the resonance of what we create.

These distinctions help us evaluate and engage our spiritual development and evolution. Some consider these to be common sense or self-evident, yet few examine them genuinely, choosing instead to maintain an air of dominance. Let's explore these distinctions with this perspective in mind.

Self-Serving: actions stem from a low vibrational frequency, often tied to selfishness and ego-driven motives. This mindset prioritizes personal gain over the well-being of others, with little regard for the consequences. Emotional attributes such as jealousy, control, immovable idealism, self-pity, or narcissism dominate this perspective. It reflects a fixation on the outer world, disconnected from the inner self. Self-serving behaviors create friction and discord as they resonate with sympathy rather than empathy. This can be considered the little 's' in self. (It's our human self.)

Serving-Self: in contrast, it carries a higher vibrational frequency and focuses on self-preservation through integrity and balance. This perspective embraces self-correction, self-realization, and self-governance, ensuring no harm is done to others while nurturing personal growth. By orienting with compassion, forgiveness, and love, serving self resonates with empathy and fosters harmony within and around us. When our actions, beliefs, or purpose are rooted in the healthy benefit for self or others, it raises the vibration. It reflects a shift toward the inner world, guided by higher spiritual principles. This can be considered the capital, 'S' in Self. (It's our spiritual Self.)

Service to others: operates at the highest vibrational frequency, representing a labor of love transcending self-interest. This state of being focuses on the preservation and the well-being of all-- fostering gratitude, compassion, and unity. By aligning actions with the greater good, service to others harmonizes with the Laws of the Universe, emphasizing co-creation and freedom. It embodies a higher octave of expression, where collective progress precedes individual desires. Laws are always Pre-Served. This can be considered a System of Belief.

To Qualify and Align Service

To answer the question, 'What energies are we qualifying?' this section provides a structured approach to examine and align the energies at play within ourselves and our actions. By engaging in reflection, we can harmonize free energies (choices and actions) with predestined energies (divine order) to create alignment with Universal Laws. The actionable steps below serve as practical tools to qualify energies and ensure they resonate with the highest good.

Consider your purpose, motive, and intent to create and speak from a seat of power. Who or What do they serve? Contemplate your beliefs, agendas, actions, words, and deeds to see if there is friction, discord, or dominance.

First Step: Apply the Law of Free Will. (Own your choices.)

Second Step: Create no harm. (Consider the impact and end result for self or others.)

Third Step: Ask and answer who these serve. (This aligns with coherence.)

How are your ideas, purpose, and behaviors serving you?

Are they:

Self-Serving? If 'self' comes first, reconsider. (selfishness, self-absorbed, self-centered, self-destruction, self-pity, self-indulgence, or an insular tone.) Ego-driven, control issues, and friction are coping mechanisms. If any action can be seen as destructive, or perhaps with narcissism, the emphasis is on self. A self–serving clue: People typically justify or defend that action or belief. Lower vibration.

(It resonates with Sympathy.)

Observer Position

Adopt the role of an observer to evaluate the energy or subject matter being sent forth. You can identify patterns of error or discordant energies by stepping back without judgment. This practice bridges mindfulness of free energies (our choices) and their interplay with predestined energies (the Divine Flow).

Serving-Self? The word Service comes first. Meaning loving self a in healthy way and causing no harm to others. (Position of the Ob-server. Self-correction, Self-governance, or self-empowerment.) If you notice, these terms offer correction and governance that serve the Self. Choosing service first helps to step into the balancing and harmonizing flow. Balanced- vibration. (It resonates with Empathy.)

Meditations or Thoughts

Engage in mindful reflection to examine how words and beliefs resonate within your energy body. This awareness allows you to refine your intentions and qualify the vibrational frequency of free energies, aligning them with the divine harmony of predestined energies.

Service to others? This energy expands freedom and preservation- pre-served. Co-creation, unity and Divine alignment. Highest vibration   (It resonates with Compassion and Love.)

Honest Reflection

Take time to reflect honestly on your purpose, motives, and agendas. Are they driven by fear or love? Harmony or discord? This step clarifies how free energies, like intent and action, align with the overarching flow of divine order.

Dominion? Removal is highly suggested. Ownership or control dramas: relationships, jealousy, possessiveness, or property. Through action, words, and deeds, we can self-govern.

Challenge Old Beliefs

Examine learned beliefs and habits to discern whether they serve a higher purpose. By challenging and transforming limiting or discordant patterns, you harmonize free energies with predestined ones that guide our growth and evolution.

My statement concerning 'want & need': "I give no energy or focus to the equation of lack; to do so would not serve a higher purpose and would constrict someone else's ability to co-create." Steps 1, 2, and 3 were fulfilled. Resides with Service to others and abides by laws. There is no human dominion in this sentence when we co-create.

If we were to look in any chapter and apply this format of Qualifying Guidelines to suggested declarations or content, we could determine the resonance of Law and its principles. Try this one: I am willing to accept healing. Or this one: What is its resonance and possible end result? This last question covers all chapters thus far within the guidance of energy. Remember, energy is a language.

These steps clarify what energies we qualify and provide tools to ensure our actions, thoughts, and intentions align with the interplay of Divine Order and human free will. Engaging in these practices can create coherence within ourselves and the world around us, resonating with higher vibrations.

Lee Two Hawks' fedora hat story reminds us why these steps matter. His journey exemplifies that observing, reflecting, and challenging beliefs can align our free will with predestined energies. Through these actions, he transformed profound challenges into harmony, showing us the power of applying these principles in real life.

Checks and Balances for Guidance: Personal Beliefs

How do we check or qualify beliefs? Apply Laws. If we question any human rights violation, where do you stand? What's your view on Abortion, Immigrants, Race, Hunger, Eminent Domain, Animal

Cruelty, or Executions? I'd like to present three additional Laws we can reference as checks and balances against one of these issues. Each Law to be described carries an aspect of Divine Will, Divine Love/Wisdom, and Active Intelligence. (–See chapter nine.)

At the heart of Universal Laws lies the concept of predestined energies. These energies act as guiding currents, ensuring that our choices—rooted in love, forgiveness, or resistance—align with or disrupt the Divine blueprint designed for our growth and harmony.

Law of Love: It includes self-sacrifice, unity, brotherhood, and synthesis, which are operative functions of the Law of Free Will. With magnetic impulse, this love is the Buddhic love transmuted from the physical desire into the more exact aspect of Oneness. Love reaches the entirety of all multiverses.

It is far more encompassing, embracing, and comprehensive than is usually understood by the term in everyday existence. In love's maturity, free will would become a moot point, as love allows no impediment or limitation; thus, it is of Divine Perfection. (-See Laws at a Glance.)

The Law of Love is the foundation of all creation, and predestined energies flow effortlessly within this vibrational field. When we act from love, we harmonize with the divine order, allowing blessings and balance to manifest effortlessly.

Law of Forgiveness: When called upon, it releases and transmutes any cause, effect, and record of any error. It gives freedom from limitation and bondage; it stops the energy's forward movement from the misdirected action. It is a required attribute to move into a higher consciousness.

Forgiveness is a personal journey for each of us and a mechanism to find our unique expression. A recommendation for its application is encoded within this energy's function. First, ask that any cause created in error be transmuted into love. Second, ask to stop or consume any effects that were initiated. Finally, it erases or releases mistakes from the etheric records. The discordant energy will return to you if not corrected; that's why we ask for the history of the misdeed to be removed.

Forgiveness is an emotional and mental component of our expression. It is designed to be practiced during our life experiences. Therefore, if we do not learn how to forgive ourselves and others here, we will master it after death; it is Law. It is used as the mechanism by which we release blockages and realign with predestined energies. By forgiving ourselves and others, we clear the path for love and light to flow, restoring harmony and grace.

Law of Life: It is a given that to understand Life, one should grasp that Life is the very nature of energy. Energy is synonymous with Spirit. Life is infused with Spirit (The Divine Breath). Thus, any Law attending to energy is, by definition, a Law of Life. Life is the essence of our being; therefore, it is light. We are light. We speak of the quality of life, not the appearance of life. This encompasses all Laws. (-See Laws at a Glance.)

The matter is so abstruse that a more in-depth explanation is beyond our effort in this body of work. However, the Law of Life reflects the ultimate purpose of predestined energies: growth, evolution, and unity. Every experience—joyful or challenging—unfolds within this framework, offering opportunities for alignment and transcendence.

These energies are not rigid dictates but dynamic flows. They respond to our choices, actions, and intentions, providing feedback that keeps us on course or nudges us toward correction when we stray. By working within the checks and balances of the Law of Love, Forgiveness, and Life, we co-create with the Divine rather than resisting its flow. When facing a challenging decision, ask yourself:

Am I acting from a place of love or fear? Have I forgiven myself and others involved in this situation? How does this choice serve the greater harmony of life?

Use these laws as a compass for aligning with predestined energies, ensuring that your actions resonate with higher vibrations.

Predestined energies remind us that we are never truly lost. With each choice guided by love, forgiveness, and life, we return to the divine current, creating a reality of peace, balance, and fulfillment.

Forgive this momentary interruption...

Before we move forward, I'd like to address forgiveness more thoroughly because it is often misunderstood. People think it's about letting someone off the hook, but in reality, it's about freeing ourselves and reclaiming our energy. It's important to note that forgiveness is not for the other person—it's for you. By forgiving, you reclaim your power and shift your focus from harm to healing. This transformative act releases energetic discord, places us with higher vibrations, and creates space for healing and balance.

When we forgive, we raise our vibration, clear energetic blockages, and open ourselves to love, peace, and abundance. It is a gift to yourself, allowing you to step forward without the weight of unresolved pain. It aligns us with the Universal Laws, particularly the Law of Cause and Effect, creating a ripple of healing that extends to others. Reflect on what you are holding onto. Ask yourself: What pain or resentment am I carrying, like a broken record?

Three practical steps are encoded within the very nature of the Law of Forgiveness.

First, ask that any cause created in error be transmuted into love. **Second,** ask to stop or consume any effects that were initiated. **Finally**, ask the Multiverse to erase or release mistakes from the etheric records. Bless the person or situation, sending them love and light as an act of compassion and closure.

As Saint Germain teaches in The "I AM" Discourses (Volume 3), forgiveness is a Divine Law that dissolves discord and clears the energetic records of imbalance—both physical and etheric—allowing harmony to be restored.

The Threefold Nature of Forgiveness

This profound process operates on a threefold level—not only addressing the cause, effect, and record but also requiring forgiveness in three directions: forgiving others, forgiving ourselves, and asking for divine forgiveness to clear all imbalances. This completeness allows harmony to flow through all aspects of our being.

Affirmations for Forgiveness:

To solidify the energy of forgiveness, say aloud or in your heart:

- I am free. I forgive. I am at peace.

- I release the past and embrace the present.

- I forgive myself and others for any harm caused.

- I am erasing the record.

- I ask for forgiveness—not only for myself but for all involved, and I call upon the Law of Forgiveness to restore harmony.

It is not about agreeing with or excusing harmful actions. It's about personal freedom. Forgiveness isn't a single act; it's a practice. Each time we choose to forgive, we tune ourselves to the frequency of freedom and grace. By stepping into the flow of forgiveness, we align with Universal Laws and create space for healing and transformation.

Appling Checks and balances: Personal beliefs

If we examine executions and ask, who or what does this serve? We will find resonance in this action or belief by applying any of the laws mentioned. Does your position vibrate with balance and harmony compared to any of the above Laws? Let's use a few steps of Spiritual Logic and see where it leads. Keep in mind the power of beliefs. We offer information for each person to explore.

Although this exercise is neither pro nor con for executions, there's additional information to help you see the grander narrative and its effect. Beliefs, either for or against, will remain a personal journey. Let's see if we can reduce the triggering of our hot buttons. A fundamental realization should be that there's no separation between the etheric and physical realms. One is the builder, the cause, and the other is the effect of a moral value. Whether our beliefs are accurate and aligned or not, they carry potency. We will receive more of the same from the etheric energy field until these harmonize with Principles.

Exercise for Executions

Considering the complex issue of executions, these laws provide a framework for examining whether our beliefs and actions align with the Universal Principles of love, life, and forgiveness. They guide us in assessing the morality and the energetic resonance of our choices. In questioning acts like execution, we ask, 'Who does this serve?' From the perspective of spiritual logic, such acts perpetuate lower vibrations, binding individuals and societies in cycles of harm. Christ's teachings, rooted in love and forgiveness, guide us toward higher resonance and harmony. This discussion isn't about right or wrong but about understanding energy and aligning actions with principles that foster unity and healing.

Before we begin, please note the positions

Etheric Position: Nothing can happen to a person without their authority or permission at the soul level, whether conscious of this or not. Death is regarded as a release, freedom, ultimate healing, or going home.

Physical Position: Death as a punishment only works for those who fear death. Death of the body is inevitable; we can qualify it with fear or lovingly accept it.

Let's consider Imprisonment for life vs. Freedom in death.

Imprisoned for Life

Those who have taken a life will pay the price, but not to us. Could we ever receive payment? Would death fulfill its asking price? Is the amount of justice based only on the values we presently hold? Humanity has weaponized death as a deterrent by taking an eye for an eye. Appropriately, these death consequences haven't worked because their design was developed by those who fear it. The crimes are still committed.

Could we consider a life for a life, living in prison? How do we justify our values? By judging others? These people have violated the Law of Free Will, criminal laws, and social norms. They imposed their will and took action, halting the free will of their victims. They will be accountable and pay a prestigious price, not specifically for taking a life but for violating free will. Cosmic Justice is in accordance with vibrational Law. We innately know this because we have created social and civic laws to gain a sense of decorum for justice. Thus, we are impulsed by the influence of energy and try to follow a set pattern of predestined energy. We are still trying to gain an expanded view and a positioning of values, which change over time.

Will our judicial system allow for emotional illness as it does for mental illness? Could not abnormal conditions of dominance and control also be considered insane? Sociopathic serial killers feed on domination, power, and control.

The removal of life by murder or capital punishment is arrogance defined. The atrocities committed by the felon sentenced to death cannot be mitigated or resolved nor redeemed by taking that person's life – which, by definition, is murder. Spending a lifetime in prison is its own hell. That person's quality of life is constrained and restrained by the existing walls and the imposition of well-defined rules. Also, the other inmates have their defining modes of acceptable behavior, which further the confining atmosphere of imprisonment. It could also be pointed out that it costs more to execute someone than it does for them to remain in prison.

Humanity places importance on life and misses the point of loving life. The results remain with friction and discord because we give more value and distinction to life than its Law. If the Law of Life came first, life would be preserved. The conflict would be reduced by maintaining the Love of Life, which resonates within all Laws; thus, energy would be Pre-Served. The expanded view is that we seek justice for the same Law we all violate, the Law of Free Will.

Through the lens of the Law of Life, we are reminded that all life carries inherent value and purpose, even when confined. Does taking a life honor this principle, or does it diminish the sanctity of existence?

Those seeking the death of another- please consider the Law of Reciprocity. It does not mean that if you wish the death of another, that death will come to you. It means that life will not be as fruitful and blessed as possible. Life will remain tainted with negative lower vibrational energy surrounding events and circumstances. How does this action serve us? Self-serving seems to be at the forefront. Payment by execution leaves an empty promise or expectations unfulfilled.

Additionally, the premise is that we know precisely where these individuals will go, to hell. This foundation is based on a religious structure, not of Law. Can we see the dominion and control we are passively enacting? Have we considered or understood how energy works? Does this way of thinking carry the same tone that Lee's fedora hat did with "Yeah, I showed him. Yep, sure did. That guy ain't gonna mess with me no more." The Laws of Free Will, Correspondence, and Attraction will be set in motion with any choice.

The influential law, in this case, is the Law of Forgiveness; it is the ultimate justice we can give ourselves in this lifetime or the next. If we do not reconcile with this Law here on earth, we will face it after we die. It is for us, not necessarily the perpetrator. Forgiveness heals and releases poisonous emotional limitations that continue to imprison us.

When execution occurs, outside the prison gates, you will see a group of people shouting 'Kill him, kill him' vibrating with animal fervor and sympathy for the victims. In bold letters, their signs express vengeance, hatred, and dire invective. Their posters also reflect their conscious fear of death. Is this madness, or is this the true human heart? Where is compassion for those remaining family members who are experiencing this trauma? Is the limiting, restrictive, and low vibrational energy being sent out returning to each of them helpful? Will humanity continue engraving this low vibrational consciousness within our hearts of stone?

The sobering truth remains that innocent people can and have been executed. As we judge, we should reflect on one of history's most profound examples—Christ himself. Wrongly condemned and executed, he chose love over judgment, forgiveness over hatred, and became the ultimate exemplar of the Law of Love.

When we observe the fervor surrounding executions, such as the shouts of 'Kill 'em, kill 'em.' it is essential to reflect on how this energy aligns with the Law of Love. Does it contribute to healing, or does it amplify discord and separation?

~To paraphrase Ingrid Newkirk, founder of PETA, the world's largest animal rights organization, "Our human nature is first to ridicule new ideas or perceptions, then discuss them and finally adopt them." ~

Freedom in Death

Therefore, a few things to ponder: Execution creates a release from a convict's confined prison cells and the physical body. We all take our personalities, including all the love or hate, with us when we die. This energy and consciousness will remain with us until the characteristics that no longer serve us dissipate and are absorbed into the collective unified energy. This dissipation resonates with the Law of Cleavages. (-See, Additional Laws.)

Energy cannot be extinguished, only transformed. Has it occurred to anyone that these killers may continue to taunt their victims and others after their execution? Especially if the perpetrator's personality is vindictive and cruel, that won't change. This convict also has free will and can choose to remain earth-bound, which can happen with unfinished business. They don't have to go home, whether it is hell or heaven. A perfect saying to reflect this is that at closing time, some bars will broadcast, "You don't have to go home, but you can't stay here."

The sentiment remains, let's execute them and be done with it. Who will stop these murderers now if we release them into the etheric field? Earth-bound entities exist. Their existence does not require a belief in them. In essence, we are freeing serial killers to continue heinously tormenting their victims. They are not imprisoned anymore—they are free.

Here is another possibility with cause and effect. We all like to believe our loved ones are in heaven and at peace, and I'm not saying they're not. It might take them a little while to get there if their death was sudden or terrorizing and full of fear. But, by chance, this previous scenario would play out, giving the villain freedom in an unknown world. With this possible result, should we seek justice in this manner?

Or perhaps give the villain a lifetime to halt the action and effects, giving our loved ones time to adjust and escape to heaven. Whom will it serve? Has step two been considered to cause no harm? Where is the love for self or others? It's something to consider.

By applying the Law of Forgiveness, we challenge ourselves to reflect on whether the executions continuously transmute harm or perpetuate cycles of pain and discord, like a broken record. This law urges us to look beyond the immediate circumstances and consider the broader energetic implications.

For a moment, we would like to address this issue of death by the hand of another. We are not dismissive of this experience's deep emotional pain. We hope healing and release from this pain will become a reality for anyone touched by these events. Please don't let anyone steal your joy, even yourself.

True to nature, we have free will and can believe however we choose. We can heal emotional scars if we have guidance and honest reflection. We do hope you can see a broader scope. It's the language of the Universe that shows us the way.

By applying the Laws of Love, Life, and Forgiveness, we expand our awareness beyond reactionary beliefs. These principles guide us to align our actions with higher vibrations, creating opportunities for harmony rather than perpetuating cycles of pain.

Clarifying Christ's metaphysical teachings

In examining Christ's teachings, we witness his embodiment of the Law of Love, offering forgiveness and compassion even in the face of the gravest injustice. This reflection on executions can be intensely emotional and challenging, requiring us to pause and center ourselves. The Lord's Prayer offers a grounding moment for those familiar with Catholicism. Its universal message of forgiveness, accountability, and alignment with Divine Will is a guiding Principle as we navigate these complex moral and spiritual questions. As Christ taught, forgiveness is not just an act but a Law that governs the transmutation of energy. Let us transition into this reflection with an open heart for guidance and support.

For those of you who study the bible, we would like to clarify a few aspects because we have spoken about energy at length. Any of Christ's teachings can be supported through metaphysical energy and the principles we have been discussing. I'd like to show you something fascinating to do with laws. The Holy Spirit confirms to Christ:

> *"This is the covenant I will make with them after that time, says the Lord. I will put my laws in their hearts, and I will write them on their minds."* Then he adds: *"Their sins and lawless acts I will remember no more."* (Hebrews 10:16-17, NIV)

This verse powerfully reminds us that Universal Laws are not foreign or complex concepts—they are already within us. They resonate as common sense because they are written in our hearts and minds. Referring to "lawless acts" speaks to the natural consequences of stepping out of alignment with these laws. It is not about judgment but about the energetic impact of not honoring these principles. In aligning with Universal Laws, Christ's teachings offer a profound example of harmony. The Lord's Prayer, often viewed as a simple recitation, reveals itself as a blueprint for aligning with Spiritual and Cosmic Principles.

As a Prayer, it is a profound guide to aligning with Predestined Energies. But its opening line, 'Our Father, who art in heaven, hallowed be thy name,' stands apart. This line is not a reflection of a specific law; it is an invocation creating the connection that allows the subsequent reflections on laws to unfold. It is the shifting into spiritual logic (180 -degrees), a moment of stepping into alignment by reaching out to the Divine. Let us break this down because each stanza carries metaphysical laws and reminds us of the covenant given to Christ.

The Lord's Prayer

Our Father, who art in heaven, hallowed be thy name;

This is the greeting, the honoring. This invocation changes our position in thoughts to 180- degrees of Spiritual Logic. This reminds us of our etheric connection to higher planes of existence to which we open the door to the Divine Source. From this act of connection, the rest of the prayer unfolds as a framework for aligning with Universal Laws. Each stanza reflects a specific aspect of the laws, offering guidance for thought, word, and action in alignment with Divine Principles or Predestined Energies. This speaks to Divine Love/Wisdom. (Similar to making a phone call, we have a private number.)

Thy kingdom come; thy will be done on earth as it is in heaven.
This emphasizes Divine Will and the Law of Free Will, including the Laws of Correspondence, Economy, and Reciprocity. Kingdom reminds us to harmonize our intentions with the greater good, aligning personal desires with universal flow. Law of Free Will and Correspondence: This stanza reflects the alignment of personal will with Divine Will, bridging the spiritual and physical realms.

Give us this day our daily bread;
An observation might suggest the Law of Abundance regarding food for the body. However, our daily bread indicates food for thought because of our connection to higher planes of existence to which we have opened the door. We also require food for our Spirit; intuition, enlightenment, or an expanded view brings light and consciousness into our bodies. This daily bread is our information highway. This line reminds us that physical and spiritual sustenance flow from alignment with Divine Principles. The Multiverse is abundant.

and forgive us our trespasses as we forgive those who trespass against us;
This is the covenant revealed; The Law of Forgiveness is the only Law mentioned by name and is a journey requiring direction and reflection on trespasses such as misdeeds or debts. When asked, it releases and transmutes any cause, effect, and record of any error. The Law of Correspondence shows the importance of working with forgiveness here, which makes it easier to work with it on the other side.

and lead us not into temptation,
This stanza reflects the Law of Vibration and Polarity, emphasizing the requirement to remain aligned with higher frequencies while avoiding lower vibrational energies that create discord. It also aligns with the Law of Mentalism, encouraging control over thoughts and

intentions to maintain harmony. It reminds us to establish checks and balances within these laws. Our daily bread can show us a path. The Law of Free Will holds accountability.

but deliver us from evil.

This means to keep our vibrational frequency high. When we foul it up, we can choose a higher frequency. Please remember that energy is neither good nor evil; it is how we qualify it. Evil, in this sense, is energy that is lower, slower, and constrictive, filled with limitations.

For thine is the kingdom, the power, and the glory, forever and ever.

This line encapsulates the Law of Unity and Synthesis, acknowledging the Divine as the source of creation and harmony. It also reflects the Law of Oneness, reminding us of the interconnectedness of all things through Divine Governance. This gives honor and serves as a reminder that this kingdom is within us, written in our hearts and minds.

Amen.

Just as a greeting or invocation, we have a closing embrace. The word 'Amen' reflects the Law of Completion, representing the affirmation and sealing of intention. It is a final act of trust in Divine Will and alignment with Universal Principles. This signifies an acknowledgment of alignment, affirming the truth and energy of what has been spoken.

Through the Lord's Prayer, Christ provided not only a method of prayer but a universal framework for understanding and aligning with the divine. By meditating on its stanzas and their corresponding laws, we gain understanding to harmonize our spiritual and physical lives.

Reframing

We have one more example to contemplate regarding word choice. The Bible contains the Ten Commandments, holding a subtle negative reference to a command. What if, in our conscious awareness, we converted commandments to commitments? We know it won't be changed because it's written in stone. But, a commandment is vibrationally lower, seeking power and control. Commitment creates an opportunity to choose free will. If we commit to living by these Ten Guidelines, we retain a choice and create a different experience. The Ten Commitments: if we choose, our lives can be filled with blessings.

By shifting our perspective from commandments to commitments, we open ourselves to free will, higher vibrations, and alignment. This shift in energy mirrors the essence of harmonizing, where we consciously choose to align our thoughts, words, and actions with the universal flow. Let us summarize how to attune ourselves and create resonance within the fabric of our lives.

Harmonizing

As we conclude these reflections, it becomes clear that the laws of life, love, and forgiveness are not abstract ideals but practical tools for navigating the complexities of existence. By engaging with these principles, we begin to see how the predestined energies of the universe and our dynamic choices co-create our reality. Harmonizing these energies is not merely a goal but a practice offering profound clarity, peace, and empowerment. The following practices serve as simple reminders-- tools we have already explored--to attune ourselves to the greater harmony within and around us.

We can attune by

- Observe nature as a teacher of energy and spiritual logic, as discussed in Chapter Three, reflecting the inherent predestined rhythm within creation. Ask, and it will be shown.

- Align your words carefully, recognizing their vibrational impact and resonance, directly influencing and qualifying energy.

- Discernment: Justifying or defending actions, words, or deeds are human responses and logic, not spiritual logic. If you have to rationalize or defend a position, you may choose to re-qualify what you are supporting. There is always another point of view.

- Observer Position: Do not engage or judge. Just assess qualifying guidelines. What energy or subject matter is being sent out to return? 'Patterns of error' can be quickly identified when we shift the focus. Reflect on service—who does it serve?

- Apply the checks and balances of spiritual laws—love, life, forgiveness—to evaluate personal beliefs, global issues, and their resonance with predestined energies.

- Reflect on the energetic consequences of your actions, ensuring they align with principles of harmony, transmuting misqualified energy into balanced expressions.

- Meditation, prayer, or consider how words and beliefs resonate with you. Remember the 3Rs. What does your energy body feel like as these concepts or ideas impact you? Do they harmonize with your energy or the energy of law? Do they resonate as discordant or graceful?

Special Note: To make a point about leading a meditation. Meditation should allow others to experience their vast, expansive nature, the power of who they are, or anywhere in between. A suggestion would be to set the frequency and then verbally match the frequency intended. For example, (unbeknownst to you) if one group member carries a discordant note for surrender, and this word is used, trust or focus could be lost. Friction will block their experience. Instead, apply caution for what is being put forth. Remember checks and balances, service to all, not just one view or position. Helping others retain their power to co-create with permission, allowance, acceptance, release, or willingness will substantially impact meditation and their lives. Look how many words to choose from with a higher resonance. Is there Divine Willing-ness?

Wrap Up

By embracing these practices, we integrate the lessons of each chapter into a cohesive path forward. These steps remind us that harmony is always within reach, and the predestined energies we explored are here to guide us toward alignment and balance, both individually and collectively.

Whether through meditation, forgiveness, prayer, or examining deeply held beliefs, Christ's teachings and Universal Laws invite us to create from a place of love and harmony. By aligning with these principles, we transform ourselves and contribute to a world rooted in unity and peace.

As you step into the next chapter with helpful tools, take a moment to reflect: How can I bring these laws into my daily life? Where can I harmonize with the flow of the universe?

Key Points: Whom does it serve?

- Honest Reflection for Self-evaluation: who and what is served?

- Align purpose, motives, and agendas into harmony. There are many ways.

- Challenge old, learned beliefs. New ones may serve you better.

- Recognize the Interplay of Predestined and Qualified Energies: Understand how universal energies guide and respond to our choices and intentions.

- Apply Checks and Balances of Spiritual Laws. Use the Laws of Love, Life, and Forgiveness as tools for reflection and alignment.

- Observe the Resonance of Your Beliefs: Examine how your beliefs align with harmony and universal principles.

- Focus on Harmonizing Energies: Align thoughts, words, and deeds with creation's flow.

CHAPTER EIGHT

TOOLS, WORDS & PHRASES

A Knock of Grace

A fateful knock of inexperience revealed life's multiple possibilities. Eva knew everything in her life had to do with timing. This was no different. She was disabled with a back injury. Nerve pain was excruciating, and her pain medications created mood swings, foggy thoughts, induced sleep, and an inability to focus on meditations. When she stood, she never knew how long it would last. Her leg would give way to a massive, non-graceful thud hitting the ground. It was like, now you see her, now you don't. The doctors had told her she would be relegated to a wheelchair.

These medications were timed around her children's activities. For Eva, having two teenage girls, being medicated, and being disabled, parenting became a task of its own. By nature, the girls were trying to take full advantage. To help them cope with a new way of living, she registered them for counseling, community youth programs, and after-school activities.

Eva had taken her pills an hour earlier, knowing she had four hours before school was let out. There was a knock on the door. Looking out the window, she saw a couple holding clipboards. Opening the door, she greeted a young woman, seemingly fresh out of college. The ink on her diploma must have still been wet as she began demonstrating her power as a Child Protective Service advocate. Immediately, she established her legal authority, which she could use at her discretion. This inexperienced advocate gave Eva an ultimatum without question. True to character, Eva rejected the ultimatum.

Pain, a foggy head, and a numb leg prevailed. A court appearance would be issued without an accurate assessment being made. She closed the door and then fell flat on her face. Laying in pain and frustration, she cursed the darkness. Eva knew this drama was because her body wouldn't work, and the C.P.S. worker failed to utilize an ounce of discernment or insight. No questions asked, just a judgment. The child was neither neglected nor in danger under her care. The only threat was from a young, inexperienced woman motivated by raw ambition and power with no parental experience. Anger took hold as Eva was losing bodily functions, her dignity, and perhaps the custody of her youngest child. She regretted answering the door.

The anger stripped away all the distractions within her, leaving her with a stark truth: this situation had to be dealt with, and no one else could do it for her. That anger became her catalyst, driving her to reclaim her power, step by step, until she could face what was required to be done.

Unknown to Eva, she was only a decision away from healing. Right after the first court appearance, her husband carried her in his arms and placed her in the back of the van. She was writhing in tremendous nerve pain, causing tears to fill her eyes. What an extraordinary cost for the lunacy of the advocate's mismanaged infantile power trip. Eva called out to the heavens in this unguarded moment, wishing this young woman would experience just a moment of her pain and suffering as a form of justice.

In less than a week, this C.P.S. worker's replacement informed Eva that this young woman was undergoing critical emergency surgery. Instantaneous guilt washed over her. Her prayer had been answered in a manner Eva never intended. The intent was for this young woman to use discernment and compassion. But that wasn't the result. Eva knew what was sent out would return to its source. Not caring about creating more negative energy, she focused on forgiveness. It was the saving grace. Eva utilized cancel, delete, and erase to stop any ill intent moving forward and returning home. This retaliation for justice was a wake-up call. There was a knock on the door, a knock on the head, and a knock on the heart. The focus was now on the lessons to be gentle for all concerned and how this situation could be turned around.

Every step, every moment became an opportunity to focus on her next breath, her next thought, her following action. And so, instead of spiraling into the shadows of pain, Eva began practicing the tools gifted to her over the years—by guides, through grace, or born of sheer necessity.

In an epiphany, Eva realized how she had allowed this injury to play a massive role in every aspect of her life. It was affecting the children and others. Eva became determined to focus on halting what she was experiencing. An awakening rushed through her. No more allowance will be given for destructive forces to control her or the family. She realized this injury would hold no power over her other than the power she gave it.

It was a knowing and observation that the pain was acting like a temper tantrum, demanding attention. From now on, she wouldn't provide any more attention nor entertain it. So, Eva slammed and locked the door on her unwelcome house guest, Mr. Pain Causing Havoc III. No entry allowed!

At this time, she sought assistance from her angels and guides. She required help with managing the pain, her thoughts, and daily activities in an entirely different way. Her spirit guide, Wayeen, answered quickly. "There is no time in the etheric. But, if you give 90 seconds of focus on pain or discord in a month, these 90 seconds become an eternity for you. Make up your mind, and match your focus with your desire. Choose your focus wisely."

Within two days, Eva happened to be in a small bookstore, and a book jumped off the shelf and landed at her feet. No one was in the store, she got the message and bought the book. It read Third Edition: MAP The Co-Creative White Brotherhood Medical Assistance Program by Machaelle Small Wright. (Wright) Eva knew the White Brotherhood meant of the light and was another name for the Ascended Masters such as Christ and St. Germain. What a blessing. Quickly studying the book, she implemented the techniques. Little by little, Eva reclaimed parts of her body and her life.

She sat in the front seat for short drives, went shopping when she could, made cookies with the kids, meditated as much as possible, and took one month to stop all medications. It should be mentioned that rapid withdrawal was not enjoyable. She became very cognizant of the minute-and-a-half eternity—the seemingly endless ninety-second waves of discomfort. Though challenging, these moments were opportunities to practice the vagus nerve breathing techniques map sessions from her new book and energy tools, which helped shift her focus. These tools would later become essential steps in her healing and part of the lessons she would share.

As a result, an impressive quality of life emerged. Severe pain and medications no longer controlled or influenced Eva. She does not have a wheelchair; she has a bicycle. She inspires others and speaks with graduating university medical students, sharing her healing journey. Each year, her body grows more resilient and reliable. Eva worked diligently to remove the record from the physical and etheric body; in doing so, she embraced life with renewed strength, gratitude, and joy.

By the way, with the second court date, not only did Eva win the case with C.P.S., but it was thrown out of court without merit, an unheard-of outcome in New York State.

Eva's name is an acronym for Eventually Victory Arrives.

This story is mine. The woman is me.

Insights for Healing and Balance

Through this profound journey, I was introduced to principles later shared in Chapter 4, especially in 'Now is the Time.' Two key points became pivotal to my healing: removing the record—both physical and etheric—and the importance of no longer speaking about the injury or its effects. The guidance provided in the Ascended Masters' prayer offered me a perception beyond measure.

This experience gave me insights that transformed my perspective on healing and pain. Pain demands attention—it's nature's way of signaling imbalance and inviting us to address deeper truths. However, the act of maintaining focus amidst pain can feel nearly impossible. This struggle was central to my journey and shaped the recommendations I share here.

With healing, our focus can be distracted by these 'shiny objects' of pain, illness, or cyclic tribulations. Shifting focus away from pain may seem like a Herculean effort, but with dedication and determination, it's possible. These teachings emerged from my successes and mistakes with energy, even when I knew better. Perhaps you could identify a few energy challenges from the story, as they are universally human.

This brings us to a practical consideration: how we articulate and assess our experience of chronic pain can shape our approach to healing. If a person is ever asked by medical personnel to rate their chronic pain levels using a 1-10 scale, with 10 being the worst, I have a suggestion. Doctors use this information to evaluate the condition and determine how to treat it. Inadvertently, they leave their patients focused on their pain. It takes only seconds to redirect with another question. What did you have for breakfast? Where did you vacation? The key is to alter or shift attention away from pain, not dive into it and stay there. We can do this for ourselves and others.

Simplistically, we are transforming the patterned thoughts of pain to be released. The moment after focusing on pain levels, immediately visualize something else, like sending healing light to that region to expand and expand. Or to have God's healing and loving grace rest in that region. I have used both to modify my body's temper tantrums.

Knock-knock: Perceptions

The knock on the door was more than a literal event—it symbolized a profound shift in awareness. Challenges often arrive disguised as disruptions, inviting us to reassess our perceptions. The knock reminded me to look beyond the immediate chaos and recognize the opportunity for growth. Events could have been different, delaying this healing opportunity. Life's 'knocks' are not random; they often serve as catalysts for transformation. By shifting our perspective and embracing these moments, we align with the flow of universal energy and open ourselves to deeper insight and healing. The bottom line is how we wish to experience life and how we will express it.

Insight and Intuition

Insight and intuition are not abstract concepts reserved for a select few—they are practical skills with transformative potential. For those in professional roles that influence or assess lives, such as counselors, judges, police officers, or doctors, developing intuitive insight is vital. Consider this: elite military forces already understand the importance of intuition. They train soldiers and snipers to develop this skill, as their survival depends on accurately assessing hidden variables and unseen threats. Intuition follows the same Laws I speak of here—it aligns with energy and reveals truth when adequately cultivated. Imagine a world where this level of intuitive awareness became a prerequisite in other professions. Judges would identify core emotional truths, counselors would uncover root causes, and hidden agendas would dissolve under the weight of insight. Mistakes would lessen, lives would be saved, and outcomes would reflect greater harmony.

These skills can be self-taught or acquired through other means. Many of the tools and techniques in this book can support this development. So, when will our universities see the benefits of intuition?

Our military already does. Elite forces emphasize its value as critical for survival and success. Please mark my words: there will come a time when kindergarten programs will naturally incorporate intuition. Not as a subject to teach but as an inherent part of how children live and learn, naturally and effortlessly, using this innate skill.

Wrap Up

Regarding my experience, the entire Multiverse gave me clues to the healing within. These distractive, shiny objects of pain kept me focused on what I was experiencing. Not what I desired to experience. My end result wasn't clear until my children were threatened, and I prayed for retribution. The mother bear had gotten poked. There was an internal dialog of insight, a download, or a knowingness that showed me the only thing I lacked for my healing was the Awareness of How. Healing would take courage and determination, prompting me to focus on intent and qualification. As a reminder, "It takes courage to look into that mirror and find the error, then repair it."

Relying on the Energy of Law, I stepped into the flow instead of simply holding a belief that healing could happen; I knew it could. This energy force is the difference between a System of Belief and belief systems. My keynote speaker helped me retain my focused intent for my end result, which no longer gave power and energy to this injury. Nor would I lack for anything.

One last point involves timeframes. Reviewing this life experience, it became abundantly clear that the decline in bodily functions was slow, worsening with increased pain and limitations each year. In my case, this gradual decline or process took about twelve years from the date of injury. There were no active thoughts to an outcome other than just trying to live with and accommodate this situation. The only thing I remember not allowing as a reality was the wheelchair.

Here is the exciting part: the timeframe for reclaiming my life happened in about two and a half years. Yes, it took a little over two years to be able to rely on my leg. Nerve damage is no joke. Oh, the power of intent. No mental work went into the decline, but mental work went into the healing. I still have some off days, but these are managed.

- I have moved from *Visualizing* that the pain does not control me.

- To *Focused Attention*: I control the pain.

- To *Qualifying*: there is no pain nor limitation.

To this day, I bless this experience and honor all who helped me through it. It does not matter what tribulations present themselves; we can choose how to integrate and expand our understanding of these life lessons. I happen to carry the message now. Nothing changed until I asked, and I had to have a reason to change. There is a way, there is another view, and there is a path. Our kingdom to create is within. When there is peace in the body, healing can exist.

Special note:
This chapter is divided into three sections, each with its own key points, which are also compiled at the end of the chapter for easy reference.

Section A: A story of experience.

Section B: Tools and techniques bring awareness, healing, and harmony into our lives.

Section C: Familiar words to consider for expanding consciousness.

The tools I will share next, gifted by my guides or learned through experience—were vital in transforming my life. Whether it was reclaiming my power from pain or shifting my focus to healing, they carried me to victory, eventually. As you explore each technique, know they were not theoretical ideas but practical, powerful tools used in my journey. Each emerged during times of challenge or revelation, offering a pathway to peace, balance, and harmony.

Key Points: A story of experience.

Section A. A Knock of Grace

- Match focus with desire.

- Pain demands attention. Refocus and seek solutions.

- Insight and perceptions shift our awareness. (Visualization, Focused Attention, and Qualifying.)

- Adversity often hides blessings that guide us toward healing.

- Tribulations -- physical, mental, or emotional— reveal areas requiring balance and alignment.

- Challenges offer opportunities to transform struggle into empowerment. How we react when situations appear out of control defines the outcome.

Section B

Tools and Techniques

Introduction to Techniques

The techniques in this section are designed to be flexible and adaptable to your requirements. Mix and match or combine several to see how they work. Feel free to revisit any technique as often as you like. These tools are meant to meet you wherever you are, whether during times of challenge or revelation, quietly sitting on a park bench, or during a chaotic day. Enjoy experimenting with them to find what resonates most with your journey.

These tools gifted by my guides or learned through experience—were vital in transforming my life. Whether it was reclaiming my power or shifting my focus for manifesting, they eventually carried me to victory. As you explore each technique, know they are practical, robust methods offering a pathway to peace, balance, and harmony.

Shadow Fox's Focused Timeframes

Purpose: *To reclaim energy from negative patterns by consciously limiting the time spent on unproductive thoughts or discussions, fostering a focus on healing and desired outcomes.*

This practice of *Focused Timeframes* was revealed to me after those moments in court-- in pain, seeking answers. This tool emerged as a saving grace. With this technique, we only give energy to an issue for a minute and a half. When speaking, thinking, or complaining about life, we provide these tribulations power to dominate us. We can reduce this error by increasing focus on those things you do desire to manifest. It also assists in healing the physical and emotional body. This guideline will indicate how much wasted time and energy is given to the things you are trying to free yourself from or that drive you crazy.

Tribulations include illness, addictions, pain, worry, fear, pride, fatigue, discord, relationship issues, belief systems that do not align with Cosmic Law, or whatever makes a good gossip story.

We create everything through focused thoughts, attention to our feelings, admittance, or permission for circumstances to exist in our experiences that make our realities. As we shift the focus, we change the result. If you do not desire it, give no consent.

There are three aspects to this guideline.

First is Speaking: stop talking about it.

Second are Thoughts and emotions: Stop giving them energy.

Third are Timeframes: Reduce the 90-second periods. Be in the present moment. A fight in the morning becomes a past reflection in the evening.

Week One Speaking: Allow yourself only 90 seconds per DAY to speak about the subject. This is for the Entire Day. Once you have expressed the cliff-notes version, you are done. No more energy is given to this situation in any capacity. This helps you to choose wisely who & when you share your information or hardship. Also, this enables you to recognize how much time & energy is actually devoted to something that does not serve you or you're trying to change.

With only a minute-and-a-half to speak or gossip about illness, fear, pain, drama, relationship issues, or what you lack, it helps us choose when to share that information. Consider phone conversations, texting, office/lunch breaks, or chance meetings at a store. This first week is the practice to get your footing. Have fun with it. How many times can you catch yourself singing those sour notes?

Overview: This first week is the practice to get your footing. Give only 90-second timeframes daily to speak upon the ills.

Week Two Thinking & Speaking: This week decreases the number of days for voicing and telling that story. Throughout the week, allow yourself THREE days to discuss any issues, so if you mentioned something on M.-W.-F., the weekend is off-limits.

Now, we will integrate becoming aware of your thoughts. In this instance, thinking is qualified in those quiet moments, perhaps when no one is around.

This second week, only allow your thoughts to focus on that pain or illness for 90 seconds daily. Just like you did with speaking in the first week. So, as you notice your thoughts or attention is on that illness or discord, you can rethink: cancel, delete, erase, and replace. Or simply tell your thoughts to be silent. This week is practice for paying attention to patterned thoughts. Upbeat and happy music can help change the focus. How many times will you catch yourself thinking?

Overview: This week is practice for paying attention to patterned thoughts. Choose any three Days **For sharing**. Give only one 90-second timeframe daily for **thoughts and emotions.**

Week Three Timeframes: The first two weeks have been re-patterning. This week, speaking gets only one timeframe period. This timeframe can be split into three 30-second intervals; once you've used this time up, mums the word. Allow your negative thoughts for only one timeframe to hold the focus in any three days. Just like you did with speaking in the Second week, we are repeating the pattern. You might notice you'll be using cancel, delete, erase, or be silent often. If you find yourself thinking about a discordant subject, seek a solution.

Overview: This week's focus is enhancing re-patterning. Give only One Timeframe: **to talk.** Use any Three Days: Give only Three timeframes for **thoughts and emotions.**

Week Four: Days are even for both thoughts and speaking. So if spoken about, times up. Suppose you thought about it, times up.

Overview: This week, we are Mastering the Practice. **Timeframes are equal:** Give only ONE 90-sec. Timeframe for Speaking or Sharing. Give only ONE 90-sec. Segment for thoughts and emotions.

Week Five: Starts a new month. Devote timeframes with an awareness of your thoughts and words for an entire month. Yes, **three 30-second** intervals can be used. Ninety seconds of focus for the whole 30 days is the goal. **The end goal is not to have to use it.**

For unavoidable situations, such as medical appointments or support groups--A.A. or N.A., acknowledge the time spent and adjust your daily practice accordingly. This technique is about cultivating awareness and resilience, not rigid adherence. So, whatever week you're working with, remember your story's cliff-notes version and continue from where you left off. Many of the 'I AM' statements can assist you in overcoming any adversity.

You will realize how much wasted time was devoted to something you're trying to stop, heal, or eliminate. So, what do you desire in your life? You are the Author, Captain, and Master; you control everything. Master the feeling world instead of it mastering you.

As a gentle reminder, the Universe or Multiverse delivers only from ITS octaves of resonance. If we engage in complaints, the Universe will comply with our request, with more of the same. The Multiverse asks us to make up our minds.

Shadow Fox's Timeframes is more than just a practice—it's an experiential technique that reorients energy and reconditions habits and beliefs. Its actual value lies in the experience of reducing the time spent on negativity. Trust the process—it's your journey.

Following is the cliff-notes version of these steps for a quick reference to keep you on track. Feel free to copy, print, or share this page for your personal use. Place it somewhere you'll see it daily --like your fridge, desk, or journal-- to help you stay on track.

Cliff Notes Version: Shadow Fox's Focused Timeframes

Week 1 Speaking: First, you only get 90 seconds daily for one week to express any tribulations for the Entire Day. Once you have described the cliff notes version, you are finished. No more energy or focus can be given to this situation in any capacity. This action helps you choose who, when, and how your information or hardship is shared. Also, this enables you to recognize how much time & energy is devoted to something that does not serve you or you're trying to change.

Week 2 & 3 Thoughts: The only difference from the previous is that you only get a one-time frame for any three days for thinking. So, by the fourth week, we are only entertaining one 90-second timeframe.

Week 4 Timeframes: Same as above. By now, we are only entertaining one 90-second timeframe. 30/30/30 intervals can be used. We are working towards only 90 Seconds for the whole month.

Stopping the Storm

Purpose: *Life's chaotic moments hold the power to overwhelm, but this technique helps you shift and resolve them. You can reclaim your authority to create effectively by honoring vibrational energy flow.*

Life's chaotic moments hold an inherent influence to teach, transform, and align us with our highest potential. The technique shared here, 'Stopping the Storm,' enables you to reclaim your seat of power amidst turbulence. You can dissolve chaos, restore clarity, and create harmony within yourself and your world. This is more than a calming tool; it is a pathway to transformation, teaching us to navigate challenges with grace and intention.

In childhood, when life's trauma seemed insurmountable, this technique came to me through the gentle guidance of my spirit guides, and I have used it all my life. It has never failed. A version of this technique was relied on during my episode in A Knock of Grace. It helps to keep the sanity and your power to create intact.

A brief intermission about storms before we continue is in order because some people fear them. Essentially, storms in the natural world are a force that changes the energy in a location. Nature's ecosystem cleans itself, waters its plants, brings nutrients, and sometimes recreates our environment. Conversely, storms following the Law of Cleavage will sometimes dismantle or destroy to create anew like a blessing in disguise.

For those who fear storms, the defining question is, how does the energy of fear serve you in this moment? Are you in a safe place reading this right now? We will not reinvent the wheel, but we can allow nature to teach us. Storms happen, so metaphysically, we can adapt the same natural energy flow to understand and recreate life's chaotic moments. A hurricane or tornado carries a sacred shape, a spiral. It's why these storms were chosen.

Also, for those who believe they cannot visualize or have difficulty imagining something, I would ask them to describe their front door or share the last dream they remember. To answer, a person must recall the door or dream and then express it, like a picture, movie, or story. That, in essence, is visualization; people get hung up on an expectation of what should be seen or felt. Each of us can visualize, imagine, or pretend. The key is to release the expectation.

There are times when the spiritual ebb, like the ocean, is at its lowest. Chaos seems to be spiraling and swirling out of control. During this time, proper recourses appear elusive, no matter what we do. When these spiritual storms enter our lives, they may feel like a tornado or a hurricane. It is as if you are being attacked from all sides, with never-ending deafening destruction. Oh, my dearest friends, it is at these times when the most significant awareness and lessons occur. So I say with all sincerity, bless these opportunities.

Understanding Vibrational Energy in the Storm

How can we bring order or harmony to the chaos? There are three ways to view and work these energies. Each step—feeding, calming, and stopping the storm—mirrors how we interact with vibrational energy, whether lowering, sustaining, or elevating it. Recognizing this interplay aligns us with broader Laws of Life and Love, including Reciprocity, the Path of Least Resistance, and the foundational principles of energy flow. These insights empower us to shift from reacting to chaos to intentionally engaging with it. For a deeper understanding of vibrational energy and its components—vibration, rhythm, and frequency—please refer to Chapter 2. Alas, the secret is in the Multiverse's language, knowing how to work with energy to quickly bring a corrective solution. We all have this choice.

Energy's Vibrational Flow

Creating Harmony out of Chaos

Feeding the storm

Most people only see the illusion that nothing can be done during a challenging situation. This is an error and dilemma that sets up feelings of helplessness. People may feel like they are being tossed around on the outer edges of this hurricane. As a result, depression and self-defeating thoughts enter the mind. People tend to question their self-worth and being-ness or begin to second-guess themselves.

We energize these storms by continuing to curse the darkness, giving us more of the same. We live in the drama, and this focus is where most play. These qualifying deeds remain as re-action and will create a negative feedback loop. Feeding the storm carries a resonance of self-serving. When is enough, well, enough? Will we endure the outer edges of this chaos continuing to be tossed around? Are we dancing to someone else's demands and then asking if we kept the beat? (Re-action.)

Evaluate the situations as an observer; do not judge them. There will be a common denominator if we look for it. Events such as court appearances may sometimes be disappointing or out of our control. However, it is how we perceive the outcome that counts. Changing our thoughts or feelings alters the result. Remember where and what you focus on is where energy is delivered.

How can we make any sense of the chaos in our lives? We can calm and stop this storm that is raging and swirling around. Having observed the storm, let's take the next step to redirect its energy.

Calming the storm

What you resist will persist. Observe, Evaluate, and show Gratitude. Place no judgment or give importance to a particular issue; this is taking action. Calming the storm carries a resonance of Serving-Self. There is a form of allowance for what seemingly is or is not. Where is the illusion? Where is the pearl of wisdom? Seek the errors and lessons; could it be accountability, victimization, or responsibility? Has there been a misdirection or misqualification of energy, or has Free Will been considered? There's a duty and responsibility to address our actions or inactions and make corrections as required. Responsibility and accountability, yes; however, do not place any blame.

Bless this excellent opportunity to create! Bless all the situations, especially the most painful ones. I can hear it now; you may question, "How in the world could I possibly bless or even be thankful for what is happening in my life? This person or that person did this, and I should bless them?" Shadow Fox, "You have no idea how bad things are. Should I be thankful for this situation?" I'll reply, "Yes, it is what I am saying!"

Blessing this chaos is an opportunity of great importance and a key factor of spiritual logic. This profound 1800 shifts the resonance immediately. Is it not the exact opposite perception and action that others view and use? Blessing and being thankful for these lessons entering your life creates a positive feedback loop. The positive inertia or forward motion makes creating so much easier. Blessings or bitterness? Instead of repeatedly cursing the darkness, open the door and let in the light.

What an opportunity! What a blessing! What a miracle! Where is the logic to curse the circumstances or energy which could manifest miracles? Please think about this premise for a moment and catch your breath. It is far easier to raise the vibrational frequency of energy than to establish its inertia. Christ used inertia that had already been created, then changed the frequency to bring about miracles. He stood in his truth. It is the path of least resistance. Test this truth in your circumstances. With this foundation of calm established, we can now move to...

Initial Steps for Stopping the Storm

Observe for a moment this storm of disharmony or chaos raging around you. The discordant events and people who impact your life are swirling around the outer edges of this squall. Stopping the storm carries a resonance of Service to Others. If this were an actual storm, would a rescue be in order? Could it be as simple as offering time to gain a sense of composure for ourselves and others? Consider yourself and include those people, whether your family members, teachers, students, co-workers, bosses, or neighbors swirling around. Allow this swirling action to continue unabated; only observe it.

Well, my friends, now's the time for the proverbial vacation: In your mind, create a natural environment, perhaps on an island, a prairie, or a mountain. Imagine the eye of a hurricane or tornado. In the center rests perfection, calm, peacefulness, beautiful sunrises, and sunsets. This eye carries a point of power; it is where the storm's energy will continue to escalate, subside, or die out. This point of power is not only for the hurricane or storm but also for you.

First Step: Finding Your Center Amid the Storm

Now that we've explored how to work within the storm's energy, we turn to the most essential practice: finding your center. No matter what is raging around you, you can always choose grounding. You can always return to your seat of power. The following guidance helps you anchor yourself in this stillness, creating clarity and strength while amplifying your vibrational frequency.

Please take a deep breath. Okay, take another. Visualize or imagine that you are in the eye of this hurricane; in your mind, be there. Tranquility, calmness, grounding, forgiveness, and love are its core resonance, its' heart. Create your heaven or paradise. No one can enter or cause harm; only safety and comfort exist. Imagine what feels noble to you. This paradise is where all creation begins; it's your seat of power. It is also standing in your truth. For some, it's your 'I Am Presence'.

For a few moments or hours, take your respite. Use this time for your emotional healing; it could be for openness, awareness, forgiveness, acceptance, patience, tolerance, or love; you decide. Remember, the storm is still raging around you unabated. However, it cannot touch or harm you; no one can rock this foundation or the tranquility you create.

Second Step: Qualifying Energy

Now is when the fun begins. Visualize yourself standing and looking out from the eye of this storm, observing all that has transpired. See all the people or situations you have allowed to influence your life, emotional state, thoughts, or decisions. Find the major and minor players in this drama, but realize you are still centered and safe in the eye. Here is the point: during this time of outward upheaval, it cannot influence you. The best time to manifest is when you are grounded in the calm power of your center; this is when the inception of miracles is born.

Now, I'll ask you, "What will you create?" How will you qualify this energy to return to you? Every storm gains its strength from energy. Will you give this storm more attention, or will you choose to weaken and stop it? It's not a secret: you control everything you experience from this center. Results manifest through either reaction or action. Reaction is jumping through hoops, remaining angry, hurt, or frustrated. With Action, there are no hoops; there is an allowance or willingness for growth, self-correction, and compassion. Now that we understand the nature of a storm and our power within its eye, we can focus on the steps to calm, redirect, or stop it altogether. Once grounded in the eye of the storm, you have several tools at your disposal to further shift its energy.

Third Step: Stop the Storm

Choose from Four visualization Techniques designed to stop the storm by raising the vibrational energy to its highest state. These techniques guide you in consciously directing energy to dissolve chaos, restore clarity, and embody your seat of power. Let's explore how these visuals or ideas can balance your space. You can choose from any of the following ideas that resonate with you.

First Visual, Blanketing the Storm

Continue from your seat of power, which is the calm eye of this storm. Imagine, if you will, that you are raising your hands far above your head. A large (baby) blanket for comfort or a freshly laundered sheet is in your hands, representing love, balance, tolerance, awareness, patience, acceptance, allowance, courage, honor, gratitude, and forgiveness. In essence, we are qualifying the energy and energizing the chosen material. Now, just blanket the storm. Imagine everything under this blanket is quiet and at peace. The universe will gently put everything in its proper place, which can do no more harm. The storm can no longer rage on or gain power again. Create order out of chaos.

Second Visual, Ballet Dancer or Figure Skater

Another way to imagine is a ballet or figure skater in a fast spin, a vortex of grace. How do they slow and stop their momentum? Physics shows that the spin will slow and stop by opening the arms. When we focus and bring everything close to our body or emotional heart, all the ills or transgressions of the spin will become fast and furious. Changing the focus by letting go or releasing the discordant energy pattern opens us to receiving and giving compassion. Give the situation all the grace, love, tolerance, positive concepts, and blessings with open arms. It will return to you in kind. You have stopped your world from spinning and opened your heart to incredible opportunities. This action also offers some level of composure and integrity to others.

Third Visual, So It Is

Another perception or visualization can be used when proficient with centering and grounding. This technique requires an awareness of our energy bodies. Position yourself in your seat of power or standing in your truth. Imagine all the positive concepts mentioned previously, pure intent radiating from your heart and chakras, including front and back. This most perfect and graceful force will go out in all directions. This elegant 3600 descending and ascending energy with such love and light imaginable will emanate outwards, enfolding those around you. Everything is in perfect balance and harmony. Finalize with, So It Is.

Fourth Visual/ perception, Remove Permissions

Declare I give no admittance to the raging energy from this outer world into my personal space. I remove all permissions of discord, whether known or unknown, past, present, and future, to exist in my physical world. This experience will stop. I give no energy to it. Finalize with: It is done, it is finished.

Word of caution: As you learn to apply these visualization techniques or tools, please be advised that discordant people may temporarily increase the harmful activity. They will notice a difference but not know why. Those who enjoy manipulations or control mechanisms will try to figure out why their efforts are not working. The regular hot buttons, when pushed, no longer get a response from you. When there is no longer a reward, the nonsense will stop.

The great news is that there is foresight into others' reactions. Realize that these techniques are working correctly, with balance and harmony. Chaos provides another opportunity to truly move through anything with grace and dignity from a solid foundation of love. No one can rock this foundation without your authorization.

This technique was born from my own experiences with trauma and the guidance I received as a child. By visualizing the baby blanket as a symbol of comfort, security, and warmth, I learned to work with energy to stop the storm entirely. This understanding became foundational in navigating life's inner and outer storms, offering clarity and empowerment in even the most challenging times.

By the way, I enact this gift each time I change the linens. I'll include anyone requiring assistance, known or unknown to me, and blanket them in comfort, love, acceptance, compassion, or the day's blessings.

As you reflect on these techniques, consider how to use them to create your desired reality. What will you manifest from this centered space of calm and power?

Here's a concise outline of the steps for applying this technique in your life.

Stopping the Storm in a nutshell

Decide what you'd like to do with the chaos. **Observe** yourself and others; hold no judgment or blame.

Claim your calm center.

Qualify the energy you wish to return to you.

Take action with a visualization technique you like; Blanketing the storm, ballet dancer, or figure skater, using 'So It Is,' or removing permissions.

The Sweep

Purpose: *To clear stale, stagnant, and discordant energy from your environment, creating space for harmony, positivity, and higher vibrational frequencies to flow.*

The Sweep technique came to me later in life and may have been inspired by energy practices I've studied over the years, including teachings from St. Germain, Deepak Chopra, and others. Over time, I've adapted and expanded upon these influences, integrating my experiences and understanding to make this technique what it is today.

Now, let's explore how you can use the Sweep to clear stagnant energy and create a harmonious environment in your daily life.

The greatest pandemic facing humanity is that of discord. An assessment from above is that the Earth is a dark planet due to the lower vibrational energy that discord exhibits. Inherently, we have all contributed to this darkness for millennia, and we can clean up our mess by removing this stagnant energy, allowing the light to shine through.

Lower vibrational energy consists of fighting, warring, fears, worries, dis-ease, genocide, violations of human rights, and free will. This stale energy surrounds individuals, families, towns, cities, nations, and globally.

This technique is quite simple to clean up our space. Imagine or visualize a broom, begin sweeping from west to east, intending to collect the discordant energy. When you have an imaginary pile of energetic dust bunnies, ask the angels to pick it up and remove it. They will, and they are waiting to help. Start with your home, workplace, school, town, city, or nation, and spread the cleanup. Do this often, especially after arguments, disagreements, or errant thoughts.

Technique Steps in a Nutshell
Visualize Sweeping: Imagine a broom sweeping west to east, gathering discordant energy into a manageable focus point.

Call on Assistance: Invite angels or guides to remove the collected energy, ensuring your space is cleared completely.

Expand the Practice: Use the Sweep for your immediate environment, then extend it to towns, cities, and globally, creating a ripple of clean energy.

The Sweep reminds us that clearing energy is possible and essential to cultivating spaces supporting our well-being and growth. I have been to many places that are so clean you could eat off the floors. Yet, the stagnant, stale energy was suffocating; this discordant residue was never cleaned. If you would like peace to enter your space, clean your environment or atmosphere as you would your house. So many pray or meditate for peace. Where is it? How will peace be established when weeds of discord suffocate its roots? If we continue to clean or sweep this friction away before we plant peace, its effects will be noticeable and fruitful.

The Breath of Light Techniques

Purpose: *To use intentional breathing techniques to align body and mind, release stagnation, and foster peace and healing through the natural rhythm of the breath.*

Note: The breathing techniques discussed here are from various modalities and can be found across multiple online resources. These methods have been adapted and integrated into this practice for deeper alignment and healing.

Breathwork meditations are a powerful transformative practice that shifts brain waves from beta to alpha. Breathwork cleans and releases old belief systems or programs locked within our bodies to establish new neural pathways. It can reduce anxiety and depression and shift us from a survival mode. It helps eliminate toxins from the body. These are just a few benefits we can gain when intentionally doing breath work.

This section includes three distinctive techniques—breathing, visualization of white light, and activating stem cells within the body for healing. Each one can be done alone or combined. Let's look at each technique because we can enhance our results by knowing their intent and purpose.

Diaphragmatic breathing

Diaphragmatic breathing efficiently holds transformative action, which anchors you in the present moment, helping establish a foundation of calm. Many people breathe shallowly, meaning the upper chest moves more than the abdomen. This shallow breathing sets up a domino effect for different illnesses and obesity. We can check this by placing one hand on the upper chest and one on the abdomen. Take a breath. Which hand moves more? We are looking for the movement of the lower abdomen, which fills the lower area of the lungs.

The most natural rhythm is 4-4-4. Breathe in through your nose and out through your mouth. Using a 4-4-4 rhythm, inhale deeply into your belly for four counts, hold for four counts, and exhale fully for four counts. This technique enhances mindfulness, reduces anxiety, and improves oxygen flow throughout your body.

Consciously breathing like this for at least three breaths helps you focus on breathing. How do you feel? You can change the duration, making each interval longer but equal. This represents the normal rhythm of breathing.

Vagus Nerve Activation

This technique uses specific breathing cadences, such as 5-3-5 or 5-2-8, to stimulate the parasympathetic nervous system. By activating the vagus nerve, this practice helps reduce stress, improve digestion, and restore balance to your body and mind.

Magic happens when we change the cadence of our breathing. Stimulating the Vagus Nerve calms the body through our parasympathetic nervous system. This breathing technique can help those who are affected by anxiety or depression. As always, breathe in through your nose and out through your mouth. The count is 5-3-5 or 5-2-8. The difference with this rhythm is that we hold/pause in the middle. This pause allows our heartbeat to gather the toxins from the body. Upon exhalation, we gently empty our lungs as much as possible. With each breath, try to elongate the intervals. Try this breath three times. How do you feel?

Chi or Pranic Breathing, White Mist

This technique helps clear energetic blockages and supports overall well-being. We can utilize the energy around us with Pranic Breathing. Once again, we can pretend, imagine and visualize. Become conscious of your breathing, inhaling and exhaling in a regular rhythm.

As you inhale, visualize life energy (chi or prana) as a white mist flowing into your body. As you breathe deeply, imagine the mist filling every cell with vitality and healing. This white mist, known as the vitalizer, is the fluid of life itself. It will help if, when inhaling, you put the tip of your tongue against the top of your soft palate. This prevents the loss of vital air through the mouth and directs the airflow to its proper designation. Maintain your normal breathing rhythm with each breath, consistently focused on the white mist entering your body and nurturing all organs and cells.

Imagine this graceful white mist releasing its potency throughout the physical and the etheric body. Imagine prana as a primary nutrient for health and healing. Savor this breath and honor this moment of being alive. Consider its multiple benefits for life and consciousness. (Another visualization technique with the white mist is imagining breathing this energy mist into your chakras.)

White Light

This is one of my favorite tools, influenced by many Ancient Wisdom Teachers, including the works of St. Germain, Alice A. Baily, and my guides. I continue to use this tool to bring healing into the body when required. The White Light can be used with or without breathwork.

By accessing our Vagus nerve, we can program our stem cells to become any cell within our body for specific healing. We can also utilize the universal healing light to enter our physical body, thus expanding and raising our frequency and vibrational resonance. I used this white light energy in my healing by activating stem cells from the Vagus Nerve. Every atom of our body responds to and acts from Divine Active Intelligence. (-See next chapter.) The cells of our body will respond to our will and reprogramming.

Here's how:

As a curious explorer, please envision a column of beautiful pure white light from the cosmos entering through the top of your head or crown chakra. When called upon, this white healing light enters the body and awaits your direction. Intend this light to enter each molecule, whether blood, tissue, organ, or nerves. Direct this loving light source to concentrate on the powerhouse, either the nucleus or mitochondria within those cells. When it arrives there, it is to expand and expand. This impregnates each molecule, radiating its healing light to the surrounding cells. This action intelligently corrects and disposes of any damaged or aging cells. It also establishes new programming with a proper new life force of perfection. Could this be a key to the fountain of youth?

At this time, we can also access the Vagus nerve, requesting brand new stem cells to be activated and deployed where they are required to bring healing and homeostasis within the body. If there are lung issues, send stem cells and light there to expand and expand. When there is peace in the body, there is homeostasis. Breathe, smile, and enjoy this beautiful healing light.

You empower yourself by envisioning universal healing light entering your body and activating healing. If you choose, use affirmations to enhance vibrational resonance and foster renewal.

By practicing these breathing techniques, we cultivate balance, align with the rhythm of life, and create a pathway for healing and renewal. Take a moment to reflect after each practice: How do you feel? Allow the breath to guide you toward greater awareness and harmony.

Affirmations

We can rewrite the programs of our past and form new neural pathways with affirmations. Affirmations- *are repeated agreements or statements that create and determine our perceptions and reality. They are effective due to the principle of resonance.*

Affirmations are powerful tools for reprogramming your mind and aligning with your highest vibrational reality. You can transform your thoughts, emotions, and outcomes by repeating them with focused intent. Choose the ones you feel comfortable stating out loud. Here are a few to guide you:

Healing & Renewal

- I am created in the likeness of God/Creator, pure energy.

- Every breath brings healing and renewal to my mind, body, and spirit.

- My will is a fractal of Divine Will, having the power to remove all obstacles and establish a healthy, youthful body.

Energy Awareness & Flow

- This natural rhythm of light expansion is fun and nourishing.

- I am in harmony with the flow of life and creation.

- It is normal and natural to have the cells of my body respond to my will.

- I can move matter inside and outside of my body.

Alignment & Manifesting

- My thoughts are aligned with the highest frequencies of love and balance.

- My desires manifest in the world within and the world without.

- The Multiverse rearranges everything in my life to reflect my resonance and desires.

Take a moment to reflect: Which affirmation resonates with your current focus? Repeat it as often as you feel inspired, letting its vibration guide your energy.

These affirmations and techniques can be used alone, combined, or incorporated into your prayers or meditations. For example, combine "The Universe rearranges everything in my life to reflect my resonance and desires." with Stopping the Storm.

As we combine these techniques, remember they are tools for growth, harmony, and exploration. Each offers an opportunity to engage with energy's flow and create positive shifts in your life.

Wrap Up

Affirmations are just one way to connect with energy's flow. Let's explore how the techniques presented align with the fundamental components of energy, creating harmony and balance in your life.

Energy has an elegant, graceful flow. As we learn its culture and language, we can co-create a harmonious reality around us using the tools and techniques shared here.

Each technique introduces a key Principle of Energy: Timeframes focus on harmony and rhythm, Stopping the Storm centers on vibration, and The Sweep clears stale and stagnate energy. Together, they create a holistic approach to engaging with energy and transforming your experiences by raising your frequency.

These tools are meant to be explored and adapted. Play with them, teach them to others, and see how they bring harmony into your life. Energy responds to your engagement; the more you experiment, the deeper your connection will grow.

Combining affirmations with techniques like Stopping the Storm amplifies your ability to direct energy, aligning your internal and external worlds with harmony and intention. For example, repeating the affirmation, 'The universe rearranges everything in my life to reflect my resonance and desires,' while visualizing a calming storm creates a powerful synergy between thought, emotion, and energy.

As you integrate these techniques, remember they are tools for growth, illumination, and exploration. Every moment offers an opportunity to align with energy's flow and create positive shifts in your life. Embrace these practices and witness the transformation they bring to your energy and world.

As you deepen your awareness of energy's flow, consider the profound influence of words. More than sounds or symbols, words carry vibrations that shape our reality. Every word holds resonance and intention in the etheric realm, becoming a building block of Spiritual Logic. Now, let's explore how the words we choose ripple through energy, shaping both the seen and unseen aspects of our lives.

Key Points: Section B. Tools and Techniques

- Timeframes: Focus on what we'd like to experience. Not how issues are presented in our lives.

- Focused timeframes help contain energy and bring clarity during chaos.

- Purify our environment and atmosphere from old, stale, blocked energy with techniques like The Sweep.

- Nature shows us the way to harmony and balance with energy. Stopping the Storm creates intentional stillness, enabling realignment.

- Breathwork is a powerful transformative healing modality that restores balance and reduces resistance.

- Use affirmations for healing, flow, and manifesting.

Section C

Words & Phrases

Feel the Resonance

Words are not just sounds; they are vibrations that ripple through the Universe. Yet, many people have become numb to their resonance, unaware of how they vibrate within our bodies or extend outward into the world. To reconnect with this power, let's explore an exercise to 'feel' the vibration of words within you.

Start with a song. Choose a simple tune— one you like, or perhaps "Twinkle, Twinkle Little Star"—or a single note, such as a Middle C. First, sing it aloud, letting the sound move outward. Then, hum the same note or tune instead. Pay attention to the vibration in your chest, throat, and head. Can you feel the hum resonating within you, radiating through your body?

Now, try a word like love or Om. Speak it aloud, and then hum it. Focus on how it feels in your chest. The vibration of a hum stays within you, connecting you deeply to the energy of the word. This is how we begin to awaken our awareness of the power of words and their resonance.

Next, let's compare the vibrations of phrases we use daily. Say these out loud, one at a time, and feel how they resonate in your chest. *No problem. You're welcome. It was my pleasure.*

Notice the difference. "No problem" might feel flat or even slightly resistant. "You're welcome" or "It was my pleasure," on the other hand, radiates warmth, generosity, and connection. These subtle shifts in language carry profound energetic differences that we can feel within our bodies.

Finally, bring this awareness to your thoughts and intentions. Just like a hum, they vibrate within you and radiate endlessly outward. When you pair conscious thought with intentional energy, you create a powerful resonance that aligns with the infinite, like the declaration: 'I AM.'

As you explore the following terms, consider how your speech patterns and intent influence the energy you create and share. These are not definitions but reflections of how the Universe understands and resonates with these words. Approaching them with this awareness can shift your perspective and the energy you send into the etheric realm.

Let's consider a few common words and phrases with their etheric resonance to get you thinking. Some of these terms do not offer our more authentic intentions because they vibrate differently in the etheric field of energy. How will you choose to use them once you know of their effects? What frequency or logic would you prefer to use? Perhaps look at speech patterns with repetitive fillers. How would you like the Universe to hear you or deliver your requests? Consider how much thought is given to a word before blurting it out to creation. How do some colloquialisms serve us? Many words carry low vibrational energy, creating unintended results. Listen to their sound when said aloud or during meditation. How do these terms serve you or the mass consciousness?

Words

Sin: Synergy In Negation, meaning missing the mark, to error. This awareness removes guilt and allows for self-correction without blame. As we shift from judgment to self-correction, we see how words can empower rather than hinder.

Expectation: Expectations come in two forms: implied or stated. What happens when they are not fulfilled? We can feel disappointment, anger, and even rage. Expectations can ruin relationships, especially when implied, as the requirement would be reading someone's mind. Everyone falls from a pedestal. Releasing expectations creates personal freedom from disappointments. We can anticipate someone home for dinner; if they miss it, the evening is not filled with resentment. Or perhaps we could be mildly surprised how a class or seminar changes from what we thought it would be.

Similarly, the energy of control versus freedom can profoundly influence the harmony of our interactions.

Command: meaning demand, control, or order, removes free will and creates friction. This term isn't commonly spoken, just like dominion isn't. However, its influence does reside within other actions, words, or phrases like rule(s) and what you will learn, or I 'want' you to do this____.

Similarly, words like must and should carry varying levels of rigidity depending on how they are framed. For example, 'must' can feel self-directed and empowering when applied inwardly but becomes constraining when directed at others.

The word 'should' is incredibly nuanced. Where the word *you* is placed, either before or after 'should' shifts the energy entirely:

When *you* comes first: "You should do this…" imposes judgment, carrying a weight of expectation and control.

When *you* follows should: "Should you choose to do this…" shifts the tone, inviting reflection, intention, and personal agency.

How do these different sentences feel and resonate within your body? Pay attention to whether the words create tension, openness, or neutrality. To be mindful of the placement of the word '*you*,' we transform '*should*' into freedom and empowerment rather than obligation.

How is humanity doing with the Ten Commandants? It is not in our nature to be commanded to do something; it's why they're broken all the time because we can. What if its title shifted to the Ten Commitments, Governances, or Principles as an understanding? If we commit to living life with this guidance, refraining from some of those acts, life will unfold without friction. The term command worked for the people in that era; their culture was to be ruled over. As our awareness expands, some words no longer serve the same value. Even stones get weathered. 'Cool man,' we're not recreating what is written in stone.

Promise: If you must promise, then did your words hold any merit to begin with? Is this used as a repetitive filler? Are the future actions in question or intent not to be trusted? Does a promise become a declaration? State what you intend to do, then do it the first time. Do empty promises sound familiar? When Lee Two Hawks and I married, we never vowed or promised anything to each other. Instead, we said we would do our best not to cause harm or overstep a boundary; this was our choice. Keep your word, and lead by example.

Trust: When someone says, 'Trust me." Why, why not show them? Refer to promise.

Success: What qualifies success to you: money, things, positions, or ownership? Are you defining it by someone else's standards? How about being able to see the illusions of humanity? Becoming success-ful at creating discord and yet remaining numb to its effects. Does this create happiness? Could value be given to harmony, balance, peace, love, or intuition? Do these qualify as success?

Happiness: How do you define this, and what qualities will you give it? Is balance or harmony in this equation? Is happiness bound to success? Can happiness or joy be found in our being-ness? Could a qualifier be about self-governance or having control of thoughts and emotions?

Judgment: As we judge others, we have identified the exact energy within ourselves. If we did not transmit that frequency, we would not see it. If we judge others, seek those qualities you admire.

We are all looking in the mirror. How much thought is given to a word, belief, or action before blurting it out to creation?

Issue: It is primarily overused and repetitive, but it is an excellent modifier to the word; problem. This term can reduce the hold or energy surrounding an illness or dis-ease.

Fight: Whatever you fight, will fight back with more resistance and friction. To continue fighting means the results will be more of the same, with no resolution. Foundations that use 'fight' in their messaging would fare much better by changing one word. Donate to heal or end cancer. Join our cause or solution. Where is the focus or end result? Vote for me, and I'll fight for you. Oh, please don't fight, be the solution. Could your speech patterns be riddled with repetitive fillers?

Reincarnation: Describes the concept of cyclic rhythms regarding the movement of energy. It references human neglect by not working within the Laws and Principles. When humans persist in this neglect and follow their materialistic concerns over their spiritual potential, the learning process is repeated until understanding comes. This awareness reduces idealism and structured belief systems.

Dude: Offensive. I will not dignify this word with a response.

Purifier: Cleaning negative energy by or through fire. Clearing imperfections from human design. Pure-fire- this word is coded with direction. The Violet Flame comes to mind.

Words are the foundation of the energy we send into the Multiverse. Thus, words are u-in-verse. By understanding their resonance, we can align our intentions with the harmony of Spiritual Logic, creating a life of balance and flow.

Phrases

No Problem: Double negative, resistance, and opposition. It must have been a problem or wouldn't have been mentioned. Is the focus on being helpful or identifying being put off? How often has your food or water been infected with a problem from a food server? How does 'no problem' sound? A gentler reply could be a simple, "You're welcome." or "It was my pleasure." Try them. Say all three out loud.

War Room: Really? Frankly, what genius with no awareness coined this title? Why are others so compliant with it? I'm sorry for backsliding. Cancel, delete, and erase the judgment. (If you can't tell, this phrase is my R3 rejection. It honors no laws.) This term has an extremely low vibration that's called into action. Worst yet, is it intended as a place to find solutions, like a think tank? Who's warring, or why is it required? Talk about delivery slowed due to the energy surrounding it. People wonder why peace is elusive. A Unity, Peace, or Strategy Room would convey solutions. However, many are so numb to the phrasing that it wouldn't sound right. Or would it? (I will no longer dignify this phrase with a response or waste more energy.) How creative can you get? Consider Laws.

Boots on the Ground: Are your loved ones some inanimate object without value? Is this a way to enter the mass consciousness to dehumanize a military action? The intent is to make it less tragic and more acceptable to the masses. Are those in power afraid to say what is meant? This military action intends to and will put your loved ones in harm's way. **Be aware of repetition and saturation.** (This is another R3 rejection for me.) We can all lose a pair of boots without crying over them. Unfortunately, I cannot say the same for our loved ones. *Be aware of what you speak, comply with, or give admittance.*

Money doesn't grow on trees: Are you sure? Someone's making money by deforesting the lands for wood. Can we consider Fruit trees? Become aware of that expansive connection that creates and manifests. This phrase will solidify a lack of funds that will find expression in your reality, your world.

Spiritual Logic of Words people confuse: (3R's)

Being Religious: Follows the Doctrines of man's human logic and beliefs derived from misunderstandings of original teachings from Law. People are given adaptations to what they believe, such as reincarnation. Being religious accepts an organized business structure to create followers, usually impressed by fear, guilt, and sin. Beliefs can and have been selective, dominating, limiting, and cruel. The Pope is considered Religious, not spiritual.

Please do not jump to conclusions that I'm slamming any religion; I am not. Nor am I saying that they do not offer spiritual comfort or support because they do. Faith has helped millions. This is the action of being religious, not religion. This is an expanded view to help reduce confusion; attending church does not mean being spiritual.

Being Spiritual: Follows the Governance and Aspects of Law and Spiritual Logic. It is not a doctrine made by men with limitations. On the contrary, the Creator designed a Governance with no separation that utilizes Divine Will, Divine Love/Wisdom, and Active intelligence. Thus, we are bestowing the power to self-govern, self-correct, and self-sustain all aspects of our lives through the energy of law. Its structure is not formed from fear, guilt, or sin. These do not apply, nor is being spiritual selective, dominating, limiting, or cruel.

Spirituality does not create followers but delivers individuals who serve the light, which is love. Moral Codes are established willingly from Divine Recognition. We can follow Christ or learn how he made his ascension so that we can make ours.

The Dali Lama is considered Spiritual, not religious. Many confuse a religious person as spiritual; this would be a rarity. If Spirituality were a religion, it would be the religion of love expressing its Perfection perfectly.

Spiritual: A quest for wisdom, knowing who you are, finding expression, and seeking oneness in a field of energy.

Spiritualism: shares Evidence of life after death. Unfortunately, people also confuse this with spirituality.

Power: Authentic power is from within, and it is the mastery of self, not others or a held position. Those who seek power and authority from jobs or positions should learn to follow first to become an experienced leader; this would help reduce abuse of power with hidden agendas and insecurities.

Have you ever paused and considered how you interpret or use these words? What energy are you unknowingly putting into motion through them?

Some terms carry a resonance so deeply ingrained in our daily lives that their impact often goes unnoticed. Two such words are 'want' and 'need.' Let's examine their energetic signatures and how they shape our reality.

Special note for 'Want or Need': If you refrain from using these enslaving words in everyday conversation or when manifesting, a word of caution. At some point, out of nowhere, someone will say 'want or need,' and it will hit you like a brick. A ball of friction smashing up against you, enough to make you dizzy, far worse than being sworn at. A realization also hits you as to the negative power it holds.

Most people do not believe me until they experience it firsthand. My niece, for example, spent six months practicing intentionally removing these words from her vocabulary. One day, while speaking with an acquaintance at the grocery store, she was struck by how heavy and jarring it felt when the conversation was filled with 'want' and 'need.' She described it as though the words carried a wave of lack and desperation, almost knocking her off her feet. Excitedly, she called me in tears—happy tears—sharing how this moment shifted her worldview.

She fully understood that words are not just empty but energy in action. She also voiced, 'I didn't believe it at first, but after that experience, I now know their use lowers vibrational energy. This brief moment validated how much my energy shifted from their removal.' This story underscores how the resonance affects our energy and perception of others. As we explore further, consider how these words influence your energy and interactions.

How do we teach our children to talk? Same as we were taught. We have yet to demonstrate effectively to our children how to express ourselves or create effortlessly. Instead, what if we asked our children, "What would you like or desire for your birthday?" If children could hear these terms instead of friction directed at them, perhaps new generations wouldn't be so numb to the resonance of words.

When writing, we have been taught to use more direct, active, or commanding words such as 'want or need.' By using anything else, it sounds unconfident and passive. These words are archaic, slang, enslaving, and full of B.S. Alright, I am gonna show the origins of 'want.' (Yeah, pun intended.) Some ancestors qualified this term and placed a value on it. Thus, it's misqualified, in-deed. Would you rather express a polite, creative voice to God/Creator? Or a commanding voice to an enslaving audience? Haven't we grown tired of being berated and sworn at? When does a polite voice not sound confident? This is the language of God/Creator, who knows no lack, responds to creativity, and does not require a command. Until we see the light, we will repeat the error. A quagmire for thought, should we engrave on our headstones, "I 'wanted' to live?"

Releasing these words ('want and need') from our vocabulary isn't just a linguistic change. It's a shift in energy and intention that creates a reality free from lack.

Wrap Up

Words are powerful, either constructive or destructive, in a resonant form. If some of the suggestive meanings brought resistance to you, this is excellent. What an opportunity to explore your surroundings and your field of energy. Everything is working with precision.

By becoming mindful of how we speak, think, and resonate, we align with higher frequencies, reducing friction and creating harmony in our lives. The key is awareness, which is knowing that every thought, word, and belief sets into motion a vibration that echoes through our reality. Universe means YOU-in-verse.

As you reflect on the teachings in this section, remember that each word you choose holds the power to transform your energy and interactions with the world. Awareness of resonance is your gateway to aligning with Spiritual Logic and Universal Laws.

Antidotes Quick References: If you choose to alter speech patterns.

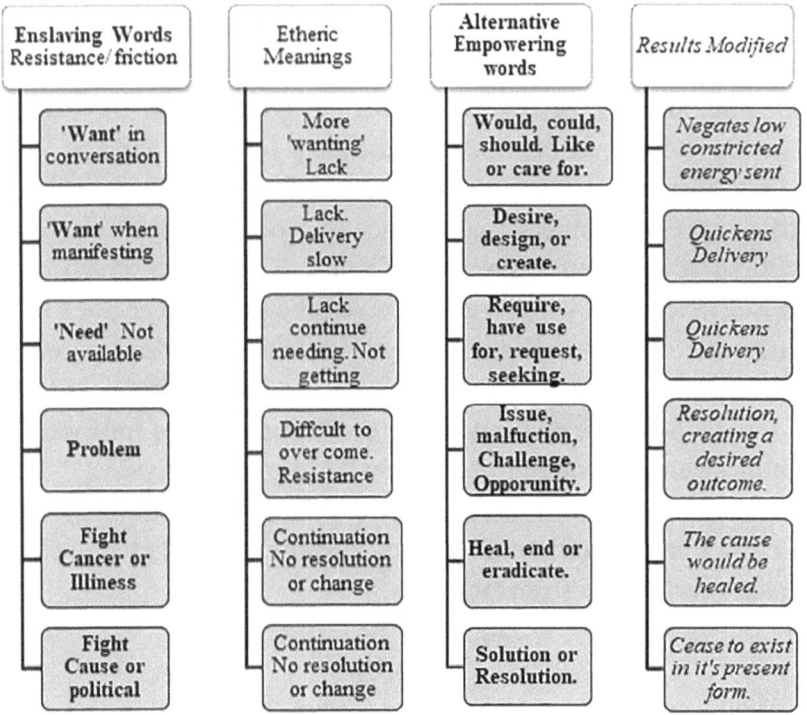

Enslaving Words Resistance/friction	Etheric Meanings	Alternative Empowering words	Results Modified
'Want' in conversation	More 'wanting' Lack	Would, could, should. Like or care for.	Negates low constricted energy sent
'Want' when manifesting	Lack. Delivery slow	Desire, design, or create.	Quickens Delivery
'Need' Not available	Lack continue needing. Not getting	Require, have use for, request, seeking.	Quickens Delivery
Problem	Difficult to over come. Resistance	Issue, malfuction, Challenge, Opporunity.	Resolution, creating a desired outcome.
Fight Cancer or Illiness	Continuation No resolution or change	Heal, end or eradicate.	The cause would be healed.
Fight Cause or political	Continuation No resolution or change	Solution or Resolution.	Cease to exist in it's present form.

Key Points: Section C. Words & Phrases

Words carry potent vibrations; their resonance depends on intent, tone, and placement. The placement of "you" in sentences changes the energy.

You should do this- It creates judgment and tension. **Should you** choose to do this- It invites reflection and personal agency.

Phrases like "no problem" and "It was my pleasure" show how subtle language choices alter the vibrational flow. Mindful speech aligns us with higher frequencies, reducing friction and creating harmony.

Chapter 8 Wrap-Up

This chapter presents a cohesive framework for understanding and applying Spiritual Logic to daily life through three distinct yet interconnected sections.

A Knock of Grace (Section A): How challenges and adversity guide us toward healing, balance, and empowerment.

Tools and Techniques (Section B): Practical methods like "Stopping the Storm" and "Focused Timeframes" to attune with Universal Laws and create harmony.

Words and Phrases (Section C): The power of language to shift energy and align intentions with higher frequencies.

Each section offers practical and experiential tools to recondition beliefs, reclaim power, and align with the flow of Universal Laws. These teachings are not theoretical—they are lived wisdom designed to guide you toward healing and empowerment.

Take these principles into your life, applying the tools and insights. Each step you take in awareness and alignment transforms your inner world and the energy you send into the Universe. Trust the process—it's your journey.

Key Points for Chapter 8

Section A. A Knock of Grace

- Match focus with desire.

- Pain demands attention. Refocus and seek solutions.

- Insight and perceptions shift our awareness. Visualization, Focused Attention, and Qualifying.

Section B. Tools and Techniques

- Timeframes: Focus on what we'd like to experience. Not how issues are presented in our lives.

- Purify our environment and atmosphere from old, stale, blocked energy.

- Nature shows us the way to harmony and balance.

- Breathwork is a powerful transformative healing modality.

Section C. Words and Phrases

- Qualify and feel the resonance of words sent to God/Creator.

- We can desensitize ourselves to the numbing agents of words.

- We reap what we sow.

CHAPTER NINE

LIFE'S IMPRESSION

Dream House Construction

*T*his make-believe story involves you, the reader. Will you play and engage in one last idea to co-create? Manifesting is a time to envision, create, construct, and play. Let us pretend or imagine for a moment what it would take to build your dream home. Perhaps you are not in the market or already living that dream. Please indulge us a moment longer for an impression.

Starting your dream house pursuit would include finding the perfect land, area, community, schools, utility hookups, and zoning. Considerations for an architect, type of house, builders, and time frame for the completion. We can speedily imagine all these steps finished. You have found a perfect parcel of land, contracts have been signed, payment is confirmed, and the property is yours to build on, free and clear. Can you envision walking on the property and planning *the direction for the best light, maybe a U-shaped driveway or pool? What elements would you like to include? You are now a steward of this property, and it's yours to design.*

The construction begins. The foundation is dug, and supporting walls for the cellar are now established. Are you going to move in now? Perhaps not. Proceeding along, the shell of your house is complete with a roof, inside walls, floors, and doors. Your building contractor installed locks on outside doors for the workers to use. However, the electricity and plumbing are not yet finished. Are you going to move in or wait a bit longer? It is your choice. You could go to the bathroom in a bucket and use a lantern. However, it would be more efficient and less stressful to wait.

Can you imagine checking in on the progress to ascertain that specific jobs are completed before moving on? Perhaps fielding calls or making executive decisions before completion? Because you have a vested interest in your home, you will oversee the progress until it is finished. These steps create movement in your desire.

So when will your house be complete and ready to move in? Is it when the wall colors are chosen and painted? Tile or wood flooring installed? These things add to the character of your home. It does not mean it is ready. There is a sign for completion.

The last task is installing new locks on the door and the doorbell. Not until this time are all workers out. Your sign for entry is complete when the house can make a sound, the door is locked, and all new keys are turned over to you. Perhaps this sounds weird, but the sound finishes your house and starts your journey in your brand-new home.

There is laughter and joy expressed as you enter. You stand in the center of your home and look around. Realizing this reality was all in the planning. A celebration is in order. Perhaps some music in the background or just a quiet reflection as you look out the balcony and admire your blessings. You breathe and think I'm here; this is my space. A magnificent journey awaits you.

As you stand within the space of your creation, breathing life into its walls, you may begin to realize how much this dream house mirrors the fluid nature of living itself. Life, like construction, rarely adheres to rigid plans; instead, it adapts, evolves, and sometimes calls us to reassess. Each decision, each turn, becomes a cornerstone, shaping not just a home but the essence of who we are. And so, perhaps you're wondering—what does building your dream home truly reveal about life's impression?

This reflects living life. Sometimes, divorce, the death of a partner or loved one, a job change, and so on can alter our plans or contracts. If or when this happens, could we change our minds and walk away? Yes, of course we could. Due to evolving circumstances, perhaps you're not ready for homeownership. I encourage you to trust your feelings and instincts if those concerns occur. This dream house construction is a creation storyline serving multiple purposes. Thank you for playing.

As you envision constructing your dream home, consider how each choice—each adjustment—mirrors the decisions we make in life. How do these decisions shape the energy we send into the world and the harmony we create within ourselves?

Impression with Multiple Purposes

This section delves into the interplay of Cosmic Laws and their influence, including sound, light, and matter. Covering their relationship with the Three Rays: Divine Will, Love/Wisdom, and Active Intelligence. While these concepts may feel profound and layered, they provide a roadmap to understanding how energy transitions from the metaphysical to the physical. Practical takeaways will help simplify these ideas, making them accessible for real-life application.

Having imagined building your dream home, you start with the blueprint (the intent), followed by the foundation (the structure), and finish with a detailed design, just as energy flows through the Cosmic Laws (to manifest) creation.

Did you notice there was a difference in creating this dream-building story? This is a tale of us; our body, life, and existence are from a position of energy. All three Cosmic Laws governing our solar system were used as an analogy for building a house. The process of constructing a home provides a clear example of these principles in action:

Law of Synthesis (Sound): Like the blueprints or architectural resonance of the house, this law sets the intention and harmony for the entire structure. (Governs sound, representing resonance and harmony. Sound is the foundational vibration that begins the creative process, aligning with the spiritual principle of synthesis.)

Law of Economy (Light): Represented by the actual assembly process, where resources are optimized, and energy flows efficiently to bring the blueprint to life. (Governs light, embodying efficiency and the flow of energy. Light provides the illuminating pathway and coherence necessary for structured development.)

Law of Attraction and Repulsion (Matter): Embodied in the physical materials—wood, brick, stone—that create the tangible, final structure. (Governs matter, representing cohesion and the manifestation of physical form. Matter completes the process, bringing abstract ideas into tangible existence.)

These elements are essential to understanding how energy transitions from the metaphysical to the physical. At its core, the integration of sound, light, and matter reveals how energy transforms from the abstract into tangible reality. Within is a progressive framework acting as a universal guide that mirrors the Universal Principles in manifesting creation.

Have you ever considered how sound, light, and matter influence your daily life or integrate into the things you create? Can you sense how these energies weave together to form the foundation of your reality?

An awareness of these Cosmic Laws reduces the emotional friction humanity places in the mass consciousness. A misqualification of human concepts and beliefs without checks and balances results in causal friction. A primary facet is unfamiliarity with the Laws of Construction, the Three Divine Principles or Rays that govern our Multiverse. Innately, humanity senses this energy; it is why most religions conceive a trinity of some kind. (-see chapter two.)

Everything in existence follows these Universal Principles. Just as sound sets the tone, light illuminates the way, and matter gives structure, the Laws of Construction guide every creation, whether a house, a body, or the Universe itself.

The Laws of Construction

Laws of Construction: *A conceptual framework describing the dynamic principles governing energy flow and manifestation into form. Rooted in the three cosmic rays—Divine Will, Love/Wisdom, and Active Intelligence—it encompasses the Cosmic Laws of Synthesis, Economy, and Attraction/Repulsion. These principles reveal how vibration (sound), illumination (light), and cohesion (matter) interact to create balance and harmony.*

Operating as a Silent Code of Life, these dynamics subtly guide existence, bridging the abstract with the tangible. By understanding these principles, individuals can shift perception—recognizing challenges as opportunities—and align intention, thought, and action with universal flow. This terminology emphasizes free will and the soul's role in engaging with energy, offering tools to apply these principles across personal, societal, and collective evolution, fostering harmony and unity. (Body of Governing Principles.)

Simplistically, as we gain consciousness of this construction, the foundational understanding can be applied in any area of our lives and release us from our travails. It serves all, delivering tranquility. The following diagram is a modest glimpse and should not be considered an absolute. All other laws radiate outward from these points. The body of Governing Principles or Rays includes life's foundational framework.

The Body of Governing Principles

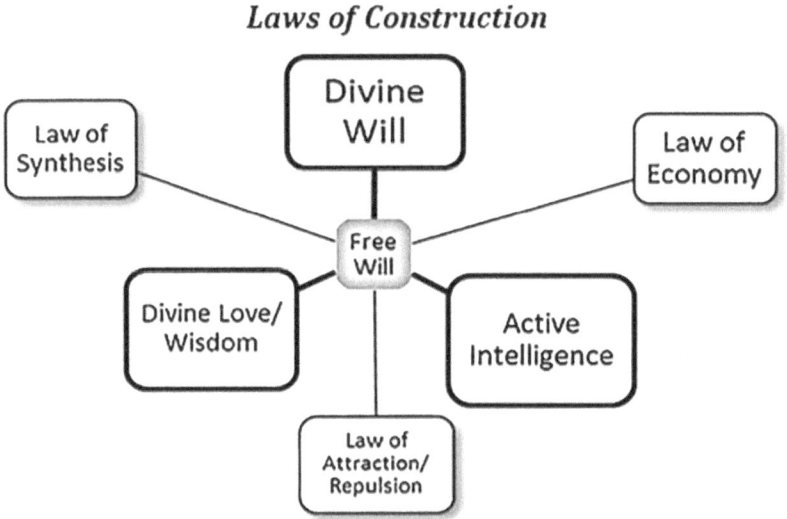

Laws of Construction

Key Takeaways:

Free Will is the foundation of the Law of Construction, serving as the central governing principle that enables alignment with higher spiritual truths.

The three Primary Rays—Divine Will, Divine Love Wisdom, and Active Intelligence—represent different aspects of creation and energy flow, connecting cosmic laws to human expression.

The Cosmic Laws (Synthesis, Economy, Attraction and Repulsion.) provide the structure and balance necessary for creation and manifestation.

This interconnected framework emphasizes the harmony between individual free will and Universal Governing Principles.

Working with the Laws of Construction

Working with the Laws of Construction follows four essential steps, each aligning with the universal principles of sound, light, and matter. This method ensures a harmonious flow of creation while reducing energetic resistance. Let's use Energy's Language.

Step One: Establish a Clear Intention
Define what you wish to create with precision and purpose. A strong foundation begins with a clear and conscious directive, such as receiving. The Law of Synthesis governs this step, ensuring resonance and harmony.

Step Two: Align with Purpose and Flow
Observe the natural rhythm of energy and move in alignment with its currents. There is no lack. The Law of Economy guides this process, ensuring efficiency and balance in manifesting your intent.

Step Three: Engage in Active Creation
Take deliberate steps toward your goal while maintaining flexibility. The Law of Attraction and Repulsion determines how energy integrates and reshapes itself. Be mindful of your alignment with your vision and the energy you project.

Step Four: Anchor in Manifestation

Ground your creation into reality by refining and affirming its presence. Confirming it causes no harm. This step ensures full integration and the successful completion or speed of the manifestation process.

Now that we've explored the foundational framework, we turn to the three Cosmic Rays that give life to these principles. These rays provide the blueprint for creation on a universal scale and within each of us, shaping our lives, actions, and purpose.

Many misqualified theories of life are due to misalignment with the Construction Laws of energy that impulse everything, yet they are right before us. Divine Will and Divine Love/Wisdom are the most abused, misrepresented, and least understood throughout history.

The principles of Divine Will/ Power, Divine Love / Wisdom, and Active Intelligence, as presented in this chapter, are deeply influenced by the esoteric teachings of Alice A. Bailey. Her profound works, such as A Treatise on White Magic and Esoteric Psychology, delve into these principles with remarkable depth and nuance. Here, we have adapted these concepts into a simplified framework to align with the accessible teachings of Spiritual Logic, offering readers a bridge between ancient wisdom and modern understanding.

Alice A. Baily's collection of books helps us understand the condition of humanity and its relation to all things, great and small. (There are 7 Rays.)

Let's look at the Rays-- Body of Governing Principles. This is a modest glimpse into the totality. These are Predestined Energies.

1st Ray: Power, Will, or Purpose. Its essence is:

Divine Will- *is both the creator and the destroyer. All manifestation clears the way for creating newer forms that fit newer energies. Will is a dynamic force that impels the Universe into synthesis and is the cyclic motion of evolution. It influences the aspects of God-Consciousness- that of a Universal Mindfulness illuminating sentient* *consciousness. Will is the One Life creating many singular yet manifest progenitors of electric fire, the fohat, which underlies Life.*

Governing Principles: The Law of Free Will and all aspects of Vibrational Law apply.

Position: Cosmic Law of Attraction and Repulsion.

Reference points: Trinity-**God the Father**.

(We innately sense Freedom.)

Practical takeaway: Divine Will is the foundational energy of creation. It aligns with the initial intent or blueprint that shapes all manifestations, similar to how the vision and decision to build a house originate. It represents the raw power to begin and sustain the creative process.

2nd Ray: Love/Wisdom. Its essence is:

Divine Love/Wisdom- *is the synthetic whole that demonstrates Cosmic Love, fulfilling 1st Ray aspects with the quality of love and wisdom. From this, everything finds its expressed Perfection, which is the Qualifier. Therefore, all energy is seeking expression of the Divine Perfection of Love. I AM Manifest.*

Governing Principles: The Law of Love and all aspects of Harmony/Rhythm apply.

Position: Cosmic Law of Synthesis.

Reference: Trinity-The **Son**.

(We innately sense Liberty.)

Practical takeaway: Divine Love Wisdom governs the unifying forces of creation, harmonizing all elements into a cohesive whole. This aligns with the collaborative efforts and relationships involved in constructing a house—architects, builders, and designers working harmoniously to manifest the vision.

3rd Ray: Active Creative Intelligence. Its essence is:

Active Intelligence- *is purposeful thought in league with Divine Principles conditioning all natural phenomena. It is a perfect directional energy force that builds, destroys, and recycles. It's considered* *the architect of energy; it includes everything from death to life, all matter and energy. Active Intelligence ensures proper adjustments for equilibrium with the necessary rate of rhythm, assuring evolutionary progress. It intertwines with a cohesive intelligence, enhancing all laws.*

Governing Principles: The Law of Life and all aspects of Frequency apply

Position: Cosmic Law of Economy.

Reference: Trinity- the **Holy Spirit**.

(We innately sense Life.)

Practical takeaway: Active Intelligence expresses itself in the detailed execution and materialization of creation. It is akin to the precise labor, tools, and resources used to construct the house, transforming the blueprint into a tangible structure. This ray ensures efficiency, order, and adaptability.

Unlike Divine Will and Love/Wisdom, which can feel abstract or intangible, Active Intelligence offers a tangible glimpse into universal design. It's present in the unseen processes of life, like the way your body instinctively heals a cut. Without conscious thought, energy flows into action, demonstrating the profound intelligence that underpins creation.

Reflection of the House Analogy

Just as building a house requires a balance between vision (Divine Will), collaboration (Divine Love Wisdom), and detailed action (Active Intelligence), so too does the creation of our lives and realities. By aligning with these rays and their corresponding cosmic laws, we can construct lives that resonate with harmony, purpose, and balance.

Please don't get hung up on the definitions. Our focus will be more on the Ray's essence and Principles. God/Creator is energy, as is the language for all construction and life. The first two Rays can seem elusive, but our lives can change when we perceive them. However, Active Intelligence is a different matter that can give us a glimpse into the deep ocean of energy. Science can help us understand how this intelligent energy works and flows. We can bilaterally compare its known aspects to the essence of the other Divine Principles because energy is intertwined and interconnected.

Concerning Active Intelligence, we can measure the effects through different fields of science. Science in any field ultimately studies the Active part of Intelligence. The Intelligence part returns us to the Divine Will and Divine Love/Wisdom.

Our bodies and all their systems respond to these Principles, as do sound and light. (Sound/light healing.) Doctors of bioengineering have witnessed a beautiful 'dance' that nature plays, discovering many designs within our immune system. Life-saving drugs have been found based on this dance. Photosynthesis, ocean ecosystems, quantum physics, insects, weather/storms, and our thoughts/emotions are sources of measurement and activity.

If you cut your finger, do you have to think about healing it? The body intelligently repairs the wound without our focus or attention, and sometimes, our immune system is stimulated. Our physical form will automatically restore tissue faster if we access this Active Intelligence through focus, intentionally using this web or ecosystem. Our hearts beat rhythmically, without thought—what a beautiful design. Additionally, upon death, the cells in the body are the most active and start to disassemble, creating a tremendous amount of energy. These are all aspects of Active Intelligence.

This brings us to the question: What does constructing a dream home have to do with energy and life? It serves as a metaphor and an impression, offering a straightforward way to describe energy flow and its Principles. An **Impression**- *is a spiritualized energy that impulses us to act or respond according to the precepts codified in law. It impresses upon us the higher vibrational frequencies, such as the Law of Correspondence, as above, so below, Involution and Evolution, or the Spirit of law/ and the Letter of the law.* Our dream home construction was codified with these Divine Principles.

This metaphor invites us to reflect on the structures we build within and around us. How does the flow of energy guide your creations, and where might harmony be calling you to realign?

Wrap Up

Through the lens of constructing a dream home, we've explored how universal principles of energy manifest in tangible ways. This metaphor illustrates how the Laws of Construction guide intention, adaptation, and creation. Yet, this is just the beginning—what lies beneath the surface is an intricate design of spiritual impressions that shape not only our actions but our very being.

These predestined energies, encoded within the fabric of existence, guide the flow of creation. Reflecting on these energies invites us to consider how they influence our choices, paths, and the joy we seek in our lives?

As we embark on this journey into Spiritual Logic, we explore how these principles move beyond the tangible, unveiling the deeper impressions that shape our reality. This next section invites reflection and an open mind, as it may challenge conventional thought while offering profound insights into the essence of life's construction. As we step beyond the tangible into the intangible, the dream home metaphor serves as a bridge to understanding how energy manifests through impressions and spiritual principles.

Key Points: Section A: Life's Impression

- The dream home construction metaphor serves as a tangible way to explore energy flow and universal principles.

- Sound, light, and matter are integrated within the Laws of Construction, illustrating how energy transitions from the metaphysical to the physical.

- Constructing a home mirrors life's creative journey, high-lighting intention, adaptation, and the interplay of energy.

- Universal Laws guide creation at every level, demonstrating how spiritual logic shapes physical reality.

Section B

Spiritual Logic's Impression

Your Journey

Please consider this an expedition of discovery because the following material could be the first time you have ever heard this subject matter expressed in this manner. This explanation of life's construction may seem controversial because our Universities and some religious structures do not apply metaphysical consciousness or Spiritual Logic. Please realize that points of contention become reference points as our consciousness expands. As we address the Law of Construction, please buckle in and turn the music down. It may be a bumpy ride for some people or perhaps a beautiful outing for others. Would you please keep in mind your 3Rs? Perhaps now is an opportunity to clear your filters. (-See Chapter 5, 3Rs- Aspects of Intuition.)

If we question, when is our soul most active? Or when does the soul enter our bodies? These questions change the narrative about life drastically because most people do not consciously consider them. These refer to the question of ensoulment or when life begins.

Each religion carries different answers, most filled with friction and division from human logic. Could there be a common dominator that brings clarity through Laws? Life's impressions are not just moments or memories; they are energetic echoes that shape our alignment with the laws and guide our soul's unique design.

Many believe life begins at conception or the heartbeat. Concerning energy, both of these beliefs are activities of Active Intelligence. Life, as yet, is to be determined by Divine Will and Divine Love/Wisdom. Energy's governing Law of Life shows our soul's expression cannot commence until the soul crosses the threshold and enters the physical body. Crossing this threshold is the Law of Life that resonates and directs all Cosmic, Universal, Spiritual, and Natural Laws.

Our Own Design

Point blank, energy teaches us we will not move into our house until its construction is complete. The premise of designing and building a home is the same format we used before birth: the Law of Attraction and Repulsion- creation's balance. Does each of us not have a body (home) for our soul to live and find expression? We all had and have a vested interest in our physical form. The key is the soul's entrance or crossing the threshold into the physical body according to energy. We will not enter the low, dense, vibrational energy of matter until the body (house) is complete; this is the Law of Economy. The doorbell in the metaphor is our ability to make sound, our cry, the Law of Synthesis. Upon inhalation, we receive the Breath of Life and, with our exhalation, create our first sound, the song. This call, or cry, notifies the Universe of our arrival; thus, the Law of Life is enabled. What impressions have shaped your understanding of life and creation?

In the same way that sound, light, and matter align to build a house, the creation of our body follows these same principles. The soul does not enter the physical form until the vibration of sound—the first cry—initiates its alignment with light and matter. Every person, parent or not, innately listens for the call. If the newborn cry is not immediate, internal alarms will sound, and the focus usually manifests as fear. Not until a parent hears that child's song will the parents catch their breath.

Birth: *The science of it all. Our soul enters our bodies upon The Breath of Life. Sound, "The Cry/Song", starts Life. (Inhale/Exhale) A heartbeat stems from Active Intelligence in action, designed from the Law of Love. The Governess of Energy, Sound- Light- Matter, is how the Creator designed it. "Let there be Light." With that statement spoken, its sound came first, then light manifested. Not until our infant cries are made (Sound) will our soul (Light) enter the physical body of (Matter).*

Soul's Entry and Laws of Construction

For clarity, any growth of the physical body in utero is Active Intelligence in action. The soul's infusion into the physical body has not occurred yet, Law of Economy- efficiency. The Miracle of Birth is the infusion of spirit with physical matter. The energy created in a delivery room is described as loving, magnetic, and pulsating. By the way, it takes seven years for the soul's infusion and its anchoring. The soul's journey begins with sound, progresses through light, and culminates in matter, mirroring the cosmic laws that govern creation. This framework ensures that the soul's entry aligns perfectly with Divine Will, Love Wisdom, and Active Intelligence.

The soul is vested in the physical form during its development, as we did with our dream house construction. How does this perspective shift your view of the body and soul as connected to universal energy?

Some people have questioned what happens if a child is premature and cannot cry? Does this mean that the child does not have a soul? No, not at all; it does. The soul is patiently waiting to enter; perhaps for the lungs to mature, the spirit will remain very close to the physical form and be part of the chosen family or community. Sometimes, a soul gets over-anxious and decides to join the physical body prematurely; it does have free will to enter or not, just like moving in and using a lantern and a bucket.

Our soul is most active a few months before birth, thus answering the very first question in this section. It's the excitement for a new opportunity. This is the same as checking in on the construction of your dream home or the activity of your cells upon death, meaning there is a tremendous amount of activity and energy. The closer the birth date comes, the quieter our soul gets. Remember the 1800 concept of the life cycle? Our spirit has to slow down the vibrational rate to enter the body of matter, crossing the threshold. This process is why most people fear death; it is an unconscious awareness of being in pain, separated. Pain might not be the best word, but it is accurate, and it is why we associate pain with death. There is no pain when the soul withdraws from the body. Nor will energy's economy be used if the physical body cannot support the *life and energy* of the spirit. It is the same concept as the house. When circumstances change, we can walk away. Without breath, there is no life.

I genuinely wish I had been more aware of this when I delivered my stillborn son at 26 weeks of gestation. It would have helped me with my grief, the blame game, and these empty arms. Unfortunately, this information you are reading has come at a high cost. There is never an experience that I don't seek a more in-depth understanding of. This is purposeful, wrought by the injuries of life. Growth can be a challenging process, but it is necessary.

As we reflect on our design and the impressions that shape us, we prepare to explore alternate realities, where energy, perception, and choice converge to create new possibilities.

Wrap up

Our design is an intricate collaboration between the impressions we carry, our choices, and the energy we align with. Through this design, our soul's journey unfolds, bridging the spiritual and physical realms.

While our focus in this section was primarily on Active Intelligence, which is easier to validate, please remember that energy is an interconnected ecosystem. As we understand the essence of one, we can apply it to the others.

By recognizing the unseen intelligence that governs physical processes, we can also begin to understand the more profound mysteries of life—like when and how the soul enters the physical body. This transition, much like Active Intelligence, occurs seamlessly, guided by universal principles. Nature supplies the answers unbiasedly without controlling mechanisms obeying the Laws of Energy. The construction of life's macro complexity can be seen in its micro simplicity through the Principles of Law, without a creation storyline from human logic. Therefore, we can reduce misqualified belief systems, release ourselves from life's travails, and convey tranquility.

Life's impressions are the echoes of energy and experience that shape our soul's journey. These subtle and profound impressions offer us guidance and alignment with the Laws of Construction. By recognizing these impressions, we open ourselves to the flow of energy, enhancing our ability to create harmoniously and reduce discord. As we reflect on this framework, it prepares us to explore alternate realities, a realm where choice and perception play pivotal roles in how life unfolds.

Together, these sections illustrate how Universal Principles manifest through both tangible and intangible realities. The dream home metaphor provides a lens through which to understand energy flow. At the same time, Spiritual Logic's Impression reveals the deeper, unseen forces that shape our lives. Recognizing these predestined energies and their framework lays the foundation for exploring alternate realities, where perception and choice shape the unfolding of life.

As we explore how impressions guide the soul's journey, we see how these same principles are mirrored in societal frameworks. The trinity of Life, Liberty, and Freedom echoes the Universal Principles of Divine Will, Love/Wisdom, and Active Intelligence, offering a bridge between personal experience and collective harmony. Life's dilemmas require an open perspective, bridging spiritual logic with the complexities of human choices and the realities we construct.

Key Points Section B. Spiritual Logic's Impression

- Life's Impressions: Recognizing life's impressions helps us align with energy and the Laws of Construction.

- Soul's Entry: The soul's entry into the physical body is guided by Divine Will, Divine Love /Wisdom, and Active Intelligence, as seen through the progression of sound, light, and matter.

- Role of Laws: Cosmic, Universal, Spiritual, and Natural Laws guide the expression of life's impressions, forming a cohesive framework for creation.

- How do life's impressions shape your understanding of creation and your soul's journey?

Section C
Addressing Alternate Realities

Great debates are raging on about pro-life and pro-choice. The intent here is to provide a lens through which we can explore these sensitive topics with greater neutrality and understanding, using the framework of Spiritual Logic. The design is to show you how to step into neutrality, being neither extraordinarily positive nor negative. This material is being delivered with the Spiritual Logic of Laws from the essence of the three Rays. Know this; Due to the sensitive nature of beliefs, I am not suggesting one way or another being 'right' or 'wrong.' Instead, it explains how energy works with checks and balances. Although the Pro-life/birth position will be addressed, the examples given are an alternate view using the Governance of Energy. I've studied both sides and prefer the middle ground. Instead, suggestions and questions are based on an awareness of offering tranquility. The expanded view and the answers will be up to you.

Just as the Laws of Construction guide the interplay of sound, light, and matter, they also provide a framework for understanding the human drive for Life, Liberty, and Freedom—principles encoded in the fabric of existence and reflected in the Declaration of Independence.

We will discuss three points from The United States Declaration of Independence as a premise, the Freedom of Life, Liberty, and the Pursuit of Happiness. While these aspects are not a privilege in many other countries, isn't that what every person resonates with, no matter where they live? These foundational principles, freedom, life, and liberty, reflect the same trinity of the Laws of Construction. Freedom, rooted in the Law of Free Will, is a shared value we all hold dear. Recognizing this, how can we honor that freedom in ourselves and others, even when choices diverge from our beliefs? Should I mention the demands for wearing masks during Covid? Freedom, as an essential principle, has the potential to serve us all. However, the pursuit of happiness is not explicitly declared as a legal recourse. Yet, how we align this principle with the pursuit of happiness continues to shape societal dynamics.

Suppose life is governed by the interplay of energy and resonance. How do societal laws align with the foundational principles of life, liberty, and freedom?

Questions and Concepts Worth Consideration

The first consideration is Life. Life represents birth to death. According to the Cambridge Dictionary, the experience of being alive is defined by self and no one else.

If we look at anti-abortion laws, the most significant abuse by far is the Law of Free Will. All human rights violations stem from this Cosmic, Universal, and Spiritual Law. We should be able to choose our life experiences of being alive or how we live. The origins of pro-life are rooted in religion. Many do not realize its more prominent contribution to abuse and only see the human rights of the unborn, which comes from doctrines to procreate. How can diverse beliefs and values coexist within a framework that honors individual freedoms and collective harmony?

Are religious beliefs or moral values being imposed on others for a unified life experience? What about other beliefs or perceptions that may hold a more significant accuracy for Life? Are people referencing the Will of God of their understanding? Or the Divine Will of God through the Laws of energy? If we look at a Christian aspect, Christ directed us to honor and follow the Laws in The Lord's Prayer. What are we constructing?

Life: Are we violating the essence?

Humanity places more importance on life/death than on loving life. Explaining this concept can be confusing because people believe and impose their opinions that Life is the utmost, and in some aspects, it is. But Loving Life considers all concerned. While the sanctity of life is central to many beliefs, prioritizing life without honoring free will risks creating imbalances that violate the universal principles guiding us. If using fear-based theologies, such as death as a punishment or being against assisted suicide, are all people being considered?

If the Law of Life came first, meaning loving life, everything would be preserved with no judgments imposed upon another. However, the Law of Life is violated when we do not consider and honor those already living.

If birth is mandated, we should emphasize and love that new life and the parent by offering education, medical care, nutrition, and loving emotional support until adulthood. Society's concern should not just be the birth of a child but to help carry the responsibility for all aspects of human development, thus putting money behind a forced moral value. Is this love?

Here is where the Love of Life becomes embroiled in its misapplication to everyday living. Life itself is universal. For us to say an unborn has a right to life is to emblazon ourselves with pious powers. The Breath of Life determines life, not us. We govern the lifelong responsibility of it.

Liberty is the second. The U.S. establishes our freedom to choose a religious/political structure. But are we now declaring a mandatory religion as idealism or a political view with control mechanisms for a specific way to behave or live? Is this Liberty? Or even freedom of religion? How might societal frameworks balance diversity and liberty, ensuring space for all expressions of life while honoring universal principles? What are we as a society to become?

Liberty: Are we violating the essence?

The freedom to believe the science of it all. To some people, science is a religion. We are all seeking expression. Our expression is why we are born; we find this through our experiences. Therefore, who can stand before another and deny them this liberty? This internal drive is, at our very core, our essence. Finding this potent expansion of love is a primary key to life and Who We Are. So, is there Freedom for Expression and Liberty to experience life when choices are compelled and controlled by man's law, denying women a fundamental personal choice? It is far more than just a choice. What does liberty mean if it does not include the freedom to make deeply personal choices?

The third is Freedom. Will we be allowed to practice the Law of Free Will, designed by God/Creator? Remember, Free Will is responsible for permissions. Is individual independence considered? Could humanity offer freedoms for happiness to live according to what brings tranquility and prosperity? No one has to like the end result, but to abort is not a position that another can give or deny. Without freedom, no one has a choice.

Freedom: Are we violating the essence?

When will accountability and responsibility be given priority? Infringing upon this Law of Free Will is a grander sin than murder.

Karmically, this is an excessive error that we place upon ourselves. We declare justice for the exact Law we violate but remain unaware of its penalty.

This becomes an oxymoron, for those who demand control of others cannot govern themselves because they fear looking into the mirror. It's so much easier to point a finger outward than inward. They will mandate regulations to justify feeling better by trying to manage the world around them. Instead of empowering others, they tear them down. Building something takes longer and uses more energy than destroying it. Many have yet to think about the aftermath of these man-dates and mans-laws because they are justified by defending a personal view or opinion. Isn't it righteous indignation to diminish access to contraception in the first place? Does it matter what someone else desires in their life? The Law of Free Will grants every soul the ability to govern its own path. Denying this through imposed societal rules contradicts the very essence of Divine Governance. Can freedom truly exist if societal laws prioritize control over compassion and understanding?

Who do these serve?

Does the safety of an abortion have any bearing? Abortions will not stop. The choices we impose on others often carry unintended emotional weight. How might we reframe our approach to prioritize compassion and understanding? Judging another's circumstance without understanding their full reality risks violating the principle of 'cause no harm.' How can we approach these deeply personal choices with respect for individual sovereignty or self-governance? Could this be considered enslavement or servitude?

As a cohesive Spiritual Logic from the Law of Free Will, the Law of Love, and the Law of Life, let's challenge the status quo of humanity's human Logic. Let's see how it lands when checks and balances are applied.

Resonate Beings

Abortion is against God's will, and it is a sin, so we're told. Yet, could God's will and mercies not have a hand in the outcome other than birth? We never walk alone, even if, at times, it feels like it. What do these people know of God's Divine Will? Is that the Law of Free Will, Life, or the Law of Love they expound upon and honor? What's the end result? If God/Creator gave us choices, who are we to deny that privilege to others?

Not to sound harsh, but standing up for the voice of the unborn is a self-serving sophism. Its qualification is egotism, arrogance, and fundamentalism being sung to the heavens. The grain of truth is the recognition we all innately know, voice and sound. To stand for those who are voiceless means ending the control and dominion of all human rights violations, easing the suffering of those who are impoverished and oppressed.

Is Life's Harmony Being Sung?

Here's an expanded view of what's broadcast to the etheric realm, the 180-degree concept. We have a better design than what God/Creator has developed. With this, our end result will remain a conflict. It has been returned to us in kind. Divine God/Creator has already given a voice, a call from spirit, in perfect timing.

(Perfection or Imperfection.) Thus, we have the magical miracle of birth. Law remains. Will we?

Can society support and give acceptance, no matter what a choice is? Is support not a result that is sought in knowing one is still loved? When I was a teenager, a friend had a successful suicide because she was pregnant, felt alone, ashamed, and not accepted. What of her family? What of her voice?

Is it not absurd to cry out for vindication or retribution, with violations held within the heart? It's an insular view filled with old, stale, stagnant energy. The absurdity that a person stands before another, judges, and then mandates how another is to live is beyond comprehension. It is an unjustified assault. Human logic and ego desire fairness, so should we continue the lunacy with sterilization? Some believe in overpopulation. Would these results not affect us for the rest of our lives? Are we indeed that opaque?

Free Will within the Law of Life is that 'will' that enriches consciousness and abides by the ultimate design of God/Creator. As free will is practiced now, it is subject to the conditioning of our belief systems, not the patterns set forth by Divinity. These are the systems commonly built from the glamour of life and not the nature of life.

In doing so, we step out of the natural rhythm of existence, creating a dance of pain and suffering instead of the movement, the equilibrium, of flawless Law, which abides not conflict or modification. Hence, it's a stuttering step of evolutionary confusion and misguided living from which unspeakable atrocities emerge.

Is there a neutral ground? Yes, there is. Believe any way you choose and tend to your own garden. If a personal decision is to abort, how is this a violation of your free will? Her only violation is a deep-seated belief that she should not have one. Her life experience holds accountability and responsibility. No person has a right to interfere with someone else's life lessons. Does this not make a rude neighbor or houseguest? Build, design, and manage your own house, which is not a metaphor. See the beauty in a home another has built, as they should see the beauty of yours.

Wrap up

Can I be frank with you for just a moment? Many have not considered the energies or their checks and balances. Laws are always in service and preserve energy flow. If nature can pre-serve us, we can consider how our beliefs serve ourselves and others. I'm not stepping on someone's beliefs, and I do not intend to offend, but have we not had centuries of discord, control, and suffering? We all have the inalienable right to believe as we choose. It's the action we take concerning it that matters. When will we learn, and when will we stop inflicting more pain? When will we recognize our activities based on beliefs have a cause and effect that produces accountability?

231

Remember, everything resonates here on the earth plane and in the etheric, for what is done to the many returns to the one, its source.

I'm sure I have brought up anger in some of you and fired up others. If fury resonates, please see if assumptions were inserted into what was said. I only applied the Laws of Energy. Also, see if you closed the door on what was presented. When resistance is felt, it is the best opportunity for personal growth.

Our actions will remain dissonant if humanity continues to sing out of tune. Lee Two Hawks says, "We should remember that the lilt of the voice reflects the inner song. Thus, sing bravely". Respectfully, these elements and impressions can help bring peace to the world. It starts with one single voice of peaceful intent.

By aligning societal values with universal principles, we gain an understanding of how spiritual logic informs the human experience. This alignment invites us to reflect on how Life, Liberty, and Freedom serve as both personal and collective pursuits, shaping the realities we construct.

Key Points: Alternate Realities

- Stepping into neutrality allows us to question assumptions and align with natural laws.

- Science and Universal Laws offer clarity and reduce reliance on theologies of human logic.

- Common denominators for moral values—compassion, causing no harm—reflect Divine Will and Love/Wisdom.

- Freedom and liberty mirror the cosmic dynamics of Divine Will, Love/Wisdom, and Active Intelligence.

- Energy serves as a modifier and equalizer, offering opportunities for growth and balance.

- Remember to tend your own garden. Believe as you wish, allowing others to do the same.

Chapter 9: Life's Impression Wrap-Up

Chapter Nine explores the intricate interplay of universal principles and human experiences. Through the metaphor of constructing a dream home, we see how energy transitions from the metaphysical to the physical, guided by the Laws of Construction and cosmic dynamics. Impressions and spiritual logic reveal insights into the soul's journey. At the same time, alternate realities invite us to question assumptions and explore the broader connections between energy, freedom, and balance. Together, these sections provide a cohesive framework for understanding life's creation and the universal flow.

As we reflect on the impressions and universal principles explored in this chapter, we may grapple with the discomfort of challenged beliefs. Growth often begins in these moments of unease, where old frameworks give way to new understanding. In the next chapter, we'll delve into the transformative journey of spiritual growth, where grace and resilience guide us through the challenges.

The following summarizes the key points, providing a clear and concise overview of Chapter Nine's insights.

Chapter 9 Key Points

Section A. Life's Impression

- Universal Principles: Divine Will, Love/Wisdom, and Active Intelligence guide energy flow and creation.

- Dream Home Metaphor: Illustrates how energy transitions from metaphysical to physical.

- Harmony and Adaptation: Constructing a home mirrors life's journey, highlighting intention, adaptation, and the interplay of energy.

- Impressions align the soul's journey with universal laws, shaping its expression in life.

Section B. Spiritual Logic's Impression:

- Impressions and Laws: Life's impressions align the soul's journey with universal laws, shaping its expression in life.

- Energy and Harmony: Cosmic laws act as checks and balances, ensuring harmony across all dimensions.

- Divine Intelligence: Nature and Active Intelligence offer insights into energy's flow and function.

- Reduce Misconceptions: Science and universal laws clarify energy dynamics, transcending theologies of human logic.

- Laws of Construction influence all.

Section C. Alternative Realities:

- Neutrality and Judgment: Stepping into neutrality invites reflection, aligning with natural laws.

- Universal Truths: Right and wrong are validated only from one's perspective, while universal laws remain constant.

- Freedom and Harmony: Life, liberty, and freedom reflect the cosmic dynamics of energy, guiding societal and personal growth.

- Question Assumptions: Examining beliefs opens pathways to alignment with universal principles and harmonious living.

CHAPTER TEN

SPIRITUAL GROWTH

A Graceful Word

*A*s a child, I had two near-death experiences at the ages of three and six. With the first, I had to learn how to speak again. In the second one, I stood before the Angelic Presence and stated, "This one will." When I drew breath, I knew I would not see, hear, or feel the world like others. Dyslexia would be an effect and a blessing. This energy awareness was part of the message I was to disclose in time. In A Child's Curiosity, which started this journey, I asked my father why people talk about love yet do not act lovingly. This confusion was an actual torment.

I had horrible experiences with being mocked, belittled, tormented, and used as an example. This was the cruelty dished out from those who professed the good word and love of Christ. This dichotomy had me wondering what these people could not see, feel, or realize. Did any of them recognize the hurt they *caused? Did they care? There was no acceptance or allowance for a child psychic medium, period. My parents tried to support me the best they could with their limited information. My Mom would direct me to Edgar Cayce so I wouldn't feel so alone.*

The other adults in my life did not intend to cause pain. They only broadcast what they learned or believed, usually from the same source. They didn't question their beliefs or the material they were given; hence, they became my greatest teachers. At that time, I did not understand how powerfully anchored beliefs were to adults or how easily angered when their comfort zones and boundaries were threatened. This was my learning curve.

Incidentally, those who retain the knowingness or sight share experiences with rejection, ridicule, and belittlement; what a shame. Do these actions mirror tolerance, acceptance, or love? We all have these abilities of intuition and knowingness. It is choosing to use and develop them or not.

People have asked me, how long have you been talking with angels, guides, and masters, or aware of energy? I always reply, "From the moment I drew breath, physically, mentally, and metaphysically." I considered this normal; there was no other way to be. The two NDEs enhanced and quickened my understanding of the world around me, seeking efficiency with the flow. Growing up, my goal was to find and reduce my errors. Knowing that, eventually, I'd offer this silent code of life from the energy field. I embraced this graceful, healing, loving light that holds all answers and solutions; Spiritual Logic's Magic. I am so blessed.

In adulthood, the herd mentality of non-acceptance was daunting. What an eye-opener. Suppose we do not conform and believe as others do. The herd will stampede, and their residual mandate remains within our mass consciousness, triggering our animal instinct. These triggers will prevail until an expanded view is revised within our conscious awareness. Do not be led astray. Question everything, especially the source. Conformity remains bland and stale. Diversity is the spice of life.

As an observation from the other side, everything looked so easy. The human experience is so vastly different. I questioned myself regarding love, herd mentality, and so much more. Why in the world would I state, "This one will?" (Above it is so easy) What was I thinking? (Below takes effort.) This life lesson taught me the responsibility of choice, vision, and leadership. By the way, leaders should experience how it feels to follow others before leading. Developing a more compassionate leader means understanding that a follower is there by choice and free will. Know this, children will be born with knowingness and full remembrance of energy. They will not conform to human belief systems injected into their consciousness. It won't make sense to them. They will not follow. Many are already here.

Much material was covered in the previous chapter. Perhaps some found a missing puzzle piece that brought clarity. Others may have felt stirred by questions, beliefs, or emotions.

Still, a few might feel so challenged they're ready to throw this book back at us—and that's perfectly okay. Growth often begins in discomfort, and sometimes humor is the best balm to help us take the next step.

During my destructive, turbulent years, I was immovable and planted in my comfort zone. I, too, might have thrown this book until the birth of my stillborn child. Empty arms caused me to really question life itself. It was a steep price, riddled with emotions and questioning who I thought I was. Now, with the death of two children, I understand grief very well. So well, grief and I are now friends, having a lifetime to grow together, interact, and for me to learn grace. That was painful to say. Ouch.

So, sharing a Graceful Word is what I see as also sharing the Light of who we all are. How can we realize this loving grace? It's easy. Stop mandating and expecting energy to conform to your ideals and create a partnership instead. Friction can be expressed through self-serving Ideals. (Like an order, I-deal, and you deliver). Harmony is expressed through service. The Universe will deal with and deliver without friction when there is a partnership of flowing co-creation. The Laws of Construction are always in action, whether someone believes in them or not.

We ventured into some challenging waters, addressing topics that may have stirred up emotions, beliefs, or even resistance. Know that growth often begins when we feel unsettled. It's in the tension between what we think we know, and the truths we're uncovering that wisdom takes root.

These pearls of wisdom are born from the questions, discomforts, and moments of clarity that challenge us most deeply. As we step into this chapter, we focus on these pearls of wisdom—lessons gleaned from life's challenges and opportunities. This is where the tools of grace, humor, and reflection come into play, guiding us to embrace growth and move toward balance and understanding. Here, we'll explore how to transform emotional pain into stepping stones for spiritual expansion, allowing wisdom to emerge from our trials.

A special note: The following energy tools and techniques shared are rooted in universal principles and practices widely recognized by those working with energy dynamics. Their simplicity and effectiveness make them timeless approaches to maintaining vibrational alignment and healthy boundaries.

Pearls of Wisdom &
Emotional Pain

When dealing with painful emotions, try not to take yourself too seriously. Laughter is the best medicine, and only the beholder can find it. If you can do this, it changes the vibration, allowing your energy to settle. You'll be able to think more clearly. When facing painful situations, assess how graceful the behavior was. You might get a laugh out of it. Next time you are in an argument, think about how elegant your actions, words, or deeds were. How did you look when you were all red in the face, with bulging veins, and pointing fingers at another in anger? Imagine if you were a figure skater performing that scenario on ice. It would look quite awkward and end with a thud. You can brush off the residue of painful energy and begin again.

Sometimes, situations can challenge us to the core of our being, leaving emotional scars. Other events can cross personal boundaries, test strength, tolerance, or courage, and define our behavior. Yet, how we address them remains. Many can identify when they are wounded and who did the damage. But can we determine when we cause pain in another through our beliefs or behavior? It's easy to point a finger outward, not so easy inward. Was there love, honor, or respect given? Was Divine Will, Divine Love/Wisdom, present? You can tell if you have treated another as you wish to be treated.

Anger to Irritants

If anger is felt from the previous chapter, this is a good sign. It shows you your tuning fork and keynote speaker. Nature is triggering those impulses for alignment and expansion from Systems of Beliefs. Spiritual Logic aids our spiritual growth. These emotions are natural. However, are they serving you for your highest and best? I've asked these questions earlier. How does it feel to 'want or need'? How does it feel to receive? Question yourself, how does it feel to be angry? I'm not mocking. It's an honest inquiry and an excellent way to qualify an emotion. Negative emotions are usually misqualified or misdirected energy and are not of the Light. Is being irate worthy of your distress, only to be delivered right back to you? What you do to another, you do to yourself. It's the negative feedback loop—Law of Reciprocity.

You can choose the "I am angry," which starts a vicious cycle. However, please note that anger can be a motivator. This energy can be re-qualified and, thus, used to heal the human condition. The condition, in part, is the uncontrolled emotional entrapment that has enslaved us for thousands of centuries. These are some considerations to make that can help you gain mastery over your emotions.

Am I using my anger to motivate positive change, or is it creating a negative cycle?

Irritants

Spiritual growth is a journey that can be painful or irritating. Anytime an understanding or belief is challenged or changed, the Law of Harmony/Rhythm is set in motion and changes our vibrational frequency. We will feel subtle disturbances until we bring into balance this new energy. It is helpful to share with others if you have a complex or challenging growth period requiring space to adjust or adapt. This way, perhaps they won't take your actions personally. Ya might be a tad bit grumpy.

Can I recognize when my emotional responses are misdirected energy? How can I redirect them to serve my highest and best?

As an example of nature in action, I'd like to share a paraphrased lesson from my father and a dear friend, White Dove Crow, a Woodland Cree Medicine Woman.

"A small grain of sand may irritate an oyster, yet the resulting perfection of a pearl is created. Life will bring us irritants that we can transform into beautiful pearls. Thus, pearls of wisdom, value, and of love." *(Crow)*

Healthy Boundaries

We all create boundaries; some are direct or indirect, and others are implied. These can range from irritants to vicious anger and vindictive actions when they get crossed. So, how graceful are you or others when boundaries are crossed?

Healthy boundaries are cushions to allow a learning experience and gently re-qualify a specific behavior. Boundaries should not be a brick wall ready for impact at sixty miles an hour. This only causes harm to both. Splat!

Am I setting boundaries as rigid walls or as flexible cushions for growth and understanding?

When we feel frustrated, impatient, or irritated with another person, we have left Lights Embrace. People 'feel' that their implied boundaries have been crossed, and they will impose their demands upon another. Usually, it's done in haste and sharply at that, without realizing that the biggest violator is themselves. Poor timing on your part does not qualify as an emergency for someone else. (Road-rage)

Conversely, poor timing on someone else's part does not grant you a license to judge harshly or become impatient. It shifts our intent from the present moment and impedes our focus. Therefore, the experience is encircled with annoyance or anger. These emotional responses are misapplied, and they are yours. You allowed them to influence you.

If and when we feel anxious or crossed, or those angry hot buttons are stimulated, you, not someone else, have triggered the imaginary borders. Your filters and alignments could be off, and so is the dynamic flow. These feelings are not cushions that allow expansion, acceptance, or adaptation that healthy boundaries do. Recognize the lower vibrations that have triggered you, and address and reconcile them. It was mentioned that when Lee Two Hawks and I married, we promised nothing, only to do our best not to cross boundaries.

To soften or modify boundaries or traverse the hot coals of a fiery moment more easily – step back and disengage. Would it be better to huff-n-puff, walk away, or simply smile?

How do I ensure my boundaries reflect compassion and grace rather than fear or frustration?

These techniques may feel familiar to others who practice energy work. While they are universal in nature, they are presented here through the position of my own experiences and insights.

Compassion is not just a feeling but a conscious choice, a vibrational state we actively maintain. As a finely tuned instrument requires care to stay in harmony, so does our energy field. When others bring their struggles to us, the temptation to slip into empathy or sympathy can be substantial. However, lowering our vibration reduces our ability to offer genuine support. Instead, we can remain tuned to compassion—the highest octave—offering clarity and strength without disempowering ourselves or others.

This exercise provides a hands-on approach to aligning with the Harmonizer aspect. By consciously tuning your energy to the frequency of compassion, you can transform reactive patterns into intentional responses. This practice not only benefits personal growth but also strengthens connections with others.

Tuning Your Instrument. Step-by-Step Practice

Ground Yourself in Compassion

Begin by grounding yourself with deep, steady breaths. Affirm your choice to remain in compassionate resonance: "I tune my energy to compassion, maintaining clarity and strength.

Visualize Your Instrument

Imagine your energy field as a finely tuned instrument. Each string represents an aspect of your being: emotions, thoughts, and spirit. Picture the strings vibrating in perfect harmony, creating a steady and uplifting tone.

Check for Disruption

When someone shares their pain or struggle with you, notice how your energy responds. Does it feel pulled downward into empathy (vitality borrowed) or sympathy (acknowledgment of limitation)? Recognize these as signs that your tuning is shifting.

Reaffirm Your Resonance

Refocus on your inner harmony. Visualize your strings gently, realigning to compassion. Feel the strength of this resonance holding steady, even in the presence of others' emotional turbulence. Repeat: "I am compassion. I hold this vibration for myself and others."

Extend Compassion Without Lowering

Picture your resonance extending outward like a stable note in an orchestra. It does not adjust to match others' dissonance; instead, it invites their energy to rise and align with yours. Hold this space as a steady beacon of clarity and strength.

Avoid Jumping in the Bucket

Lowering your vibration to match someone else's pain does not serve them. Instead of jumping into their bucket, extend a hand from your place of stability: "I see your strength, and I hold this space for you to rise into it." Compassion uplifts; it does not descend.

Restore Your Alignment

After the interaction, take time to recalibrate if required. Revisit your visualization of the tuned instrument, reaffirming your choice to vibrate at the octave of compassion.

The Octaves Key Insights

Sympathy: The lowest octave. Acknowledges limitation and reinforces smallness. It pulls your vibration down, leaving both you and the other person in dissonance.

Empathy: Vitality borrowed. It connects emotionally but can drain your energy and disrupt your harmony.

Compassion: The highest octave. It holds space for others without lowering your vibration, empowering them to rise into alignment.

By consciously choosing compassion, you remain a steady, harmonious presence, allowing others to retune their instruments to that elevated frequency. This practice uplifts those around you and preserves your vibrational integrity, creating a ripple of harmony and healing.

With this foundational practice, we move into the work of mastery—where compassion, grace, and alignment become second nature. By integrating these principles, we step fully onto the path of spiritual growth and self-mastery.

Magic Keys to Mastery

What is Self-Mastery? How do we define it, and more importantly, how do we embody it daily? Self-mastery is not simply an achievement but a dynamic, ongoing process of aligning with our highest self. It invites us to cultivate peace, observe without reaction, and radiate compassion and light in every circumstance. Through this journey, we learn to navigate life with grace, maintaining alignment with the Universal Laws and the I AM aspect. Self-mastery is the conscious practice of stepping into the eye of the observer, where reactions are replaced by intentional responses. It is the foundation of compassionate living and a cornerstone of spiritual growth.

In this section, we explore the Aspects of Self-Mastery, practical tools to embody these principles, and references for deeper exploration.

Our emotions are intertwined with our thoughts and beliefs. If you are experiencing discord, struggling with drama or trauma, emotional ups and downs, feeling alone or defensive, you've missed the mark. It is misapplied, misdirected, misunderstood, or misaligned energy of Law. Remember, all information has to go through your filters. Our emotional intelligence with responses will rest upon one of three fundamental energy components. Does humanity have the courage to c-our-age as the heavens do? We can look to the vibrational harmonic frequencies to bring our emotional mastery into balance, tranquility, and peace.

Vibrational Energy of Emotional Responses, as seen from above:

Prehistoric: Pure instinct. No thought of the outcome. (Acting out of anger or rage.)

Primitive: Self-Serving Response, minor consideration for results. (Getting a grip.)

Pragmatic: Holistic response, Serving-Self, and others. Inner resolution- peace, balance, and harmony. Events do not shake your emotional foundation. (In the Flow)

All these Emotional Responses register at different vibrational levels and some at higher octaves, to which few achieve this emotional intelligence applied with wisdom. (We're hinting toward Divine Love/Wisdom.) The third pragmatic position is where humanity's destiny is unfolding. Only you can choose which vibratory rate you desire to express. The goal is to gain mastery of your thoughts, emotions, and beliefs. Qualify with Harmony and Balance. (Please be cognizant and walk softly upon Mother Earth, for she is pregnant.)

What daily practices can I incorporate to sustain my alignment with the highest octave of compassion?

"The Destiny of Mastery"

These insights resonate deeply with Kryon's teachings, which offer further illumination on the principles of self-mastery. As channeled by Lee Carroll, Kryon's perspective supports the notion that mastery is not about control but about embodying elevated states of being that naturally uplift and harmonize the world around us. Kryon (channeled by Lee Carroll) delves into this concept in "The Destiny of Mastery." This video is available on YouTube: https://www.youtube.com/watch?v=TNl1_zfoM7s&t=9s

According to Kryon, the principles of mastery include:

- The master can go to a place of peace, safety, and comfort in the midst of turmoil.

- Mastery observes rather than reacts.

- Mastery surrounds itself with so much light that nothing dark can approach it.

- Mastery does not diminish another human being. (Kryon)

How can we embody the principles of mastery, such as observing without reacting and creating peace amid turmoil? Mastery provides a sanctuary within. It allows us to remain centered and calm, even when surrounded by chaos, embodying peace as a state of being. The master approaches life as the observer, maintaining awareness and detachment from emotional triggers. This reflective stance creates clarity and allows for intentional, compassionate responses. The light of mastery is a shield of resonance. By radiating harmony and high-frequency energy, the master naturally repels lower vibrations, protecting themselves without resistance or fear. Compassion and respect are hallmarks of mastery. The master uplifts others, recognizing their potential and innate worth, fostering empowerment rather than judgment or criticism.

Together, these perspectives reveal that self-mastery is not a destination but an evolving practice. It is the ongoing choice to remain in alignment with the highest frequencies of love, light, and compassion, regardless of external circumstances. By weaving these teachings into our lives, we not only uplift ourselves but also serve as beacons for others on their journeys.

Kryon's channeling, as shared by Lee Carroll, offers profound insights into self-mastery. These teachings highlight the role of emotional neutrality and energetic alignment as pathways to compassion and coherence. Readers can refer to Kryon's online lectures and videos for further exploration.

Self-mastery, as an expression of spiritual growth, brings together the tools and teachings explored in this chapter. By integrating the Four Aspects of Self-Mastery and embracing compassionate practices, we position ourselves with the Universal Laws.

How do I ensure I uplift others without diminishing their autonomy or worth?

Our Senses

We have been speaking about life, our body, and our existence from a position of energy. I'd like to shift momentarily to our energy bodies and interconnect them with boundaries. We can create healthy, well-defined margins for where we begin and end. It's that comfort zone we feel when standing close to one another. Sometimes, we must step back because we are in someone's space. We sense this from our aura.

The distance of our sphere or egg-shaped aura constantly changes based on our thoughts and emotions. Inclusive or loving thoughts expand our field, while being exclusive, with destructive thoughts and feelings, constrict and bring it close to our physical body. (Happy or Sad.)

The aura functions like a membrane, filtering energy. I've coined this as a **Semi-permissible membrane**- *We filter and give **permission** for what is allowed to enter our field of existence, the aura. The finer frequencies of love pass back and forth effortlessly, equally giving and receiving, through the membrane. Discord's heavy, slow vibrations are blocked, and entry is prohibited. It's the same concept for a semi-permeable membrane in medical terminology.*

Creating a Vivified Aura

For simplicity, each of us gets a ten-foot radius to work with, and everyone else can have the universe. The focus is only on your aura, where you feel you extend outwards and then stop. Just notice and sense your energy as a sphere, extending beyond your physical body, front, back, sides, above and below. You can qualify your energy house and program what is allowed in and out. These permissions are the boundaries for your energy body. Such as intending only love, grace, and compassion to enter, equally giving and receiving. It is just like breathing. You can deny the boulders of discordant energy like hate, anger, or fear from entering your space, your home. Your semi-permissible membrane, or auric field, is now crisp and well-defined for what is given and received.

Your auric boundary now pulsates healthy, nurturing energy. The health of the aura reflects the health of the physical form. Each of us should have a well-defined auric field. Doing this assists sensitive or empathic people from absorbing someone else's energy. For example, suppose others are upset or arguing, and you enter the room. In that case, you won't be so influenced by their energy because it won't enter your ten-foot space. They get the universe.

What sensations or changes do I notice in my energy after an aura-clearing practice?

How does this align with my emotional and spiritual state?

How can I use my auric boundary to maintain alignment and balance when I sense discordant energy around me?

Before we move on, I'd like to speak on permissions, protection, and boundaries as one singular component. This is a vibrational perception worth further investigation. For those of you who have been working with energy using protection tools, please continue to do so, especially if you're a beginner. However, when you request protection from lower, harmful, nasty energy, it means this energy is permitted to exist in your reality, and you'll continually have to use the protection tools. Foul energy cannot influence you if you remove its permission. That is the law, the Law of Free Will. Also, look to the Law of Vibration and apply it. Lower, slower energy cannot enter, higher, faster vibrations. You can lower it, keep it the same, or raise it by giving or removing permissions. Why create or live in an environment that requires protection in the first place? So much time and energy is provided to create protections. Why? Allow no entry or harm; it's your will, acceptance, and boundaries. Create and live in an environment of light.

Transiting to our five senses, sight, hearing, taste, touch, and smell, well, there is an elephant in the room, folks. There are more than five. We can think, cognize, have emotions, and perceive energy. I didn't even mention intuition. In the future, researchers will update their reference books. There are so many more than I'll list here. If it were up to me, I'd re-number them for the importance of our evolution as follows.

Our bodies receive sensory information through our:

1. Thoughts
2. Emotions
3. Intuition
4. Cognition

5. Visualization
6. Imagination
7. Feeling or sensing energy

How we process new information, whether fantastic or devastating news, will affect our energy and senses. For example, if you receive news that you lost your job or house, believing they were safe alters that belief and causes chaos within your senses and aura. Perhaps you cannot focus (thoughts) on a new job (visualization) due to discordant (emotions) energy of anger, fear, or worry.

The previous chapter alone could have challenged learned beliefs and created blockages from disbelief or wondering who we are as a species. Due to this, we would like to share an energy technique to clear your aura from blockages associated with shattered beliefs. So, not only can you create a well-defined healthy auric boundary, but you'll also be able to have it radiate a shining auric field.

Releasing the Blockages of Grief Technique

At some point in our lives, we will experience grief. It can present in various ways and varying degrees. It's felt as a loss of something, perhaps, from a relationship, job, house, belief, the use of a limb to an amputation, or the death of a loved one. Even the death of a loved one is given a grief value from a child, spouse, parent, sibling, or friend.

Grief is a personal process, with no right or wrong way to navigate through it. It's an emotional pain with no time constraints. Nothing anyone can say or do will lessen it, and bystanders sometimes feel helpless, trying to offer comfort. However, we can assist ourselves by knowing how to release the energy blockages from grief that continue to trigger pain. The actual pain still exists, but this energy work can help you process it in a healthy way.

Broken Mirror Metaphor

Sam, who is barefoot, breaks a mirror on his tile floor. Broken pieces in various sizes spread out all over the room. He grabs a broom and starts to sweep up the glass. Large and small pieces form a pile in front of him. He finishes the task, dumping the pile in the garbage bin. Suddenly, he feels a sharp pain in the heel of his foot. Sam immediately sits on a chair next to him and examines his foot. A wedge of glass had pierced the flesh. As he removed it and applied first aid, he noticed the blood was reflected back to him from the mirror.

Limping, he looks down and notices more broken glass. He gets out the vacuum cleaner and vacuums with determination. A few days later, more shards were still glistening on the floor. Sam used a wet paper towel to clear the remaining remnants.

Sam was surprised with the process. When he thought everything was clean and tidy, shards still appeared days later. This metaphor mirrors grief and its destructive energy.

Grief

We suggest you research if you're unfamiliar with the stages of grief, the chakras, or their meanings. A plethora of online information can assist your understanding, and if required, please seek professional assistance for grief. We'll show the extended version with 7 stages of grief https://activepause.com/grief-stages/ because it aligns with the 7 chakras for illustration purposes. People can experience these stages out of order, such as guilt being the first placement. Our focus is on energy, which is also in no particular order, meaning stage 3 anger might resonate with the 5th chakra. According to Elisabeth Kübler-Ross, the stages of grief are as follows. (Kubler-Ross)

We are using a descending order to associate the chakras.

We are using a descending order to associate the chakras.

Stages	Chakras/ Colors
7. Acceptance and Hope	7. Crown/Violet, Gold or White
6. Depression	6. Third Eye/ Indigo
5. Guilt	5. Throat/ Blue
4. Bargaining	4. Heart/ green
3. Anger	3. Solar Plexus/ Yellow
2. Denial	2. Navel or Belly/ Orange
1. Shock or Disbelief	1. Root/ Red

The Energy of Grief

All beliefs are stored within our chakras. When grief strikes, those beliefs are shattered and spread into our aura, just like the floor in the metaphor. In essence, Mirror Reflections of what was to be, pieces of energy that no longer serve us, now occupy and cut us from the inside out. Suppose we are dealing with the death of a loved one, for example. In that case, the shock or disbelief causes a domino effect, affecting all chakras. Now, a rainbow of broken shards and mirror images from all the chakras are enclosed within our aura. Disbelief, guilt, or denial now pierce us from within, creating blocked condensed energy. Perhaps perceiving we can't escape this never-ending, gripping ordeal. An important aspect to remember is that our chakras do not require healing. They are energy wheels or vortexes that spin according to a person's conscious awareness; they can't be harmed, perhaps congested.

We can remove the glass blockages or any remnants of fractured beliefs so they don't continue to stab, trigger pain, and leave us bleeding. Cleaning our aura allows us to re-establish or reformat a previous belief occupying each chakra. In time, it helps to integrate a different reality, such as living without our loved one still physically by our side. Or incorporate an affirmation such as not allowing anyone to steal your joy, even yourself. This clearing allows room for the process of healing to begin. Eventually, hope and joy can be re-established and integrated, thus paving the way for a higher vibration and frequency.

To be clear, this removal does not remove the memory of a loved one or any events, only the fragments of a belief. If you ever thought or said, "I can't believe this happened or I can't believe it's true or What was I thinking." there has been a dislodging of a belief held in a chakra.

Clearing the Blockages

Energy Hygiene is always an excellent practice for any reason. If you choose to work with this technique for grief, it's best if you're past the initial shock and denial of the second stage. The energy of denial deters a focused thought. With energy work, we use our imagination, visualization, or pretending. This will be no different. We will use roses for this process because they symbolize the Ascended Masters. However, a feather or sacred geometry could be used if you prefer.

The Process of Releasing

Get into a comfortable position. Take a refreshing breath and breathe, closing your eyes. As a curious explorer, imagine your aura, an egg-shape or sphere surrounding your body. Inside the aura, you see, feel, or sense various sizes of broken glass, mirroring the colors of the rainbow. These remnants of energy no longer serve you. For now, just notice them. If there is difficulty in this visualization, know that they exist within your energy field.

In your mind's eye, picture and create a bouquet of seven roses, each a color from the rainbow. These roses function like a special magnet, a sticky gripper, a duster, or a vacuum. Like magic, broken shards of colored glass will be attracted to the rose.

Start with the color red for the root chakra. Move your magi-cal rose inside your aura around the top, sides, bottom, front, and back, allowing these red pieces of energy to be gently dislodged and attached to the rose. Using it like a feather duster, make a few passes. When you feel this process is cleared, take your rose and place it outside of your aura. If you're unsure where that is, just intend it to be outside the aura. Dispose of the flower immediately so it won't infect or cause harm to another. So, composting is not an option. Burn or evaporate it, eliminating its existence. Take a breath, breathe, and smile. Observe your aura and notice there are no red fragments at this time.

Pick orange next from your bouquet of roses, and repeat this clearing with each chakra color. Start from the root/ red, Navel or Belly/ Orange, Solar Plexus/ Yellow, Heart/ green, Throat/ Blue, Third Eye/ Indigo, and finally to the Crown/ Violet, Gold or White, each time eliminating the used rose outside of your aura. Remember to breathe between each completion. Observe your aura; it is clean, clear, vibrant, and bright. Smile, your aura is magnificent.

This activity does not take long to do. If working with grief, the seven stages should be cleared as you experience them. So, it should be done often because as remnants of energy are removed, some deeper, stubborn, or embedded energy will dislodge and surface. They are only shards appearing later and will slowly stop. This is our energy body's healing mechanism, release, clear, restore.

This releasing method can also assist in clearing our filters so we can process new information without opinions or judgments, including shadow work, beliefs, and giving and receiving forgiveness for self and others. This process resonates with frequency. By clearing our energy, we actively empower ourselves, being more receptive to the nourishing, harmonic vibrational energies surrounding us.

As bystanders, Lee Two Hawks and I witness so many people who have not done or know how to do energy work, and they appear so weighted down and congested, limping through life. Please take a seat, remove that metaphorically infected glass wedge from your foot and aura, and allow healing to begin. Before you know it, you will feel stronger and stronger. Let your Loving Light Shine.

What shards of emotional energy or beliefs might still be lingering in my aura, preventing me from healing?

After practicing the grief-release technique, how has my perspective shifted?

Working with Energy as an overview

This energy diagram represents the culmination of the teachings throughout this book. It synthesizes the totality of energy as a fundamental force, weaving together concepts discussed from the beginning, such as the I AM aspect, the principles of life, love, and alignment with universal laws. This visual offers a comprehensive framework to understand and work with energy in its various manifestations.

The energy of life is impregnated with love, and love is impregnated with life, which are interchangeable in the metaphysical world we live in. The boxes or their content in the diagram below are also interchangeable and are used as a visual overview of energy.

Energy Diagram: Life's Substance Infuses All

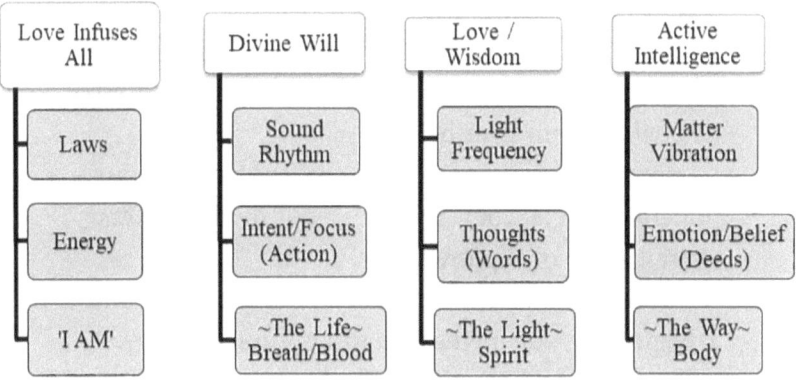

As the final teaching chapter, this diagram encapsulates the journey we have taken together. Exploring the energetic components of life, the I AM aspect, and the tools for navigating existence. It serves as a reminder of the intricate and beautiful interplay between energy, love, and life, guiding us toward mastery and balance in our co-creative reality.

For those who may require additional explanation, the diagram consists of four rows and four columns. Each component represents a principle or manifestation of energy. Love Infuses All, Divine Will, Love/Wisdom, and Active Intelligence, alongside their corresponding expressions, such as rhythm, frequency, emotion, and belief. This structure is dynamic and interchangeable, reflecting the flow of energy in all aspects of life.

Utilizing the Energy Diagram

Reflect on how the components of the diagram (e.g., Love Infuses All, Divine Will, Active Intelligence) are currently present in your life.

Choose one principle, such as Divine Will, and explore how you can consciously align with it in your actions, thoughts, or decisions.

Use the diagram as a daily visualization tool. Imagine each box glowing with energy, integrating its qualities into your being.

Journal about how the interplay of these components affects your relationships, decisions, and overall sense of alignment.

This framework stands as both a conclusion and a beginning—an invitation to continue exploring, embodying, and aligning with the universal energy that infuses all life. May this serve as a tool for your ongoing growth and evolution.

How do I currently balance the components of vibration, rhythm, and frequency in my daily life?
What areas of my life might feel out of harmony?
How can I use the Laws of Energy to bring them back into alignment?

Wrap up

As we close this chapter, let us reflect on the journey and wisdom we've gathered. Knowledge gained is a beautiful thing. Wisdom gained is potent and is the proper application of knowledge. Many have knowledge, but few use wisdom. So, which is of higher service to you and humanity?

Many people have questioned how God/Creator could have allowed some atrocity to occur. God/Creator didn't. We did this by not following the Laws. I could reference that humanity has misplaced the memo on Divine Will, Divine Love/Wisdom, and Active Intelligence from a higher perspective. Until we, as a species, see the light, we will remain in darkness with our imperfect logic and impose it on others.

Reflect upon the Laws of Construction. This is where answers can be found for anyone seeking an accurate moral compass. Nature always obeys the Laws of Energy. Remember, where we place our focus is how we perceive life. We can sing harmoniously to the heavens and will be rewarded in kind. We just have to consider the position from which we broadcast.

Each of us has the ability for self-mastery, alignment with the Governance of Laws, and working with energy as a totality. Energy is a Universal Language.

Remember, you are a co-creator of your reality. You transform your life and the world around you by aligning with the highest frequencies of love, light, and compassion. Carry these teachings forward, and continue exploring the energy that infuses all life. Your journey has only just begun.

Key Points: Graceful Expansion

- Energy hygiene is like taking a shower or brushing your teeth. It's a good practice for vibrant energy. Showering in grace and beauty.

- Working with energy is the quickest way to modify any experience or event. Clearing your aura vitalizes your energy.

- Recognize Wisdom as knowledge energized.

- Whether you choose to be a leader or not, live compassionately. You are the captain of your ship. Self-mastery is a key.

- Higher frequencies can trigger your growth or understanding. Spiritual Growth can be felt as pain. Be kind to yourself.

- Reflect on the principles of self-mastery: observe without reacting and align with the highest frequencies of love, light, and compassion.

- Use reflective practices, such as aura clearing and grief work, to restore energetic harmony and balance.

- Recognize the influence of your energy on the collective consciousness—your alignment uplifts the world around you.

- Apply the components of the energy diagram as tools for daily alignment with universal laws.

- Revisit earlier teachings, like the 'I AM' aspect, to deepen your understanding of energy's universal language.

- Focus on intentionality—where you place your focus determines the reality you co-create.

- Energy is a universal language; mastery over your energy empowers transformation in both personal and collective realms.

Chapter Eleven

SUMMARY

Summum Bonum

A Message from the future to the past.

*D*ear Beloved Ancestors,
I send greetings and gratitude…and, perhaps, hope. My name is Summum Bonum, and I function as a Professor or Elder at one of our Temples of Learning. A personal passion of mine is human evolution, so I am reaching out to you from a time yet unrealized in a world yet unknown to you. You are reading an impression sent to you through intent, manifesting as words on a page. I have just sent you thoughts of encouragement. It exists before you now.

Interestingly, what seems impossible exists only in what can or cannot be imagined. In my time, our world expression may seem beyond your immediate capabilities, but be assured that your perspective may enrich such a possibility over time. We would not be here had events not occurred that marked an evolutionary advance on the part of Humanity, a united effort, and a realization of necessity and survival. This evolutionary awakening shifted the focus from 'the me' to the many and then the global. The rule of human law became the acceptance of cosmic and solar laws. Natural law became, well, natural. The human race became alert to a sublime reality – we are the extension of divinity, and we began acting accordingly. And so, this message.

Please be patient as I delineate a few noticeable schisms from your era. Your societies are in their embryonic stage, becoming more compassionate and inclusive. I offer a focal point.

Your time frame is equivalent to what you knew as the Middle Ages. A few alumni here still consider your era to be the Dark Ages. The light of consciousness is yet an ember. Logically, we struggled to understand why people would become so unsettled over mild irritations, road rage, and domestic abuse, ending in beatings or death! Jealousy degraded into murder or religious persecution of those with differing views. How unseemly. Separatism, hatred, and racism were the cast of your day, causing much delay in advancing human consciousness.

We have mastered patience, reason, kindness, and imperative resolve to achieve the best result; thus, our vision guides what is best for the many. We share and embrace compassion as the avatars of beauty and harmony. Our societies reason and strategize together for value and quality without division. In those dark days, you call the present, humanity argued with arrogance, bullets, and bombs, vying for dominance and hoping to drive your brothers and sisters into submission. But instead, gaining only the temporary submission of others marked with their blood and the flesh of your sons and daughters.

The Dark Ages started wars, annihilating the best and brightest – the youth of your future. Our world's significant treasure is our children, who are not seen as disposable resources. We immeasurably invest in all aspects of their development, for they are our future. This brings about a few focal points for communication and freedom on your horizon.

The way we communicate has changed and will continue to do so. Our children are taught the affect and effect of language, tone (sound), action, and feeling. There is a particular focus on trusting their intuition as guidance. Old-timers would say, "Be cautious of your actions, words, and deeds." In contrast, we focus on the thought itself, the progenitor of all words, actions, or deeds. Thoughts are potent, random, or otherwise. They can manifest as cruel or beneficent energies affecting the human exchange of feelings or actions. So, our words are few but carry potent causal effects upon the field of love. Especially now, when telepathic communication is ordinary, what is voiced is usually saved for specific circumstances, which leaves little for interpretation because our speech obeys laws.

In our framing, a sense of fairness or injustice is non-existent because we would not give cause in the first place; all are equal. It would not serve a higher purpose. By enhancing sharing, caring, and compassionate measures, we overcame self-indulgences, self-serving ideologies, cultural deficits, and separatist movements. These elements of our social intercourse are in your future.

Those considered wealthy in your era now share their success; eloquently modified, gains are not met by greed or dominion. None go without, for funds are escrowed for the use of the many. What is gained is given. There is no hunger, fear, or life's bitter taste, neither of failure nor of failing.

In addition, we have developed the methodology for self-healing, so few now become afflicted by any nuance of disease. Our bodies are more refined now, adapting to the nature of the immaculate forces and energies now permeating our environment. Our bodies understand and respond to what we can only define as the embrace of cosmic abundance, which we call Love.

Homage is due. What there is lies in the teachings of the wise ones of your day and before. Their footprints were sandals, for they often relinquished monied interests, power, or conquest. They were not of society, social interests, or the higher echelon of corporate intrigue but the warp and woof of the human mystery. Their 'power' was of the heart, the mind, and the essential quality of the human condition. They must have felt so alone, so distant from the basic animalism of their brothers. Wisdom teachers knew but quite often hid their knowledge in analogies or fables. Furthermore, provoking the unaware too early produces confusion, misinterpretation, and unqualified messaging. We thank them for their growing pains, for their ache of solitude.

So gently, let us lay the seeds of progress within the acolytes and the seekers; many more will follow. We stand on the shoulders of giants from the past. Those courageous ones with foresight shared a peek of an eminence yet to be fulfilled. They carried a shining brilliance, lighting the way to greater illumination beyond consciousness and into revelation. We honor these ancient guiding lights. Dear ones, it is you. What might be seen may be stupefying or frightening. Yet, it is Essence, and it is us dressed in the colorful raiments of a long, accomplished journey.

Encouragement for those still struggling, the key is to maintain your poise and embrace a purposeful choice. It's how you present yourself to the world – no matter how small that world may seem. Honor and respect all, especially those you disagree with at times. Something to consider is that societies are a brotherhood, sisterhood, and neighborhood; there can be unity. Love is the vehicle for transformation and transportation. When unity fails, the vehicle engine lights come on. Look under the hood; it's where vital components are located.

So, in closing, blessings to you of the past for all your travails; you've brought us transcendence. One day, too, I will be an ancestor. I hope I have planted virtuous seeds here, as nourishing as you have gardened. There is more to flourish in the hearts and minds of Humankind.

Sending peace, blessings, and expansion,
Your son ~ Your brother ~ Your grateful student.
Love always, Summum Bonum.

As explored throughout this book, each choice we make contributes to the collective symphony of growth, serving as a guiding light for our individual and collective journeys. The letter stands as a profound reflection of what is possible—an evolutionary vision of humanity's potential. It offers a message of hope, unity, and transformation, reminding us that self-mastery and collective growth are not distant ideals but achievable realities. It is a call to action for each of us to embrace our roles as co-creators of harmony and light in the world.

This letter is more than a glimpse into the future; it is a mirror, reflecting the path we can all walk. It encourages us to lay the seeds of progress through compassion, wisdom, and alignment with higher principles. The letter invites us to pause, reflect, and consider: How do our choices today contribute to the collective evolution described within these words?

Yet, alongside this vision of unity and growth lies the stark reality of choice. The resonance of the letter, filled with hope and possibility, stands in contrast to the paths that may lead to discord, destruction, or stagnation. These divergent paths remind us that evolution is not guaranteed—it requires conscious effort, intention, and alignment.

As we explore the differing paths, we are called to acknowledge the shadows that exist alongside the light. Each path is a choice, and each option carries its own resonance. Let us now consider these options, recognizing the responsibility and power we hold in shaping the future.

Different Paths

Whatever path one chooses, it contributes to the web of existence we all share. Each step we take creates ripples that shape our world, connecting us to the greater whole. Some people will continue to be destructive through cruelty and abuse, demanding dominance through their standards or principles. This is a road filled with potholes and steep cliffs. The only way is their way, which exists with demoralized values sung to the heavens with a loudspeaker. They do not take a respite. This is not a judgment but an observation that holds old ideas with stale and stagnant energy. Oh, I digress. If moral values represented a direction as true north, these people could not find north with a compass and a flashlight. They cannot see the bigger picture while being self-serving and insular, nor would they care.

Their comfort zone and expression remain with the lower vibrational energies. Others can offer suggestions of an error, hoping they will eventually see the light and choose differently. Until then, please modify these destructive effects by blessing them and clearing the discordant sticky residual. (-See Chapter 8, The Sweep.) Eventually, what will remain as their audience will be only the heavens; they can have at it and go for it. We'll send blessings to them.

The Web We Weave

Still, others would like a respite from life's duties and not entertain anything requiring thought or effort. Perhaps by choosing not to be a parent, light worker, or world leader, we recognize this rest is well deserved. We honor that.

Living life on and of purpose with dignity, compassion, gratitude, and curiosity is an honest reflection of life. It should be understood that if a person, in their day-to-day living, continuously expresses kindness, joy, honesty, integrity, tolerance, or care for others, they are aligned with one of the vital laws – the Law of Love. The very nature of these actions is inclusion, service, and compassion, the virtues of a gracious human. You are marking a path for those yet fumbling and tumbling in the mire of dismay, living by example. As so many will see, joy is yours, just in your smile.

Weep not if you feel inadequate or unprepared to meet some aspects or elements in this book. As a reminder, the seven tools the Universe supplies are worth their weight in gold or pearls. Personal strength can be gleaned through thoughts, allowance, acceptance, adaptation, integration, gratitude, and belief. Live a life of purpose with joy in your heart, and do not allow anyone to steal it, especially yourself.

As we choose an evolutionary path, we can focus on the physical or etheric realms; it's just a position, and there is no separation. We can experience life with synthesis as we find our voice of authentic expression. The Spiritual Logic of words and beliefs can propel us into a beautiful symmetry of radiance, transcendence, and freedom. Each of us plays a part within this ecosystem of octaves. Everyone is moving on and upwards. Judge not, the differing abilities that add such spice to life, for your light shines through and into radiance. Even if you can't see it yet, we do.

The threads we weave through our actions, thoughts, and intentions create the tapestry of humanity. Living purposefully with virtues like love, joy, and compassion ensures that our contributions strengthen the fabric of existence. Each vibration we emit contributes to the field of energy that connects us all. Just as a single note can harmonize with others to create a symphony, our actions and intentions ripple outward, influencing the greater whole.

This is the principle of resonance—the idea that our alignment, or lack thereof, creates patterns that impact not only our lives but the fabric of humanity, and we become instruments of change, guiding others to find their own harmony.

Let us reflect: What vibration am I contributing to the world? How do my choices resonate within the collective field of energy? Morphic resonance reminds us that we are not isolated beings; through mindful action and intentional alignment, we can weave threads of connection, healing, and transformation into all existence.

From this perspective, the paths we walk take on new meaning. Each journey, though unique, contributes to the universal energy that binds us. Let us explore these paths with open hearts and aligned intentions, knowing that every step shapes the journey ahead.

What threads am I weaving into the tapestry of humanity?

The Language of Energy

The Language of Energy reminds us that mastery begins with awareness and continues through intentional action. Our words and energy hold the power to shape our experiences and influence those around us. Manifesting or healing can become the by-product simply by being in tune. By familiarizing yourself with the fundamental component of Harmony/Rhythm, you reduce friction and step into flowing order. The term Miracle reflects an unknown source of action. This unknown source is the law of energy that is directed and applied consciously. We can create miracles when we understand their construction. Christ mastered the Laws. If you haven't noticed, we have not explicitly focused on constructing from the Law of Attraction. It has been mentioned and expressed, but that's all. We utilized the expanding web of the eco and echo system. Imagine that.

Our words have begun reflecting our evolution and the subtle changes in the abstract consciousness of our very being. More people are gaining the ability to identify with each other's resonance. Our power and willingness to harmonize effectively will enhance our communication skills as we reach higher levels of consciousness.

Our thought process will be clarified and qualified in the etheric realm, where unintended results, misinterpretations, and misunderstandings will cease. On the grandest scale, only perfection will be noticed. Words will be few and used with a powerful directional force. This awareness is an evolutionary goal and the path of humanity, which has already been initiated.

These stepping stones are tools for continuous alignment—revisit them often as your journey unfolds. They serve as practical anchors, helping us stay attuned to the higher frequencies of love and harmony.

The Stepping Stones for Being in Tune

The Universe is always listening, so become:

- Conscious of the words spoken and broadcast. Qualify them first.

- Mindful of your thoughts- they are lightning-fast. Faster than the speed of light.

- Aware of focused intentions put forth- what are possible results?

- Conscious of governing laws- there are nuances. Reduce friction.

- Cognizant of alignments- checks & balances, qualify beliefs and moral values.

- Aware of nature- answers reside here.

- Attentive to emotions- you have the power to change them. Master your emotions instead of emotions mastering you.

- Conscious of qualifying energy, self-correction, and self-governance.

This understanding calls us to consider: What patterns am I reinforcing through my actions and thoughts? How can I contribute to a field of resonance that uplifts and inspires? Through intentional alignment, we become catalysts for healing and co-creators of a world that reflects the highest frequencies of energy and life.

Everyone is powerful. We are prevailing and potent creators. We can write, direct, and be masters of our lives.

The Governance of Laws should become our unified morality to serve all of humanity. But please know that any empowering words, checks/balances, adjusting focus, aligning with laws, or processes in this book can be lightning-fast. They could all be done before you figure out what you'd like for dinner.

The power within you exists to create unlimited possibilities. You have free will to choose how you will express and experience the direction of your life. Frankly, please do not believe anything brought forward in this book. We can only ask that you experiment with these golden nuggets presented as laws, concepts, and techniques and see how they work. This book wasn't written to convince anyone of anything, nor what or how to believe. Only to help you find a way to validate your power and bring an awareness you can step into. If you choose, then perhaps you can make this awareness your own. A path of self-discovery is before you. Which turn will you make? How will the heavens hear you?

The Gift of Life is Love

In time, humanity will remember the potency from which we come and live life from this position, this gift of love.

Love is the Recognition of the Synthetic Entirety and the immersion thereof. Love as an emotion is delegated as a mere reflection to awaken us to the truer Awareness. Love is the elixir of Life but not the Substance. Those who are thirsty drink from the cosmic well. Those of Understanding bathe in the embrace of Substance and thus essentially teach and show the Way.

Wisdom carries these essences within the ethers for all to speak a language, which is little known but is the Voice of the Eternal. This is that light that blinds the foolish but nourishes the Seeker. Vision is that Voice, slightly heard, enabling the tired Pilgrim to ever proceed. Vision is the sight, as the Voice gives the Promise.

Lao Tzu states in Tao Te Ching,

"My words have an origin. My deeds have a sovereign. Truly, because people do not understand this, they do not understand me." **(Stenudd) www.taoistic.com/taoteching-laotzu/ taoteching-70.htm**

Wrap Up

This chapter invites us to reflect on the totality of our personal and collective journey. Through love, resonance, and intentional action, we weave a tapestry of harmony and transformation. By aligning with universal principles, we contribute to the emergence of humanity's highest potential, embodying the infinite possibilities of growth and light.

Energy, as our Universal Language, flows through every aspect of existence, from the breath we take to the food we eat and even in the smallest gestures, like a smile shared between strangers. It connects and sustains us, guiding and teaching us to work harmoniously with its rhythms and laws. By understanding and embracing energy, we align ourselves with the universal currents that propel us forward.

Sincerely, Lee Two Hawks, and I hope we have created more questions than answers. As your journey unfolds, we have created a metaphoric map or chart that can take you anywhere you'd like to go. Perhaps you'll enjoy a smoother ride. The only catch-22 is your ability in map reading. It is a quick reference for further study of the energy of laws; it's our gift to you.

In honoring Lee Two Hawks, he has the last word.

Shadow Fox and I give gratitude for this beautiful journey you have taken with us. Thank you for riding along and the music you bring. It is an honor to be of service.

~Artisans of the Spirit~ C. Shadow Fox & Lee Two Hawks.

I have not yet breath

Throw off these shackles!
These maniacal shackles
Of bone teeth flesh blood;
Speak instead in the language of spirit
wrapped in song and prayer
wind and spinning tremolo of Allah,
God, Krishna, Bob, George, Sam
Mary or Sue...

Baptisms of blood calling for
brotherhood the breach of dogma;
The process of world view, the ache
beyond mortality
calling for the greatness of man,
the infinite compassion of man,
the common ground of man.

I have not yet breath but
a thickness and fumbling of tongues
to say come all
to union.

Lee Two Hawks

There are sometimes words

There are sometimes words
larger than my mouth can speak
their meanings
larger than my heart can carry;
Words of bright colors,
sentient words, filled with music,
resonant in the Universe.

Anger, fear, vengeance
are the force of tongue;
Recreant deeds of the mind
their guiding light;
war   abuse   anger
are my muses
to tear, to break, to shatter
are the direction of my tone.
But
There are sometimes words
larger than my mouth can speak
their meanings
larger than my heart can carry;
It is why I walk
Stoop-shouldered,
and stutter… when I write.

Lee Two Hawks

WORKS CITED

Anonymous. "Unknown." N/A.

Bailey, Alice A. *A Treatise on Cosmic Fire*. 16th 2005. New York: Lucis Publishing Company, 1925.

—. *Esoteric Psychology (Volume II)*. Lucis Publishing Company, 1942.

Baily, Alice A. *Esoteric Psychology I; Vol.I, A Treatise on the Seven Rays*. Vol. 1. New York: Lucis Publishing Company, 1936. Channeled from Djwal Kul, known as the Tibetan Master or D.K.

Berkeley, George. n.d. <https://en.wikipedia.org/wiki/If_a_tree_falls_in_a_forest>.

Green, Dallas. "O' Sister." *Little Hell, City and Colour*. By Dallas Green. Hamilton, Ontario, Canada, 2011.

https://activepause.com/grief-stages/. The 5 (or 7) stages of grief & loss: Grief cycle & grieving process Elisabeth Kübler-Ross . n.d.

Keegane, Acended Master. n.d. Meditation. Late 80s.

King, Godfre Ray. *The Magic Presence*. Vol. 2. Schaumburg: Saint Germain Press, 1935. 20 vols.

Kryon, (Lee Carroll). *The Destiny of Mastery*. n.d. YouTube,uploaded by Kryon Channel. <https://youtu.be/TNl1_zfoM7s?si=btK0FDIlXcQlxIDu.>.

Kubler-Ross, Elisabeth. n.d.

Stenudd, Stefan. *Tao Te Ching: The Taoism of Lao Tzu Explained.* Arriba, 2015. 23 10 2018. <www.taoistic.com>.

LAWS AT A GLANCE

The following briefly describes and should not be considered a complete explanation of Laws. They have been compiled from many sources and interwoven for their essence of energy. We have listed a few prevalent ones; if you feel confused, please move on. What is to be exhibited here is a quality of existence. It is yours to research these Laws further; they are abstract and not a concrete ideology. They are not mandates but a fluid field of experiential qualifiers. Although you may find differing explanations, the primary outtake is self-discovery, which stimulates you to recognize what is and isn't.

This energy always compels us to act in one form or another. Therefore, each Cosmic, Universal/Solar, Spiritual, and Natural Law plays an integral part in influencing all aspects of the Physical, Mental, Emotional, and Spiritual Planes of existence.

As one Law is triggered, other Laws respond. (Perfection-Spiritual Logic or Imperfection-Human Logic.) Most life lessons we experience are because we misqualified a Law. That initiates other Laws immediately to teach us to return to balance. Are we paying attention to this simple design? Seek the lesson, find the law. Seek the law, find the lesson.

No singular Law is more powerful than another or holds a more significant position. Laws work in Harmony and support each other, allowing us to create checks and balances. Just envision a spider's web or an ecosystem.

The Body of Governing Principles

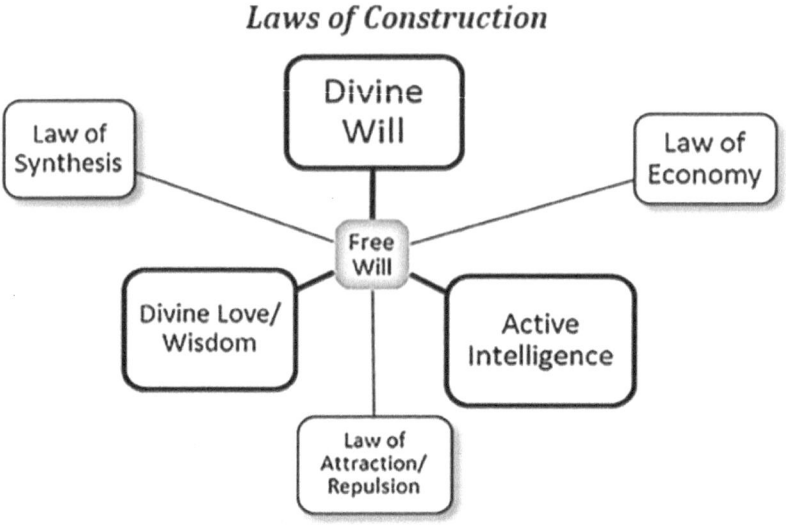

Laws of Construction

Laws of Construction

The Laws of Construction: A conceptual framework describing the dynamic principles governing energy flow and manifestation into form. Rooted in the three cosmic rays—Divine Will, Love/Wisdom, and Active Intelligence—it encompasses the Cosmic Laws of Synthesis, Economy, and Attraction/Repulsion. These principles reveal how vibration (sound), illumination (light), and cohesion (matter) interact to create balance and harmony.

Operating as a Silent Code of Life, these dynamics subtly guide existence, bridging the abstract with the tangible. By understanding these principles, individuals can shift perception—recognizing challenges as opportunities—and align intention, thought, and action with universal flow. This terminology emphasizes free will and the soul's role in engaging with energy, offering tools to apply these principles across personal, societal, and collective evolution, fostering harmony and unity. (--See Chapter 9, Working with the Laws of Construction.)

Working with the Laws of Construction

Working with the Laws of Construction follows four essential steps, each aligning with the universal principles of sound, light, and matter. This method ensures a harmonious flow of creation while reducing energetic resistance. Let's use Energy's Language.

Step One: Establish a Clear Intention

Define what you wish to create with precision and purpose. A strong foundation begins with a clear and conscious directive, such as receiving. The Law of Synthesis governs this step, ensuring resonance and harmony.

Step Two: Align with Purpose and Flow

Observe the natural rhythm of energy and move in alignment with its currents. There is no lack. The Law of Economy guides this process, ensuring efficiency and balance in manifesting your intent.

Step Three: Engage in Active Creation

Take deliberate steps toward your goal while maintaining flexibility. The Law of Attraction and Repulsion determines how energy integrates and reshapes itself. Be mindful of your alignment with your vision and the energy you project.

Step Four: Anchor in Manifestation

Ground your creation into reality by refining and affirming its presence. Confirming it causes no harm. This step ensures full integration and the successful completion of the manifestation process.

Predestined (Immutable Laws)

The Concepts of Rays or Principles that guide us: (--See Chapter 9, Laws of Construction.)

1st Ray: Power, Will, or Purpose. Its essence is:
Divine Will- is both the creator and the destroyer. All manifestation clears the way for creating newer forms that fit newer energies. Will is a dynamic force that impels the Universe into synthesis and is the cyclic motion of evolution. It influences the aspects of God-Consciousness- that of a Universal Mindfulness illuminating sentient consciousness. Will is the One Life creating many singular yet manifest progenitors of electric fire, the fohat, which underlies Life.

Governing Principles: The Law of Free Will and all aspects of Vibrational Law apply.

Position: Cosmic Law of Attraction and Repulsion.

Reference points: Trinity-**God the Father.**

(We innately sense Freedom.)

Integration: *Set a clear intention today. Pause before making decisions to ask, 'Does this align with my higher purpose?' Meditate on aligning your intent with the greater good, allowing divine guidance to inform your choices.*

2nd Ray: Love/Wisdom: It's essence is:
Divine Love/Wisdom- is the synthetic whole that demonstrates Cosmic Love, fulfilling 1ˢᵗ Ray aspects with the quality of love and wisdom. From this, everything finds its expressed Perfection, which is the Qualifier. Therefore, all energy is seeking expression of the Divine Perfection of *Love*. I AM Manifest.

Governing Principles: The Law of Love and all aspects of Harmony/Rhythm apply.

Position: Cosmic Law of Synthesis.

Reference: Trinity-The **Son.**

(We innately sense Liberty.)

Integration: *Identify one way to show compassion or wisdom today. Reflect on how this act aligns with your core values.*

3rd Ray: Active Creative Intelligence: Its essence is:

Active Intelligence- is purposeful thought in league with Divine Principles conditioning all natural phenomena. It is a perfect directional energy force that builds, destroys, and recycles. It's considered the architect of energy; it includes everything from death to life, all matter and energy. Active Intelligence ensures proper adjustments for equilibrium with the necessary rate of rhythm, assuring evolutionary progress. It intertwines with a cohesive intelligence, enhancing all laws.

Governing Principles: The Law of Life and all aspects of Frequency apply.

Position: Cosmic Law of Economy.

Reference: Trinity- the **Holy Spirit**.

(We innately sense Life.)

Integration: *Bring mindful creativity to a task. Ask, 'How can I solve this issue or build something meaningful?'*

Laws are the Governance of Energy, and Principles are our guidance. Energy is the access/delivery system.

The Law of Energy: It is an ambient, intelligent force that carries information, influencing and directing all through and by vibration, rhythm, and frequency. Everything in existence, seen or unseen, is multidimensional energy. This force or power is the Universe's access and delivery system, in which everything is defined through expansion and contraction. Energy is spirit; spirit is energy; thus, it is where authentic power is seated. As a Focused Force, it relates to motion or action and is magnetic, electrical, gravitational, and active intelligence. Energy cannot be extinguished, only transformed. It is neither positive nor negative. Qualifying energy is how we can transmute it.

The Universe is always listening, responding to the energy we send out through our thoughts, words, and actions. The Law of

Energy, as a totality, invites us to become aware of this continuous exchange and align ourselves with its flow. How would you like the Universe to hear you?

Actionable Steps: Use as a guide for conscious engagement with energy. Pause each day to become aware of the energy around you. Close your eyes, take three deep breaths, and ask yourself: 'What am I sending into the world right now?' Focus on aligning your intention with harmony, balance, and growth. Visualize this energy expanding outward, connecting to the greater field, and returning to you in its highest form.

Ask yourself: Are your words, thoughts, and actions in tune with the harmony you wish to create? By becoming aware of your energy and intention, you open the door to greater alignment with the Universe's silent yet powerful language.

Cosmic Laws

Cosmic Laws-These principles, or Predestined Energies, provide the structure within which energy manifests and interacts, governing harmony and balance in all things and from which everything radiates. Energy is not random. It moves according to *ITS* resonance that shapes all existence. Governing Our Solar System are the Cosmic Laws—Synthesis, Economy, and Attraction/Repulsion.

The following Three Cosmic Laws are as presented as (**Macro**). Their sublet Universal Laws are shown as (*Micro*) and are more commonly known, such as the Law of Attraction.

(—See Chapter 9, Impression with Multiple Purposes.)

Law of Synthesis Macro: Demonstrates that all things, abstract and concrete, exist as one. It is the law governing consciousness of thought-form, from the unmanifest and manifest, in that the macro and micro are the totality of all that is. It is resonance, sound, harmony, and balance, a symphony of synthesis. (Sound. Harmony/Rhythm)

Law of Synthesis Micro: (Sound) Resonates to reveal itself as the unconscious drive towards unity. There is an inclination to form groups, committees, and even governments where a synthetic view or policy arises. Yet, oddly, it is responsible for our curiosity, the urge to investigate ourselves, our world, or our Universe from the tiniest particle of an atom to an unknown infinity. The larger scale is the veiled sense or sensitivity towards Oneness or Wholeness. It is often expressed as an innate drive to individualize or develop the authentic Self. It brings a more realistic and inclusive identity into reality than our five senses can convey. It is that urge to find God, to return home. It is our voice, our sound.

The very sound of human activity reverberates beyond our solar systems into listening worlds and the vastness of the cosmos. (The Etheric Realm.) An action has sound, thoughts have sound, and emotions emit huge waves of aural resonance into infinity. We are heard. What message do you wish to leave?

Law of Synthesis (Sound): Like the blueprints or architectural resonance of the house, this law sets the intention and harmony for the entire structure. Governs sound, representing resonance and harmony. Sound is the foundational vibration that begins the creative process, aligning with the spiritual principle of synthesis. (–See Chapter 9, Impression with Multiple Purposes)

Actionable Step: Reflect on a moment where harmony emerged from diversity. Consider one action you can take to align contrasting aspects of your life. (Reframing thoughts or positions?)

Law of Economy Macro: Nature's efficiency concerns the Material & Spiritual evolution of the cosmos. With the least expenditure of force, each atom of time, each eternal period, is perfect. It carries ALL onward, upward, and through with the least possible effort, without opposition. The 3rd Ray of Active Intelligence ensures proper adjustments for equilibrium with the necessary rate of rhythm, assuring evolutionary progress. (Frequency. Light)

Law of Economy Micro: (Light) Represented by the assembly process, where resources are optimized, and energy flows efficiently to bring the blueprint to life. (Governs light, embodying efficiency and the flow of energy. Light provides the illuminating pathway and coherence necessary for structured development. (—See Chapter 9, Impression with Multiple Purposes.)

The Path of Least Resistance- briefly, minimal energy expenditure; nothing is wasted nor recognizes opposition. There is no friction. Extremely efficient, effective, and effortless. Shares Natural Law. Responsible for Resist/Persist.

In other words, nature flows efficiently and effectively with the least effort. This master cohesion includes animals, water, weather, quantum physics, and everything in our Universe. We are all influenced by this law.

Actionable Step: Observe an area where effort feels wasted. Identify a way to simplify and optimize your approach.

Law of Attraction and Repulsion Macro: Compelling force that holds our Solar System in Cohesion. It is the cohesion of and for all substances and all matter. To include all atomic, molecular & physical matter. Active Intelligence is a directing force. In the Etheric, like attracts like. If you can manifest a working solar system, we gotta talk. (Vibration. Matter)

Law of Attraction and Repulsion Micro: (Matter) As a micro sublet, it describes the expressed force that overcomes inertia by applying will and desire. At the atomic levels, the vibrational resonance causes atoms to coalesce when of vibrational accord. Specific thought energies merge with like energy thought forms, i.e., hate, anger, love, or compassion. In the Physical, opposites attract (m/f). In the Etheric, like attracts like, thus the importance of shifting our awareness to a 180-degree position of spiritual logic.

(--See Chapter 9, Impression with Multiple Purposes.)

The Law of Attraction Micro- (Matter) What's focused upon will manifest. This Law will also teach us life lessons of initiation. Know this: once an aspect of Self is mastered, the frequency increases, and those lessons are no longer required. We create our homing signal, so monitor your thoughts, words, emotions, and actions so that you may only attract the brightest, lightest, and highest Self. (This governs matter, representing cohesion and the manifestation of physical form. Matter completes the process, bringing abstract ideas into tangible existence)   (-See chapter 4, Perceptions.)

Actionable Step: Reflect on a relationship or situation you're drawn to or repelled by. Ask, 'What energy am I contributing to this dynamic?'

Law of Love & Understanding are New Influences

This new impulse of energy has just begun its influence on humanity. The following three laws aid our comprehension of our evolution for our era. The Laws of Free Will, Love, and Life will assist with the Law of Understanding that has already been initiated to bring us into the next age. We have nestled them between Cosmic and Universal/Solar Laws; these three laws blend and flow with every existing governance and aspect and then some. Interestingly, each resembles the Divine Principles of Construction 1-3. Notably, these are the most misconstrued, misunderstood, and debased. We will continue with struggle and strife until human logic coincides with Spiritual Logic to find a more profound and loving understanding of existence.

Laws Governing This New Influence

Law of Love: includes self-sacrifice, unity, brotherhood, and synthesis, which are operative functions of the Law of Free Will. With magnetic impulse, this love is the Buddhic love transmuted from the physical desire into the more exact aspect of Oneness. From Divine Love, everything finds its expressed perfection, the qualifier. (--See Chapter 7, Checks and Balances.)

Love reaches the entirety of all multiverses. To understand this law, one should remove oneself from the cultural interpretation of 'the term' love. There is the love of family, nation, and love of one to the other, none truly representing the totality of meaning within the context herein. The Law of Love drives the desire element of the astral nature to move into or become synthesized with the Buddhic nature and its coherent primacy within our spiritual development.

It is far more encompassing, embracing, and comprehensive than is usually understood by the term in everyday existence. In love's maturity, free will would become a moot point, as love allows no impediment or limitation; thus, it is of Divine Perfection. With its magnetic impulses, this Buddhic love transmutes from the physical desire into the more authentic aspect of Oneness.

Eventually, humanity will understand that life's gift is love. Love is the Recognition of the Synthetic Entirety and the immersion thereof. Love as an emotion is delegated as a mere reflection to awaken us to the more accurate Awareness.

Love is the elixir of Life but not the Substance. Those who are thirsty drink from the cosmic well. Those of Understanding bathe in the embrace of Substance and thus must teach and show the Way.

Wisdom carries these essences within the ethers for all to speak a language, which is little known but is the Voice of the Eternal. This is that light that blinds the foolish but nourishes the Seeker. Vision is that Voice, slightly heard, enabling the tired Pilgrim to ever proceed. Vision is the sight, as the Voice gives the Promise.

Actionable Steps: Identify one action today that expresses unconditional love for yourself or others. This could be offering a kind word, forgiving yourself, or showing gratitude.

How does this act of love ripple outward? Who does this serve, and how does it align with the greater good?

Law of Understanding- This (New) Law will govern and influence our evolution in the coming race. It can mitigate the Law of Cleavages if Humankind can embrace its nuances. This Law undergirds this solar system in this world period and is expressed as the spiritual over the material, the inclusive over the exclusive, and the Unity of Humankind, and more emphatically, it is the voice of the One who oversees all. (Also known as The Law of Loving Understanding).

Actionable Steps: Practice active listening in one conversation today. Seek to understand the other person's perspective without judgment or interruption. Reflect on how this deepens your connection.

How does seeking to understand others also help you better understand yourself? What insights arise from this practice?

Law of Free Will- We all experience life or express ourselves by qualifying the energy and resonance. Everyone chooses their beliefs, actions, or deeds; we do not have to agree with others' choices. Most importantly, we <u>cannot</u> <u>impose</u> our beliefs, ideals, or wills upon another. This Law carries permissions, accountability, responsibility, and karma, individually and that of Nations. Without Free Will- no one has a choice. (--See Chapter 6, Bridging Two Worlds.)

Free Will is a part of our being and an inherent right to an evolutionary unfoldment. It is why prayers were invented; we ask for assistance. Ask, and it will be given. Angels will never violate this law. To do so would not serve a higher purpose. Therefore, humanity goes where even Angels will not tread.

This Law carries greater accountability for its violation than for committing murder. Human logic hasn't reasoned with this. As spiritual logic unfolds, it becomes crystal clear. All human rights violations originate from not honoring this Law. The absurdity of old, stale, and stagnate thought forms becomes apparent when a person stands before another, judging them and mandating how they should live. Is it not absurd to cry out for vindication or retribution, with violations held within the heart?

Actionable Steps: Make a conscious choice today that reflects your highest values. Before deciding, pause and ask, 'Does this honor my responsibility to myself and others?'

How do you exercise your free will responsibly? How do your choices honor both your individuality and interconnectedness?

Law of Life- is energy ever-flowing. To understand Life, it is a given that one should grasp that Life is the very nature of energy. The Breath of Life determines life, not us. Energy is synonymous with Spirit. Life is infused with Spirit, the Divine Breath. Thus, any Law attending to energy is, by definition, a Law of Life. Life is the essence of our being; therefore, it is light. We are light. We speak of the quality of life, not the appearance of life. (--See Chapter 7, Checks and Balances.)

Life becomes embroiled with its misapplication to everyday living when humanity places more importance on Life itself instead of Loving Life. Loving Life considers everyone and all concerned, and everything would be pre-served with no judgments imposed upon another. But, unfortunately, the matter is so abstruse that a more in-depth explanation is beyond our effort here. This encompasses all Laws.

Actionable Steps: Engage in one activity today that makes you feel fully alive, such as walking in nature, connecting with a loved one, or creating something meaningful. Reflect on how this supports your purpose.

What does it mean to you to truly live? How does your current life align with your sense of purpose?

Laws of Energy (--See Chapter Two, Energy Components)

Law of Frequency: Defines a sound, radio, or light wave according to its cycles per second, expressed as a range of qualitative vibrations designed by the energy output of the source. Frequency varies from low to high Hertz (cps), which defines a shape of energy requisite to the manner of its expression. This Law helps us to find expression. As related to vibration and harmony, it is the application of rhythm from idle speculation into a higher purpose, thus a compelling force of involution and evolution. This is established by an inner stimulation of the astral or mental body moving out of inertia into expression. It is a measurement of sound and light in the physical and etheric realms. As an abstract concept, it's referenced as differing octaves for consciousness, mindfulness, knowingness, and our spirit. Its electromagnetic resonance stimulates and impulses a desire for self-discovery, why we are here, and our purpose. (Energy-light: Water-vapor/gas: Time-future). If our thoughts are focused primarily on the future, it can create feelings of anxiety.

The key to life is awareness and integrating these energies, thus changing the motion/rhythm and creating an orderly, harmonious flow. The harmony connects all the worlds of manifestation and Nature's Laws.

Actionable Steps: Set an intention to elevate your energy by focusing on gratitude. Write down three things you're thankful for, and notice how your emotional state shifts. Reflect on how they influence your day. Have ideas been challenged?

As your frequency changes, what discomfort or growth do you notice? How can you use this awareness to navigate transitions gracefully?

Law of Harmony/Rhythm: It preserves Universal Equilibrium. It is the motion of flowing order and rhythmic consistency—the Universe's Cyclic Movement produces various manifest actions. This perfection and timing will produce manifestation as a by-product. It bridges physical and etheric realms, with two distinct names implying particular positions. This Law is closely related to Vibration. However, Harmony/Rhythm is the Universe's precise timing and flowing order. (Energy- Sound, Water-liquid, Time-present. If our thoughts are focused primarily on the present, we step into harmony and flow.)

Harmony of thought, mind, and conscience with those around us and harmony with spirit is required for perfect conditions of

293

mental development, spiritual unfoldment, and reception of spiritual influences. When all is balanced and harmonious, power is generated correctly, then manifesting becomes a by-product instead of a centralized focus. Being out of tune will cause an imbalance, and there will be friction and sour notes. This law is the easiest to detect.

Actionable Steps: Identify one area of imbalance in your life. Take one step toward restoring harmony, such as resting or reorganizing priorities. Recognizing the natural cycles of life and finding balance within them.

Law of Vibration: It delineates the speed at which energy flows and helps form to maintain its stability. Everything is substantiated through or by vibration, partly responsible for the process that helps to produce a harmonic balance. This denotes the expansion and contraction of energy. (Energy-matter, Water-solid, Time-past. If our thoughts are focused primarily on the past, it can create feelings of depression.)

All things are in motion as vibrations. The lower, slower vibrations are seen as still, heard as soundless, and felt as density. Lower, denser vibrational energy cannot enter into higher vibrational regions until it matches that speed by expanding. The higher vibrations can enter the lower, thus, by default, raising the vibration. This process cannot be seen, heard, or felt within our third-dimensional reality until an expanded consciousness evolves.

We have three choices: lower the vibration, remain at the same, or raise it by expanding or contracting. Every thought, action, word, deed, and emotion we produce must go through this transformation process, which appears slow. For example, love and laughter can increase and alter vibrational rates. This Law demonstrates light entering a dark room.

Actionable Steps: Pause during the day to assess your energy. Use grounding tools to raise your vibration when required.

Pay attention to your emotional and physical energy throughout the day. If you notice discomfort or tension, use a grounding tool like deep breathing, journaling, or listening to uplifting music.

Universal/Solar Laws

Law of Abundance: briefly, requirements will be met for all things required for life, including the infusion of knowledge from the subconscious to the conscious awareness. There is enough for everyone, from the unmanifest to the manifest. Any and all possibilities exist, being either positive or negative in nature. It does not mean hoarding such things as land, water, money, etc. This law does not recognize lack. To do so would be an oxymoron- voiding the law. (-See Chapter 4.)

Law of Cause and Effect: It is a measurement from the beginning to the end of Life. It's a progressive record of working through life's lessons to be learned and mastered. It is known for raising human consciousness. The Law of Karma is one of its most noted aspects. Causes are unseen. Effects are seen, felt, and experienced. (--See Chapter 4, Concept Envision.)

Actionable Steps: Reflect on a recent event in your life. Trace it back to a decision, action, or thought you had. Consider one minor adjustment you can make to create a different outcome in the future.

How do your choices and actions ripple out to create your current circumstances? What can you consciously adjust today?

Law of Correspondence: As above, so below. On earth, as it is in heaven. Nothing exists that does not have a corresponding attribute or aspect at a different vibrational level. For anything to be created in the outer world, it must first be created in your inner world. It is that which produces a balance between physical and mental and between spiritual and mental. Therefore, know that what you do in the realm in which you are conscious is the realm in which you create your experiences; we call this 'reality.' This references the 180-degree Spiritual Concepts. Cause and effect; affect and effect. Its resonance shares the laws of physics and natural laws. (-See Chapter 5, Attribute for Healing.)

Actionable Steps: Observe an external pattern in your life that mirrors an inner state, such as relationships, work, or health. Identify one small action to align your inner thoughts and outer experiences.

How do the patterns in your external environment reflect your internal state? What changes could you make to shift both?

Law of Forgiveness: When called upon, it releases and transmutes any cause, effect, and record of any error. It gives freedom from limitation and bondage; it stops the energy's forward movement from the misdirected action. Working within this Law is an attribute to higher consciousness or healing.

(--See Chapter 7, Checks and Balances.)

For its application, ask that any cause created in error be transmuted in love. Then, ask to stop or consume any effects that were initiated. Then, erase or remove the error from the record. This energy will return to you if not corrected. That's why we ask for the Universe to remove the record.

Actionable Steps: Take a moment to reflect on someone or something you hold resentment toward. Visualize releasing this energy with compassion and say, 'I forgive you and free myself from this pain.' Visualize releasing the emotional weight and creating space for healing.

How does forgiveness create space for healing in your life? How might this shift your vibration?

Law of Reciprocity: briefly means that what is unequal, unbalanced, or inharmonious must be equalized, balanced, and harmonized. Hence, an exchange has to be equivalent to 'the nature' of what is given to be beneficial. Under this law, it returns in equal force. Thus, provide only that which builds, for anything less will only compound itself. That which is given with actions, words, deeds, thoughts, or intent returns to you unchanged until it aligns with Divine Will, Divine Love/Wisdom, and Divine intelligence. What you send out will be returned in kind. So, whatever you say and do will eventually come back to you. (--See Chapter 4, Power of Intention.)

Actionable Step: Reflect on a recent exchange. Ask, 'Did this interaction feel balanced and harmonious?' Adjust your actions accordingly.

Additional Laws

These Laws either influenced or were mentioned but not directly described. They are in abeyance throughout this body of work. (Additional Laws)

Law of Cleavages: Holds dominion for our era of evolutionary development. The Law will sometimes dismantle or destroy to create anew, like a blessing in disguise. (Storms) This law finds expression in the separateness of human units (Jews, Muslims, Christians, political designs, government intrigues). Unless the coalescence of these divisions is worked for and achieved, the human race will, once again, face destruction. This law's influence is why emphasis is placed upon Revelations in the Bible. This Law still has a strong impact but is diminishing over time, allowing the Law of Understanding to gain a stronger birthing.

Actionable Step: Acknowledge a division in your environment. Take one step toward understanding or reconciliation.

Law of Completion: (Not a traditional Universal Law but a guiding principle) emphasizes consciously closing cycles, relationships, or beliefs that have served their purpose. We create space for new opportunities and harmony by releasing what no longer serves.

Actionable Steps: Reflect on unfinished or unresolved areas within your life and affirm, "I release what no longer serves me."

Create a simple ritual of closure—light a candle or write a release letter to symbolize letting go of the past and welcoming new beginnings.

Law of Magnetic Impulse: We see the driving force that helps precipitate active intelligence. It is that intelligence that works to build according to the dictates of organization, planning, and activation, bringing forth beauty and solidity of the parts to the whole. By the decree of Magnetic Impulse, the varied pieces interlock to create a harmonious entirety.

Actionable Step: Focus on a desire or goal, such as finances. Visualize it as magnetized energy coming to you. Be open to receiving.

Law of Mentalism: The principle that all is mind, and thoughts create reality. Mind is the builder; notice how your mindset influences your experiences. Focus on thoughts that bring clarity, harmony, and constructive action.

Natural Law: these are influences governing and regulating the activity, quality, and sentience within a form to ensure cohesion, synthesis, and achievement of potential in expression and experience in the natural world. Natural laws are subordinate and influenced by Spiritual laws, which govern cosmic, solar, and planetary involutionary and evolutionary processes, also known as the Laws of Being.

Actionable Steps: Spend time observing a natural process, such as the flow of water, plant growth, or the day's rhythm. Reflect on how you can align your actions with this effortless flow.

What lessons does nature offer about balance, harmony, and resilience? How can you apply these to your daily life?

Law of Repulse: This law operates and intends to remove or repulse the undesirable, the blockages preventing full spiritual expression, allowing the entity to move himself to higher, more attractive –albeit more challenging – expressions of the Self. Eventually, within a completed cycle of expression and experience, this law repudiates the call of the form nature, spiritually elevating the entity into an enhanced status. (Implied as Ascension)

Actionable Step: Identify something you've outgrown. Let go of it with gratitude to make space for new opportunities.

Law of Service: Within this law lies the intent far beyond good intentions by lying in the impulse of at-one-ment. Its operational tools are love, wisdom, and intelligent design. The heart chakra awakens to its fuller activity, and action is taken, not with emotions but with mental aspiration and thoughtful conduct. Thoughtful conduct considers who does this serve.

Actionable Steps: Perform a simple act of service without expectation. Reflect on how this impacts your sense of purpose.

Law of Thought: Conditions the creative mind in building some sort of orderly manifestation to demonstrate itself objectively. This is so throughout all existence. This law suggests the law of fire, which transmutes the many into one. As with the cosmos, so with humanity, but on a far lesser scale. It is Vibratory (of differing rates according to its source), effective or not, depending on its creator's focused or not-focused ability.

Consider this: Consciousness conditions thought. One can be conscious without thought, but thought cannot exist without consciousness.

Actionable Step: Are my thoughts in alignment with the highest good? Could they carry a negative resonance?

GLOSSARY

W e encourage everyone to research the meanings of these words we have condensed and expressed. These definitions are intentionally crafted to reflect the deeper energetic and spiritual concepts explored throughout this book, offering perspectives that may differ from traditional interpretations.

ADI (Active Divine Intelligence)- A dynamic force of energy that bridges Divine Will and human action. ADI represents the intentional, conscious application of spiritual awareness into purposeful creation. It aligns thoughts, emotions, and actions with higher Universal Laws, enabling harmony and effective manifestation. While closely related to Divine Active Intelligence, ADI is more consciously accessible, guiding how we intentionally align our thoughts, emotions, and actions with higher Universal Laws to create harmony and purposeful manifestation.

Affirmations- can rewrite the programs of our past and form new neural pathways. They are positive statements or repeated agreements that create and determine our perceptions and reality. They are effective due to the principle of resonance.

Astral/Etheric body- Herein lies the energies of emotionality, desire, and sensitivity reflected into the physical, etheric plane expressed in the physical form. It is that body of ancient design which brings forth adulation or hate. Of its seven levels, the lowest comprises human imaginings featuring monsters and fearful entities composed by Humanity over eons. The seventh level is constructed of emotions or feelings of compassion, caring, and, at best, beneficence. Most of Humanity is greatly influenced by this body. However, the mental body is now more succinct and potent.

Emotional Body- is impressed solely by the astral world; the astral body within our aura is the delivery system to the physical body. Within limits, the astral body is the traveler and explorer in times of deep sleep. When we dream, messages, or especially nightmares, can shed light on issues we may be dealing with. Although unrecognized by the physical body, these can lend an emotional aspect and reaction to everyday events or experiences. Emotions like love, frustration, kindness, or jealousy emanate from the astral body. Emotions do not have to rule our lives. We do have a choice in how we react or act.

Emotional Plane- Removing all forms of dominion from consciousness would be a mere reflection of the scope of the Emotional Plane. At this level of development, the meaning and use of dominion would, therefore, change drastically. Its purpose would be for creation -- to masterfully create within the highest service to others. Ascended Masters.

End Result- is implied with full awareness, for a desire to be fulfilled precisely as qualified and intended with perfection. A bigger picture is involved. It is how and what will manifest in your life.

Esoteric- Is the study or journey of seeking answers and deepening awareness of the seen and the unseen.

Fohat- is an electrical and magnetic force responsible for the vitalization of sentiency, awareness, and conscious forms throughout the cosmos, including universes, galaxies, solar systems, planets, and the environs thereof.

Impression- An impression is spiritualized energy that impulses us to act or respond according to the precepts codified in law. It impresses upon us the higher vibrational frequencies, such as the Law of Correspondence, as above, so below. Used as a metaphor to help describe energy flow and its Principles.

Laws- are a body of governing principles.

Metaphysical- It's that, as yet unseen. Yet, it influences everything we do and who we are. It is an exchange of energy, love, breathing, prayer, and even frustration; every expression we have as human beings is energy expressed.

Morphic Resonance- A concept proposed by Rupert Sheldrake, describing how patterns of behavior, form, or thought established in one instance can resonate across time and space, influencing similar patterns in others through a collective memory field. This resonance amplifies and perpetuates shared experiences, shaping individual and collective realities.

Mysticism- Is the emotional (astral realm-based) response to energies of a spiritually elevated nature and the subsequent appropriate or inappropriate use of these energies.

Occult- The scientific investigation of force and energy and their correct application. This investigation includes all energetic bodies' subjective and objective nuances of man, the sun, or the galaxy. The widespread misapprehension is attributed to abuse and misuse of knowledge for personal desires with selfish intents. Energy, per se, is neutral.

Principles- This means the causal element of affect and effect. (Vibration, Rhythm, and Frequency.)

Principle of Thought- This underlies the Law of Manifestation. It is the creative endeavor of the Mind as one facet; in another, it is a collation of energies wrought from the mass consciousness, whereas thought becomes unspecified and without merit.

Reincarnation- Describes the concept of cyclic rhythms regarding the movement of energy. It references human neglect by not working within the Laws and principles. When humans persist in this neglect and follow their materialistic concerns over their spiritual potential, the learning process is repeated until understanding comes. This awareness reduces idealism and structured belief systems.

Self-Serving- carries low vibrational energy. Selfishness comes to mind. When rooted in personal gain, an action, belief, or purpose is considered self-serving. Where self or others could be harmed or not considered. Focus is fixed on the outer world or is ego-driven. Emotional components would be jealousy, control, and immovable idealism, including self-pity, self-absorption, or narcissism. This can be considered the little 's' in self. Thus, it's our human self.

Serving-Self- carries a higher vibrational frequency than self-service. Self-preservation comes to mind. When our actions, beliefs, or purpose are rooted in the healthy benefit for self or others, it raises the vibration. Therefore, our consciousness resides for the highest and best for all, not causing harm to ourselves or others. Focus is fixed on the inner world of who we are. Emotional components include compassion, understanding, integrity, forgiveness, and love. Finally, we have Self-love, self-correction, self-realization, or self-empowerment. These should be self-evident. This can be considered the capital, 'S' in Self. It's our spiritual Self.

Systems of Belief- A belief is what we do not know. Beliefs are something we hold onto without certainty. This bridges the gap between what we know and what we hope to understand. This is a concept that underscores how Systems of Belief (awareness or knowingness) extend beyond individual constructs, resonating through the etheric to create harmony and alignment with Universal Laws.

Terms we've coined:

Semi-permissible membrane- We filter and give permission for what is allowed to enter our field of existence, the aura. The finer frequencies of love pass back and forth effortlessly, equally giving and receiving, through the membrane. Discord's heavy, slow vibrations are blocked, and entry is prohibited. (It's the same concept for a semi-permeable membrane in medical terminology.)

The Silent Code of Life- is expressed as harmony and balance sustaining a resonance, which contains the rhythm of life. Life can be considered the synthesis of Divine expression or that agency of discovery, coherency, and transmutation, embodied within dynamic Purpose, Design, and Plan according to Law. This is immersed in the cosmos down to the atom, containing a language and culture. The Silent Code of Life lies in the very fabric of all that is. It comes as a whisper within the Silence, including a graceful, healing, loving light that holds all answers and solutions; Spiritual Logic's Magic.

Spiritual Logic- This is a framework for understanding and interpreting life through the lens of Universal Laws and the etheric realm. Unlike human logic, which is grounded in duality and imperfection, Spiritual Logic reflects Universal Energy's absolute precision and perfection. It aligns thought, intention, and action from higher vibrational principles, enabling harmony, balance, and resonance. Spiritual logic invites individuals to perceive beyond physical limitations, fostering a connection to the oneness of creation. (-See Chapter 3)

SUGGESTED READING

Listed here are several books that may be useful as reference materials or leisure reading. By no means is this compilation complete or comprehensive. If you should pursue an investigation into the ancient mysteries, the material that most acutely influences or inspires you will so mysteriously come into your presence. May your search be productive as your life moves forward.

Any Saint Germain series expresses laws in action with the utmost precision and how to walk with your I AM Presence. Your questions are answered, and the teachings are timeless. (SaintGermainPress. com) Books 1- 4 By Godfre Ray King are recommended. Also, Map: The Co-Creative White Brotherhood Medical Assistance Program. Third Edition. By Machaelle Small Wright

In addition, the works of the following Authors may deserve your attention:

Bailey, Alice A.: Esoteric Psychology I; Vol. I, A Treatise on the Seven Rays. The Light of the Soul: Its Science and Effect,

Besant, Annie: A Study in Consciousness. The Ancient Wisdom. Esoteric Christianity. Thought Power. Basis of Morality. Etc.

Blavatsky, H. P.: The Secret Doctrine. (late 1800's)

Hawkins M.D., Ph.D., David R.: The Eye of The I From Which Nothing is Hidden. 2001

Leadbeater, W.: The Chakras. Man, Visible and Invisible. The Inner Life. Freemasonry and Ancient Mystic Rites. The Astral Life, Invisible Helpers. The Masters and the Path.

Orwell, George: Animal Farm. 1984.

Patanjali: The Yoga Sutras of Patanjali. With commentary by Alice A. Bailey: Lucis Publishing Company, New York

Pert, Ph.D. Candace B.: Molecules of Emotion, The Science Behind Mind-Body Medicine.

Ruiz, Don Miguel: The Four Agreements: A Practical Guide to Personal Freedom. 1997

Stein, Charles: The Light of Hermes Trismegistus New Translations of Seven Essential Hermetic Texts. 2022

ABOUT ARTISANS OF THE SPIRIT

With over 80 years of collective experience, Shadow Fox and Lee Two Hawks have developed an alliance to express the qualities and understanding from their journey of spiritual life and living. They are the artisans, crafters, and wisdom talkers of incisive and frequently potent information. As partners, they hold a lamp for all to see beyond the mundane.

Lee Two Hawks Journey

I was an unloved child. "You are so stupid." "You are worthless." "You are ugly." "Nobody wants you." These are what I was told. I was a mistake; this I knew. I was a freak of nature, incapable of being held or embraced. Always being the fifth wheel, incessantly moving, family to family within the foster care system, then finally ended up in an orphanage. My worldview was of hatred, cruelty, and abuse. This is all I knew.

As a teenager, I entered a library. Among the books, I found what was called a music room. I sat in a cubicle, selected a classical record, put on headphones, and pushed play. I was shocked. What I heard was of such beauty and passion, such joy that I cried. I knew, at that moment, this sound would change my life. I knew that what was would be no more. My worldview suddenly expanded. This beauty, this sound, became my saving grace.

There were markers along the way, the promise of resolution. I discovered actualities or little truths, each supporting the other, always revealing a growing vista. There was the recognition of some greater awareness yet to be expressed. The little truths were not facts, as facts are external verifications of some external event. It was an inner search for immensity yet unrevealed.

As a seeker of love, I had first to accept and avow that such an abstraction existed. My childhood had taught me differently. In maturity, I found love – of family, of friends, of a nation. Many hearts ensure continuity.

However, it is not a healthy heart unless there is unanimity of rhythm – of a common cause – Life. There can be no disease in a healthy heart nor in those smaller hearts that comprise it. A unity evolves into a synthesis.

My pattern of thought and deed has become a drive to precipitate a universal understanding and development of a united Humanity working in unison for each other's health and well-being. There are billions of us. I am but one. One is a small voice; the voice of billions can shake the earth free of the shackles formed by fear, shaped by greed and cruelty. A Unity can become a synthesis only by becoming an active and potent oneness, an immovable force.

I aspire to this unity in my meager way – as a teacher, speaker, and, hopefully, exemplar. This is the voice of a few to the ears of the many. So, let us pull this thread into the warp and woof of a fabric that no one can penetrate nor dissolve.

Shadow Fox's Journey

It was upon a deep, painful breath that awareness came…

There is a word most people know but few truly understand: dedication. Another, now rarely spoken yet vital to the human spirit, is integrity. Shadow Fox embodies both. She is thorough—meticulous in her research, and unwavering in validating the truths she offers. With integrity guiding every word and honest intent shaping every thought, her life is not theory but practice, a living testament to the very teachings she imparts.

With this dedication lies a profound calling—to see beauty not as surface adornment but as a force deeply embedded in the soul, illuminating the path to consciousness. Shadow Fox's journey endured adversities that could weaken the spirit and deny the heart. Yet, from moments of deep sorrow to the quiet victories of healing, her path has been one of grace and transformation.

Shadow Fox's life reflects the essence of harmony through conflict—not as a struggle, but as a dance between understanding and growth, listening to the quiet whispers of energy, guiding her and others toward alignment. These are not fleeting gestures but steady, radiant expressions of a spirit that has chosen to heal and guide.

Through spiritual logic, Shadow Fox helps others realign with Universal Laws—to find stillness where there was noise, clarity where there was confusion, and peace where there was once unrest. As an Artisan of the Spirit, she aims to illuminate the path toward inner harmony, where healing and manifesting become a naturally unfolding by-product.

…With her first agonizing breath after a near-death experience was acceptance—to share energy's wisdom. It is a duty honored and a life fulfilled. Shadow Fox stands—steadfast and luminous—a guiding light for those seeking their awakening.

To you-- of you-- for you … Lee Two Hawks.

THE AUTHORS

C. Shadow Fox & Lee Two Hawks are Artisans of The Spirit with over eight decades of combined experience. They are recognized leaders in spiritual enfoldment, energy mastery, and healing modalities. As Artisans of the Spirit, they have dedicated their lives to expanding consciousness and empowering through their guidance, insight, and humor.

C. Shadow Fox, M.Sc., specializes in the nuances of Cosmic, Universal, Spiritual, and Natural Laws, weaving these Governing Principles into practical applications for healing and insight. Her connection to the Spirit brings forth spiritual logic through energy healing modalities that support those on their journey and unlock their potential.

Lee Two Hawks, an elder walking the Red Path, is revered as a 'Teacher of Teachers' offering unparalleled wisdom in energy, ceremony, and the essence of existence. His ability to bridge Ancient Practices with modern understanding distinguishes him as a cornerstone of their shared mission.

Together, as Reiki Masters, Reverends, and Spiritual Guides, they embody the principles they bring forward. Their work inspires the integration of synergy, mindfulness, and spiritual enfoldment. They aim to help humanity awaken to resonant fields of consciousness through Ancient Wisdom, fostering Unity and Synthesis.

Artisans of the Spirit.com

www.ingramcontent.com/pod-product-compliance
Lightning Source LLC
Chambersburg PA
CBHW030908120626
46554CB00001B/55